Endorsements for *The Divided States of America?*

"Dr. Land sheds light where others—from left and right—sow confusion. One can disagree on specific policies and still laud the author's dedication to America's founding values and his grasp of the proper role of religion in public life. *The Divided States of America?* is essential reading for fair-minded people."

—Madeleine Albright, former U.S. Secretary of State

"Baptists in America have a vibrant tradition of defending freedom, and religious freedom in particular. This thoughtful book demonstrates how that tradition helps us to think in fresh ways about the foundations of freedom."

—Dr. Richard John Neuhaus, Editor-in-Chief, *First Things*

"Looking for a book to help a liberal understand and respect a conservative Christian perspective on current issues? *The Divided States of America?* is it. Richard Land patiently counters the left's assumption that Christians are would-be dictators. He also upends some evangelical tendencies to see America as the new Israel. With so many books and orators, left and right, screeching to their respective choirs, it's great to see a thoughtful and faithful work."

—Marvin Olasky, Editor-in-Chief, *World*

"Richard Land is a brilliant, conscientious, and good-hearted advocate for religious conservatives in America. This book helps re-establish Baptist political theology at the center of the church/state debate."

—Steven Waldman, Editor-in-Chief and CEO, *Beliefnet*

"Richard Land has always been too much of a thinker and much too committed to biblical standards to simply go along with anything and everything proposed by conservative activists. On the crucial questions, *The Divided States of America?* is a candid and enormously helpful look at the mistakes of both the left and the right from the perspective of one of the greatest advocates of religious liberty in our country today."

—Dr. Paige Patterson, President, Southwestern Baptist Theological Seminary

"Richard Land has strong views on God and America and has long been well-placed to influence the opinions of many who care for both. In this new book, he speaks a welcome and necessary word of passionate caution, content neither to preach to the choir nor yell at ideological opponents in the destructive culture wars. Both liberals and conservatives will profit from the analysis and tone of this book, an altogether constructive contribution to an important debate too frequently marred by ranting and posturing."

—Peter J. Gomes, Harvard University

"This book could not be more timely. Richard Land has made a decisive contribution to the contentious debate about how religious believers ought to relate their faith to politics. In a reasonable and measured fashion, he offers constructive advice to both conservatives and liberals. My hope is that it will be read widely by those on the political Right and Left, because the necessary correctives offered here will improve everyone's understanding on a topic that is woefully misunderstood by religious believers and nonbelievers alike."

—Michael Cromartie, Vice President, Ethics & Public Policy Center

"This is a lucid statement of a reasonable position on the place of religion in public life. While the author writes from a committed Evangelical standpoint, his views on church/state relations will be plausible to many who do not share his religious commitment. The book will also be useful in dispelling negative stereotypes about Evangelicals due to its mellow, nonconfrontational tone."

—Peter L. Berger, Director of the Institute on Culture,
Religion and World Affairs, Boston University

"Finally—a book that sets the record straight on some of the most contentious issues of the day. Richard Land has written a brave and important book that has much to say to liberals, conservatives, and persons of all positions in between. *The Divided States of America?* has surprises for everyone, and it shows a keen and dedicated mind at work. . . . Richard Land combines brilliant analysis with his personal charm and deep convictions. You had better read this book soon—everyone is going to be talking about it."

—Albert Mohler, Jr., President, The Southern Baptist Theological Seminary

"One of the clearest, most tightly argued, and informative accounts of religion in the public square today by an especially intelligent and well-informed evangelical leader. From a man who has been active behind-the-scenes, even when not caught sight of in public, Land's book is an eye-opener. Anybody who claims to know American political life without having read it is missing a lot of the story."

—Michael Novak, American Enterprise Institute

"What is the proper place of religion in American public life? In *The Divided States of America?*, Richard Land ably defends the original vision of our nation's founders: the institution of the church and the institution of the state must be strictly separated; yet Christians and other people of faith can and should bring their religiously-informed judgments of morality and justice into public debate on the great questions of the day—whether slavery in Abraham Lincoln's time, segregation in Martin Luther King's, or abortion and human embryo-destructive research in our own. Dr. Land shreds the arguments of militant secularists, on one extreme, and theocrats, on the other."

—Robert P. George, McCormick Professor of Jurisprudence, Princeton University

THE DIVIDED
★ STATES ★
OF AMERICA?

What
Liberals AND
Conservatives are
missing in the
God-and-country
shouting
match!

RICHARD LAND

THOMAS NELSON
Since 1798

thomasnelson.com

To my ancestors who fought to defend our God-given freedom
in the Revolutionary War, the Texas War of Independence,
the Civil War (on both sides), and World Wars I and II;
and to all men and women who have honorably worn the uniforms
of our nation's armed services in defense of that freedom.

Published in Nashville, Tennessee by Thomas Nelson, Inc.

Thomas Nelson, Inc. titles may be purchased in bulk for educational, business, fund-raising, or sales promotional use. For information, please e-mail SpecialMarkets@ThomasNelson.com.

All Scripture quotations, unless otherwise indicated, are taken from the Holy Bible, New International Version (NIV). Copyright © 1973, 1978, 1984, International Bible Society. Used by permission of Zondervan.

Other Scripture references are from the following sources:

Holman Christian Standard Bible (HCSB). Copyright © 1999, 2000, 2002, 2003 by Holman Bible Publishers. Used by permission.

The King James Version of the Bible (KJV).

New American Standard Bible (NASB). Copyright © 1960, 1977, 1995 by the Lockman Foundation. Used by permission.

Editorial Team: David Moberg, acquisitions editor; Thom Chittom, managing editor
Cover Design: Matt Lehman
Page Design: Mandi Cofer

Library of Congress Cataloging-in-Publication Data

Land, Richard D.
    The divided states of America? : what liberals and conservatives are
missing in the God-and-country shouting match / Richard Land.
        p. cm.
    Includes bibliographical references and index.
    ISBN-10: 0-8499-0140-5 (hardcover)
    ISBN-13: 978-0-8499-0140-9 (hardcover)
    1. Christianity and politics—United States. 2. United States—Church history. I. Title.
BR526.L345 2007
322'.10973—dc22
2006101081

Printed in the United States of America
07 08 09 10 11 QW 5 4 3 2 1

★ Contents ★

CONTENTS

★ Acknowledgments ★

An undertaking of this magnitude requires an enormous amount of work, and I am truly grateful for the significant contributions of the many friends and colleagues who shared the burdens always associated with such creative projects.

I am especially grateful to my writing partner and colleague, Kathy Helmers. Her gifted contributions of prayer, perspective, research, writing, discussion, debate, editorial expertise, and patient deciphering of my dysgraphic scribblings were literally "invaluable." This book has been immeasurably enhanced by Kathy's myriad gifts.

Also, special thanks are due to Robbie George of Princeton University; Michael Cromartie of the Ethics & Public Policy Center; Walter Russell Mead and Nancy Roman of the Council on Foreign Relations; and Paige Patterson, president of Southwestern Seminary and my close friend of nearly forty years. Each took time from an extremely busy schedule to read the first drafts and make many significant and helpful suggestions, greatly improving the final text. Of course, the responsibility for any mistakes and errors in the finished product is mine alone.

Another special category of people who supported me attentively through the completion of the book and to whom I am indebted includes David Moberg, my publisher; Thom Chittom, editor; and Debbie Nichols and the entire team at Thomas Nelson who worked so diligently to pull this book together.

Over the years, I have been extremely blessed to have so many dedicated and gifted people to come and to serve alongside me in the accomplishment of significant ministry projects like this one. Consequently, I want to express my gratitude to my staff, who labor above and beyond the call of duty. God has

ACKNOWLEDGMENTS

blessed me with an incredible ministry team. Their diligent support, commitment, skill, encouragement, and servant hearts have been a continuing inspiration to me. Thanks go to Kerry Bural, Doug Carlson, Rob Chambers, Amber Chesser, Pat Clark, Karen Cole, Barrett Duke, Jacob Fentress, Harold Harper, Dwayne Hastings, Matt Hawkins, Chadd Hodges, Barbara Jester, Lana Kimbro, Judy Lawson, Jill Martin, Bobby Reed, Beth Sartain, Tom Strode, Rachel Wiles, and Sulyn Wilkins.

From a more personal perspective, I am forever indebted to Becky, my dearest friend, my wife, and my ministry partner for nearly thirty-six years. I cannot honor her enough. The most important reason that I am able to devote my entire life to the Lord's work is because Becky embraces joyfully her calling as wife, mother, and servant of our Lord (including serving as chief check balancer and general chief operating officer of our household). Her love, encouragement, and self-sacrificial support have been the essentials that have made all else possible.

I owe an enormous debt of gratitude as well to my mother and father, which a lifetime could never repay. My parents always taught me to love my country and respect my heritage—and always to love and respect God even more.

I must add a special word of gratitude to the late, great theologian Dr. Carl F. H. Henry, who long ago began to challenge me persistently to take up the task of grappling with the major issues involved with Christians and their engagement with their society—a challenge to which this book is a partial reply.

Most of all, I am grateful for my Heavenly Father and God's Son, my Savior, the coming King, the Lord Jesus the Christ. May He use this book for His Kingdom and His glory, and may He continue to bless the United States of America.

Richard Land
Nashville, Tennessee
Spring 2007

★ Foreword ★

By Senator Joseph I. Lieberman

In *The Divided States of America?* Richard Land makes a strong case for rescuing the "values" debate from the extremes and moving it toward a common-sense middle where people of all faiths and no faith can calmly, candidly, and constructively talk to each other about how to make our lives better. Dr. Land's thoughtful and hopeful effort to change our national conversation about faith and values should be read by people of all faiths.

I believe that our nation is in the early stages of a third "Great Awakening" of religious faith and activity as a counter to the current erosion of our values and the coarsening of our culture. The "guardrails" that have guided our culture toward moral and civil behavior have been removed, and the lines between right and wrong have become blurred. For example, parents know they must be constantly wary about an entertainment culture that extols permissiveness, undermines civility, and promotes violence.

Most of the American people want these trends reversed. To do so in their own lives, they turn to their faith, their family, and even sometimes their government. But in the latter they too often find partisan division and demagoguery.

When the left hears the right talk about "values," they hear it as a code for intolerance and censorship. When the right hears the left talk about "values," they hear it as a code for sectarianism and permissiveness.

These polarized responses do not represent the beliefs of the majority of

Americans. Most people I talk to believe we can uphold our common values without trampling on anyone's rights or faith. What we need is a political awakening of shared values and unity to accompany the current spiritual awakening.

Encouraging the respectful dialogue among people of many faiths and beliefs that can facilitate such an awakening is the very heart of *The Divided States of America?*

Dr. Land writes that our Founding Fathers did not set out to create a Christian nation, though almost all of them were Christian. But he also reminds us that they did found their new nation on faith in God and intended it to be a country in which religion was honored and freedom of religion was protected.

Dr. Land is right. The United States is a faith-based institution. You see it right at the beginning in the first American document, the Declaration of Independence, where our Founders said they were forming their new government to "secure" the rights to life, liberty, and the pursuit of happiness, which were (and are) the "endowment" of our "Creator."

I see American history as a journey to secure those rights. It is a journey in which faith-based groups have fittingly played very progressive parts. The abolitionist movement in the nineteenth century and the great fights for social welfare and civil rights in the twentieth century were each led by religious leaders and their faithful.

To this day, religion plays a larger role in the lives of Americans than almost anywhere else in the world. According to the Pew World Attitudes Project, nearly 60 percent of Americans reported that religion was "very important" in their lives, compared to 33 percent in Great Britain—the second highest of the eight developed nations surveyed.

It is folly to believe that in a nation where so many hold religious beliefs, that those same people won't bring to the public square the values their faith has taught them. To try to separate America and its people from their faith in God and the values it engenders is an unnatural and unnecessary act.

What is crucial is that when we bring our faith and values to the public square, we do it with respect for all. Dr. Land writes that ". . . no one has a right to say, 'We *have* to do this because the Bible says so.'" But everyone, he argues, has a responsibility to include people of all faiths—or no faith—in our national dialogue.

Foreword

In this book, Richard Land uses a constructive and instructive dialectic approach, first examining the extremes on both sides and then building a middle position of reasonable "accommodation."

Whatever our political differences, we all share the values that underlie our freedom and democracy. Unity based on those values is imperative now because our nation is under assault from the totalitarian movement of Islamist extremism. In fact, one of our best defenses against that extremism is the interfaith diversity and dialogue that has long been characteristically American, and which Dr. Land advocates in this book.

In 1790, George Washington wrote a letter to the Jewish congregation of the Synagogue of Touro in Newport, Rhode Island, declaring that the rights of all to worship as they choose was no longer a matter of just "toleration," as it was in Europe, but a fundamental right in the new nation that could never be taken away. He closed his letter with a benediction that speaks to us and our time.

"May the children of the Stock of Abraham, who dwell in this land, continue to merit and enjoy the good will of the other Inhabitants; while every one shall sit in safety under his own vine and fig tree, and there shall be none to make him afraid."

In the same spirit, in *The Divided States of America?* Richard Land asks us to overcome our divisions and lower the barriers that prevent us from becoming again the United States of America. For that, he deserves our praise and attention.

★ 1 ★

What's God Got to Do with America?

It is imperative that we begin speaking plainly about the absurdity of most of our religious beliefs.

—SAM HARRIS[1]

With God officially expunged from America's public life, can guns be far behind? . . . Without guts, guns become museum pieces, and God becomes a nostalgic memory. In other words, lose one and you lose all three.

—CHUCK BALDWIN[2]

Rolling down one side of America's cultural highway is a Lexus RX hybrid with a "Love Your Mother (Earth)" decal discreetly placed in the lower left of the rear window. Below, a bumper sticker features an illustration of Rodin's famous sculpture *The Thinker*, next to the quotation, "I think; therefore I am a liberal." Headed in the opposite direction across the double yellow line is a Dodge Ram Hemi pickup truck with a gun rack mounted in the cab, a Confederate flag pasted across the back window, and a bumper sticker proclaiming, "God, Guns, 'n' Guts Made America Free!"

On their way home to Blue and Red America, these two road warriors are unwitting adversaries in a titanic clash of conflicting worldviews—often called the culture wars.

What's God got to do with America? The woman in the Lexus behind designer prescription sunglasses thinks God has nothing to do with America—past, present, or future. The dude in the Dodge wearing a Skoal ball cap thinks God has a lot—if not everything—to do with America.

Could they both be wrong? God may very well have more to do with America than liberals may think and less than conservatives often assume.

THROWING "RABBIT PUNCHES" AND
LOW BLOWS LEFT AND RIGHT

America's political divide has generated plenty of heat and hot air, and voices on both sides have been needlessly strident. The nonfiction best-seller lists in the last decade chart the partisan pendulum swings. Ten years ago liberal comedian

Al Franken threw down the gauntlet with his crass-as-you-can *Rush Limbaugh Is a Big Fat Idiot* (Delacorte, 1996). Conservative television host Bill O'Reilly hit the list a few years later with his pull-no-punches diatribe *The O'Reilly Factor: The Good, the Bad, and the Completely Ridiculous in American Life* (Broadway, 2000). Emmy-winning reporter Bernard Goldberg turned up the volume by blowing his shrill whistle *Bias: A CBS Insider Exposes How the Media Distort the News* (Regnery, 2001), recounting tale after tale of liberal censorship in the way the media control and shape the news.

Leftist muckraker Michael Moore—best known for his "documentaries," such as *Roger and Me* and *Fahrenheit 9/11*—grabbed the book-shaped megaphone with *Stupid White Men . . . and Other Sorry Excuses for the State of the Nation!* (ReganBooks, 2002), a screed about how "Thief-in-Chief" George W. Bush and his Republican power elite allegedly stole the 2000 election from Al Gore and the Democrats. Authors David Hardy and Jason Clarke countered with *Michael Moore Is a Big Fat Stupid White Man* (ReganBooks, 2004), which drew praise from conservatives (and not a few liberals who confessed they couldn't stand Moore either).

Ann Coulter further lowered the level of "discourse" with *Slander: Liberal Lies about the American Right* (Crown, 2002). Franken hit it big again with *Lies and the Lying Liars Who Tell Them: A Fair and Balanced Look at the Right* (Dutton, 2003). Not to be outdone, Bernard Goldberg encored on the best-seller list with *100 People Who Are Screwing Up America (and Al Franken Is #37)* (HarperCollins, 2005), which featured Michael Moore on the front cover, among other "America Bashers," "Hollywood Blowhards," "TV Schlockmeisters," and "Intellectual Thugs." Meanwhile, Ann Coulter kept up her best-selling attacks on the Left, including *How to Talk to a Liberal (If You Must)* (Crown, 2004) and *Godless: The Church of Liberalism* (Crown, 2006), swinging verbal punches in her books and in interviews with the articulate, yet no-holds-barred, abandon of a roller-derby queen. Talk show host Michael Savage continued to live down to his name with best-selling tirades, such as *Liberalism Is a Mental Disorder: Savage Solutions* (Nelson, 2005).

A little book that never made the best-seller lists employed a compendium of liberal pundits to take down all the voices on the Right in one volume, one target per chapter, in *The I Hate Ann Coulter, Bill O'Reilly, Rush Limbaugh,*

What's God Got to Do with America?

Michael Savage, Sean Hannity . . . Reader: The Hideous Truth about America's Ugliest Conservatives. The back-cover copy hits the sneering tone of the political culture wars with pitch-perfect prose.

> Sick to death of the right-wing blowhards and bullies who dominate our media? This collection exposes the hypocrisy and lies of the reactionary jerks, hate-mongers, and sycophants who foul the public's airwaves. Get the goods on hateful hatchet woman Ann Coulter, who disdains facts as much as she does ordinary Americans. Check out the titanic hypocrisy of talk-radio loudmouth Rush "drug users should go to jail—except in my case" Limbaugh. Stand amazed at the antics of pompous, rage-filled bully Bill O'Reilly as he stoops to new lows to serve his corporate masters and his own gigantic ego. Observe lunatic thugs Sean Hannity and Michael Savage as they drag our public discourse through the gutter for their own selfish ends.[3]

The problem with nasty shouting matches is that eventually they get boring for all except the few principals juicing their adrenaline and the followers feeding off the vicarious thrill. The most thoughtful inevitably turn down the volume simply by turning away.

The major media outlets in this country bear a significant responsibility for shaping the debate in these stark, most-extreme-position terms and then labeling it "balanced journalism." Most Americans—unless they have been interviewed for a radio or television program—are not aware of a nefarious practice called the "pre-interview process." In this screening procedure, the media interview potential candidates for their suitability in filling the preordained slots of extreme-Right and extreme-Left positions they have already identified. They often cull out the individuals who have balanced views and who try to discuss the issues in a reasonable way. Instead of bringing on two people with divergent views who are trying to forge some common ground, they feature adversarial opponents and try to maximize the distance between them. This strategy distorts the individual positions while misleading the country into thinking there is greater divisiveness and less common ground than actually exist.

I know this prescreening process like the back of my hand, because I have been culled out hundreds of times. I remember being questioned for an interview in which the producers wanted me, as an Evangelical, to say that Pope John Paul II—one of the greatest historical and religious figures of the twentieth century—was the head of a "false religion." I was not prepared to say such a thing because I don't believe it. Rather, I said, the pope is the head of a doctrinal understanding of the Christian faith with which I disagree—a position that disqualified me from participating.

During another pre-interview I was asked if I, as an Evangelical, believed that Islam was an evil religion. I said, "No, as a Christian, I believe that Islam is a wrong religion—Christianity is right about the truth, and Islam is wrong." I described "evil religion" as somebody doing something evil in the name of religion, whether the Ku Klux Klan burning crosses to terrorize African-Americans in a blasphemous distortion of Christianity or terrorists recruiting children to be suicide bombers in the name of Islam. That response wasn't what they had in mind. It was far too reasonable and not nearly extreme enough. "That's not really what we're looking for," the producer said to me, "but thank you for your time."

One of the primary reasons I am writing this book is to circumvent media prescreeners (and their "adversarial extreme" model of journalism), to penetrate the din generated by societal screamers, and to invite you, the reader, to a conversation concerning these critically important questions: What does God (or religion, if you prefer) have to do with America today? What has God had to do with our past? And what role *should* God play in our nation's future?

Interestingly, it appears that the media themselves are aware of their tendency to distort religious issues. A Public Agenda study on American attitudes toward religion found that the media admit their coverage of religion is anything but evenhanded: "Of the 219 journalists surveyed—reporters who cover straight news stories, not those who exclusively work the religion beat—35% agree with the statement 'On the whole, the news media do a very good job of covering religion and religion issues.' Almost six in ten (59%) journalists express concern that 'the news media are especially eager to report scandal and sensational news when the subject is religion.'"[4]

Current best-seller lists suggest that the liberal-versus-conservative screeching to the choir seems to be passing its peak of popularity, for which no doubt some of us will be thankful while others fidget impatiently for the next political smack-down contest. As the hot air drains out of the culture-war winds, however, the debate continues to shift over to the new tide of rising interest in religion. After ignoring this elephant in America's living room, mainstream media have finally caught on that religion is a major force in American life, not a fringe curiosity of political fanaticism.

I have been called upon in media interviews as a conservative Christian countervoice to leftist ministry leader Jim Wallis, familiar for decades in Christian social justice networks through his *Sojourners* magazine and national Call to Renewal movement. Those who followed his antiwar activism during the Vietnam War era know that his critique of American capitalism and free-market economies is long-standing. When Vietnamese refugees fled their country in the 1970s in the wake of the newly victorious Communist regime, Wallis declared, "Many of today's refugees were inoculated with a taste for a Western lifestyle during the war years and are fleeing to support their consumer habit in other lands."[5]

Recently Wallis has become a fixture in mainstream media through his best-selling book *God's Politics: Why the Right Gets It Wrong and the Left Doesn't Get It* (HarperSanFrancisco, 2005), which agitates for his left-leaning social and political agendas while critiquing positions espoused by conservative Evangelicals. The degree of regularity with which "God's politics" seem to agree with Wallis's politics is amazing.

The popularity of Wallis's book has coincided with a rising tide of media attention to the greatly increased interest in religion in America. The attacks on our country on 9/11 were part of this impetus, thrusting questions about religious fanaticism and extremism into public consciousness. Added to such flash-point issues as abortion and same-sex marriage, already laden with religious content, have been controversies that pose the question in the most direct possible way of what role God should play in American public life: not just school prayer, but references to God in our Pledge of Allegiance, on our currency, in our public assemblies, and in the self-expressed faith convictions of candidates for public office.

Everywhere, it seems, the question is being raised, *What's God got to do with America?* The question of whether, how, and why God is—or isn't—involved with this country has been on the lips of our leaders and citizens since the very beginning of English settlement on this continent. However, the most recent versions of this question have roots in the enormous transformations that have taken place in this country since the cultural sea changes of the 1960s.

HOW THE REPUBLICAN PARTY
GOT RELIGION (AGAIN)

Our political system is based on two major parties. Third parties formed around particular issues or individuals inevitably rise and fall as tangential to the two that are dominant. If a crisis occurs in which neither party will accommodate itself to a social movement that has reached critical mass, history shows we will not get a third party. Rather, what will happen is that the weaker of the two major parties will die, and it will be replaced by a new party. That has already occurred once before in our history, when both the Whig Party and the Democratic Party tried to be pro-choice on slavery. The antislavery movement had reached critical mass, and the weaker party—the Whigs—died and was replaced by the Republican Party, which became the party of the antislavery movement.

In the latter third of the twentieth century, the social issue reaching critical mass was the pro-life movement. On January 22, 1973, the U.S. Supreme Court's *Roe v. Wade* decision changed our social, political, and moral landscape by declaring almost all restrictions on abortion unconstitutional. I am convinced that if the Republican Party—critically weakened in the wake of the Watergate scandals of the Nixon administration—had not accommodated itself to the pro-life movement (which was reaching critical mass in the period between 1976 and 1980) and had not adopted a pro-life plank in its platform, it would have died and been replaced by a new party, formed in large part around the burgeoning resistance to abortion.

What happened in the period between *Roe v. Wade* and 1980 that contributed to the Republican Party's revitalization? One of the things that happened was that an odd-looking little man named Francis Schaeffer began writing and speaking against abortion-on-demand. He became arguably the most influential conservative, religious activist of the modern era. He wielded enormous influence in getting Evangelical Christians involved in the political system, especially in response to *Roe v. Wade*.

Schaeffer believed in truth with a capital *T*—"true truth," he called it. That meant it was true not just on Sunday, but also on Monday. It was true not just at home, but also at school and at work and in the public arena. Christians had an obligation to be "salt" and "light" as the Bible says (Matthew 5:13–16).

Schaeffer helped Evangelicals jettison a deep strain of pietism that had misled them to believe they shouldn't be involved in politics and other "worldly" activities. He helped an entire generation of Christians to understand their biblical responsibility to be salt and light in society—and, of course, salt has to touch what it preserves; light has to be close enough to the darkness that it can be seen. Among the questions that Schaeffer repeatedly posed (usually in the context of the abortion issue) in his books, such as *How Shall We Then Live?*, *The God Who Is There*, and *A Christian Manifesto*, were these: If not you, who? If not now, when? If not this, what?

Resistance to abortion is what brought about the phenomenal and unprecedented alliance between Evangelicals and Roman Catholics that marked the 1980s and beyond. This ecumenical cooperation did not happen just at the national level; it happened at the local level as well, in neighborhoods as Protestants and Catholics worked together in crisis pregnancy centers and walked side by side on protest lines. They began to get to know each other in new ways and discovered more common ground than differences in their worldviews on social issues.

Foundational to the common ground that Protestants and Catholics were discovering in each other was the belief that human beings are accountable to a transcendent moral authority. Therefore, individual choices are limited by divinely ordained moral imperatives regarding the beginning and end of life. There has always been a strong religious element in the conservative movement in the United States, and in the late 1970s the religious core of the Republican Party was galvanized in large part by the abortion issue. At the same time, the Democratic Party was becoming the party that believed in the Ten Suggestions rather than the Ten Commandments.

In recent decades, the conservative-liberal divide has widened over this very issue of moral authority. One of the foundational planks of conservatism is the belief in a transcendent moral order: in other words, there are—dare I mention the word?—*absolutes*. Some things are always right, and some things are always wrong, and truth is not always relative. In fact, truth is *never* relative.

For liberals, however, personal autonomy and freedom of choice have been the highest values, along with a denial of transcendent moral authority—thus the pro-choice side of the abortion issue. In the absence of truth with a capital

T, each individual is free to manufacture his or her own moral universe. In the absence of absolutes, personal freedom and individual rights become the highest values (though, as philosophers have observed, the moral grounds for any person to respect another's freedom and rights are undermined eventually).

Georgetown professor and Brookings Institution senior fellow E. J. Dionne Jr., commenting on the new religious divide in this country between traditional religious believers and those with no religious faith or a more liberal, "modernist" faith (evidenced in the 2004 election, when regular churchgoers voted overwhelmingly for George W. Bush and nonchurchgoers voted heavily for John Kerry), cites this underlying clash of worldviews: "James Davison Hunter, a sociologist at the University of Virginia who introduced the culture-war concept to a wide audience, defines the orthodox or traditionalist view as 'the commitment on the part of adherents to an external, definable, and transcendent authority.' In progressivism, on the other hand, 'moral authority tends to be defined by the spirit of the modern age, a spirit of rationalism and subjectivism.'"[6]

This is a clear picture of the religious divide in this country: on the one side, those who are committed to a transcendent moral authority; on the other, those whose moral authority is defined by rationalism and subjectivism. *Rationalism* is the view that we know the world only through our rational faculties of reason and observation—something is true if you can understand it and measure it. Either there is no such thing as the supernatural, or it is irrelevant, and religious faith, which takes it seriously, is misguided and naïve. *Subjectivism* views reality through one lens: the self—it's true if it's true for you. There is no reality outside of your own experience. You can have religious faith or not, as long as it has nothing to do with some absolute reality beyond the self, because the self is the only ultimate or absolute reality.

Let's illustrate the clash of these views on an obvious subject: sex. The traditionalist view says that how we think and behave about sex is defined by a moral authority transcendent to ourselves. We can't simply do what feels good, because we are accountable to a higher being—God, who created sex for specific reasons and gave it to us as a gift. The progressive view says that sex is a personal experience, and anything is permissible as long as it involves no coercion or deception. Sex is simply an appetite that consenting adults can indulge at will as long as it doesn't "hurt" anybody else.

Even liberals have begun to admit (mostly when their daughters reach the teenage years) that the so-called sexual revolution of the 1960s has had unfortunate, unforeseen consequences. The ravages are there for all to see—the rising poverty rates among unwed mothers, the sexual abuse by nonbiologically related males living in the home, and the exponential spread of sexually transmitted diseases—just to name a few. A friend of mine, a practicing therapist who happens to be a liberal feminist, tells me of the steady stream of young women she sees from the university campus nearby who come into her office over and over again with the same basic lament: "I just want sex to *mean* something." I don't think there is any other area of human life as utterly and overwhelmingly *de*meaned by the do-your-own-thing subjectivism of our age as sexuality. And now, thanks to the Internet, no corner of our society, inside or outside the church, children or adults, is safe from the horrific plague of pornography that has descended upon us.

What God has to do with America starts with what Americans have to do with God. Is there a God or not? If there is a God, is He the God of the Bible, of the Torah, of the Qur'an, or a god we can "find within," entirely defined by how we experience that god? Is there a source of moral authority beyond ourselves, or are we the supreme rulers of our own bodies and souls? Does sex really *mean* something absolutely or not?

Keep this in mind, because first we are going to plunge into the God-and-country shouting match to see what each side is saying and what each side is missing. Only then can we dig down deep enough to identify what God should and shouldn't have to do with America, why it matters so much, and how we can find a solution that honors our country and empowers each of us to serve faithfully and freely as citizens of this remarkable nation out of the deepest, God-honoring convictions of our lives.

AMERICA—SHOULD GOD LOVE IT OR LEAVE IT?

Steven Waldman of Beliefnet.com and John C. Green of the Pew Forum on Religion & Public Life have identified what they call the "twelve tribes" of American politics, a configuration based on moral values, spiritual affinities, and religious affiliations. Their research yields intriguing insights into how and why people vote in particular ways on "moral values" issues and in relation to the religious convictions of political candidates.[7] However, in the general clamor of the God-in-America debate, the noisiest voices seem to coalesce (predictably) around two opposing viewpoints, conservative and liberal.

Roughly speaking, the conservative view could be summarized as the traditional God-and-country position: "We've been taking God out of this country, and we need to put Him back in—where He's always been before we headed down this godless road." For example, here is a warning from radio talk show host and Christian minister Chuck Baldwin:

God (at least the God of the Bible) has been expelled from America's schools and from America's culture. "Merry Christmas" has been replaced with "Happy Holidays." Major corporations and government entities are openly hostile to virtually any form of Christian expression. Furthermore, the Ninth Circuit Court of Appeals recently ruled the phrase "under God" in our Pledge of Allegiance to be unconstitutional.

With God officially expunged from America's public life, can guns be far behind? Well, the same Ninth Circuit Court of Appeals appears ready to rid our country of them, also. . . . Here is the point: the assault weapons ban signed by Bush the Elder is scheduled to expire during the next Congress unless Bush the Younger decides to extend it. This is why the timing of the Ninth Court's decision is so important, which brings us to the third member of our triumphant trilogy: guts. . . .

Without guts, guns become museum pieces, and God becomes a nostalgic memory. In other words, lose one and you lose all three.[8]

At the other end of the spectrum is the liberal view, which we could basically summarize in this way: "Separation of church and state means that God shouldn't have anything to do with American politics and public life, so we need to take God out of this country—and keep it that way."

Sam Harris, author of *The End of Faith*, condemns any belief that is not subject to rational, evidence-based reasoning. Thus our religious traditions are "intellectually defunct and politically ruinous," he maintains, and religion is "nothing more than bad concepts held in place of good ones for all time. It is the denial—at once full of hope and full of fear—of the vastitude of human ignorance."[9] It is not enough for Harris simply to denounce religious faith as irrational, however. Citing religious war as the inevitable consequence when opposing belief systems clash, he calls for an end not just to religious extremism, but to "the very ideal of religious tolerance—born of the notion that every human being should be free to believe whatever he wants about God" as "one of the principal forces driving us toward the abyss."[10]

Harris would argue for more than simply taking God out of public debate in America; he calls for the literal marginalization of those who stubbornly persist in believing in God: "It is time we realized that to presume knowledge where one has only pious hope is a species of evil. . . . Where we have reasons for what we believe, we have no need of faith; where we have no reasons, we have lost both our connection to the world and to one another. People who harbor strong convictions without evidence belong at the margins of our societies, not in our halls of power."[11]

Do you think Sam Harris is a lone voice crying in the wilderness of liberal extremism? His book has become a best seller, garnering accolades and winning awards such as the prestigious 2005 PEN/Martha Albrand Award for Nonfiction. In the *New York Times*, reviewer Natalie Angier commended Harris's depiction of "major religious systems like Judaism, Christianity and Islam as socially sanctioned forms of lunacy." Further, she hailed his willingness to write "what a sizable number of us think, but few are willing to say in contemporary America."[12]

What's God got to do with America? The voices in today's heated arguments provide wildly opposing answers. However, regardless of how any of us respond, the question itself immediately confronts us with a few realities preceding our individual opinions.

From the standpoint of the past, the answer to this question is unequivocally, "Quite a lot." Any study of American history necessarily involves understanding what Americans thought God had to do with them. We will be exploring more of this legacy later on—what it meant then, what it means for us now, and why there's so much controversy over America's religious past.

From the perspective of the present, the answer also would seem to be, "God has a lot to do with America," because that is the majority opinion according to numerous polls. Seven of every ten Americans say they want the influence of religion in our society to grow.[13] It's well documented that a majority of these individuals are referring to a religion centered on "God" as traditionally understood in the Judeo-Christian tradition.

And looking ahead, if trends hold, America's future will continue to involve "God" prominently and publicly because more people are becoming more religious or "spiritual."

But these realities don't address the question of what God really *does* have to do with America—why, how, and in what forms and ways? And how can we possibly answer such a question when so many Americans differ so widely on their views of God (or no god), how their views influence their private and public lives, and how they feel *others'* views about God ought to impinge on personal and public areas of their lives?

For understanding the nature and shape of American society past, present, and future, I can hardly think of a more relevant question to pursue—thus this book. But I also believe it is an important question to ask and seek to answer because there is currently so much confusion over this question. We must seek to answer this question because so much is at stake in what we determine the answer to be.

The conservatives too often assume that God is on America's side, making patriotism idolatrous and the country an idol. That is the Right's besetting error. Liberals too often don't believe it matters whether God has a side in public policy debates, or they believe such questions are disqualified from consideration by a supposed constitutional mandate of church-state separation. That viewpoint makes a particular judicial interpretation of the Constitution an idol. That is the Left's besetting error.[14]

What's God got to do with America? The country needs a better way to think about this question, because both sides of the worldview wars are missing the mark in some very crucial respects. And while I confess that I enjoy a good round of verbal jousting, I don't have much appetite for shouting matches. When neither side is interested in listening to the other, but each side responds by shouting so loudly that its opponents either can't or won't listen, both sides generate a lot of heat, but very little light.

Clearing the confusion is not just an exercise in getting policy right, having the "right" views, or trumping the other voices with a more clever solution. And neither do I presume to have the full-orbed biblical perspective on the question of what God has to do with America. Ultimately, only God knows what the complete "biblical" position is, but if Christians fully commit themselves to Him in Christ, I believe He will graciously lead us to a more complete understanding.

However, I am earnestly invested in proposing an appropriate and fruitful way of addressing this question because the future of our nation will be shaped by how each of us answers it. If we don't identify what each side of this debate is missing and why, we're going to waste precious time and resources on yet another shouting match that will take the place of the kind of moral and spiritual reformation we so desperately need. We can't afford to get sidetracked in yet another screeching-to-the-choir wrangle that will only leave opponents more embittered and hostile to each other, with increasing numbers in the middle deciding, "This whole God thing is just a personal matter, and anyway, nobody really knows for sure."

If we allow confusion or frustration to deflect our best efforts, we will miss what the underlying crisis truly is—a titanic clash of the worldviews masquerading as a political correctness debate about whether I have the right to impose my religious views on you, or whether you have the right to tell me what I can and can't say or do when I step into the public square. My friends, underneath this debate are critical assumptions that will radically shape the future of this country for good or for ill, and it is high time we realize what they are and learn how to respond to them in ways that will cut through our cultural impasse and lead us to a better future for all Americans.

So let's take a closer look. What's God got to do with America? Well, not everything . . .

> but far more than liberals may think,
> and a lot less than conservatives may assume,
> in much different ways than either side acknowledges,
> and for far more important reasons than you might imagine.

$$\star\ 2\ \star$$

What Liberals Are Missing

The great enemy of truth is very often not the lie—deliberate, contrived and dishonest, but the myth—persistent, persuasive and unrealistic.

—John F. Kennedy[1]

The woman in the Lexus RX hybrid is driving down America's cultural highway convinced that any discussion of what God should have to do with America is a dangerous erosion of the separation of church and state. She gives money to organizations such as the American Civil Liberties Union and People for the American Way to help ensure that the "Religious Right" cannot take over the nation's public schools, community boards, and political offices and try to force their religion and moral values on others.[2]

She might well approve of this call to abolish references to God—in the form of all institutionalized religion—from public life:

> Words like "God" and "Allah" must go the way of "Apollo" and "Baal," or they will unmake our world.
>
> A few minutes spent wandering the graveyard of bad ideas suggests that such conceptual revolutions are possible. Consider the case of alchemy: it fascinated human beings for over a thousand years, and yet anyone who seriously claims to be a practicing alchemist today will have disqualified himself for most positions of responsibility in our society. Faith-based religion must suffer the same slide into obsolescence.[3]

This condemnation comes courtesy of Sam Harris, who equates the violence of Muslim suicide bombers with believing in the literal truth of the book of Revelation—"or any of the other fantastical notions that have lurked in the minds of the faithful for millennia."[4] Because human beings have now invented weapons of mass destruction—chemical, biological, and nuclear—Harris contends that we can no longer afford to indulge the illusions of any religion that purports to have received an infallible word from the one true God. Even moderate religious faith poses a threat to our survival, he maintains, because it permits exclusionary beliefs to breed religious extremism.

LOOK WHO'S TALKING ARROGANTLY NOW

Harris certainly does not speak for all liberals, for which we can be thankful. The "liberal" spectrum is a broad one, from the extreme of secular Fundamentalists who see all religion as dangerous to the so-called Religious Left, smarting from what Jim Wallis describes as the feeling that "our faith has been stolen, and it's time to take it back."[5] Interestingly, virtually all liberals are united in their disdain for conservatives' "moral arrogance." Listen to this standard-bearer for conservative-phobes:

> [Fundamentalists] have become increasingly influential in both religion and government, and have managed to change the nuances and subtleties of historic debate into black-and-white rigidities and the personal derogation of those who dare to disagree. At the same time, these religious and political conservatives have melded their efforts, bridging the formerly respected separation of church and state. This has empowered a group of influential "neoconservatives," who have been able to implement their long-frustrated philosophy in both domestic and foreign policy.
>
> The influence of these various trends poses a threat to many of our nation's historic customs and moral commitments, both in government and in houses of worship.[6]

Let's summarize what this critic is saying about Christians with conservative views:

- *They are becoming increasingly influential.* Last time I checked, the core idea of democracy is that the majority view prevails. We have checks and balances to ensure that the majority does not run roughshod over the rights of minorities, as is too often the case in "mobocracies." So what is wrong with increasing influence? Nothing—unless you dislike the *kind* of influence it represents.

- *They are rigid instead of nuanced and subtle.* Here's a classic stereotype: conservatives believe some things are right and some things are wrong, and that makes them rigid. Liberals are sophisticated enough to pay attention to nuances and subtleties. Black-and-white is bad. Gray is good. Of course, this represents a black-and-white caricature of conservatives, but never mind.
- *They put down those with whom they disagree.* There's a sweeping statement: conservatives are mean to other people. And that makes liberals . . . nice people? Take another look at the passage quoted above and ask yourself, "Who is putting down whom?"
- *Religious and political conservatives are eroding the separation of church and state by working together.* One would hope that this statement also would apply to Christians on the left who are joining their efforts with political liberals—which, in fact, is what this critic's book is advocating.
- *Their success in influencing the country through democratic means is bad for our government and our churches.* The sweeping condemnation in this statement is breathtaking, but it is the logic that is problematic—again, the confluence of religious and political conservatives poses a threat only if it is antithetical to what one presumes to be "our nation's historic customs and moral commitments, both in government and in houses of worship"—and that is a huge presumption.

Would it surprise you to learn that this critic is a self-professed "Evangelical Christian"—a Southern Baptist like myself, even? Former President Jimmy Carter, for all the fine work he has done through such ventures as Habitat for Humanity and the Conflict Resolution Program, can be less than tolerant of those who disagree with him. And he has spoken out of both sides of his mouth on the religion-in-public issue: he says we need to bring faith into politics, and then he says we shouldn't bring faith into politics. He says we have to have separation of church and state, so while he has private views, he can't bring those views to bear on public policy. Then he writes an op-ed piece in the *New York Times* against the liberation of Iraq based on his understanding of biblical principles.[7] You can't have it both ways, President Carter. You can't say on one side that there has to be a separation of church and state and therefore leave your Christian convictions aside when you deal with public policy issues such as abortion, yet take a public stand against the liberation of Iraq because you think it's against Christian principles. There are two words for such behavior: the charitable one is *inconsistency*; the less charitable one is *hypocrisy*.

President Carter also makes a classic liberal error in assuming that his positions are the norm and conservative positions are the extreme. The title of his book *Our Endangered Values* indicates that he is equating his values with America's values. That is quite an assumption, even for a former president. He doesn't say "my" endangered values, but "ours." Apparently, they weren't the values of the American people based on what the majority of the voters thought when he ran for reelection. Apparently, they weren't the values of his fellow Southern Baptists, 84 percent of whom voted for George W. Bush in 2004.

Those who are saying that Republicans in general and Christians in particular need to construct a bigger tent are upset by the so-called Religious Right because their assumption of moral superiority is being challenged. They can't forgive the Religious Right for challenging causes such as the pro-choice position on abortion, which they have already proclaimed the morally superior position.

The liberal Left can't forgive the Religious Right for refusing to accept its claim to moral hegemony. Let's try a test question: is it more or less moral to say that three thousand six hundred American women every day should have a right to abort their babies? Religious conservatives say it's less moral. Society has a moral responsibility to protect unborn children. In a civilized society, no human being, even a mother, should have the absolute right of life and death over another human being.

Jack Danforth, former U.S. ambassador to the United Nations and three-term U.S. senator (R) from Missouri (and an ordained Episcopal priest), has jumped on the liberal bandwagon of criticizing conservatives for attempting to influence the Republican Party to adopt their views. Based on his views, I guess he would have been unhappy with the abolitionists who were the founding core of the Republican Party.

> Jack Danforth wishes the Republican right would step down from its pulpit. Instead, he sees a constant flow of religion into national politics. And not just any religion, either, but the us-versus-them, my-God-is-bigger-than-your-God, velvet-fist variety of Christian Evangelism.

As a mainline Episcopal priest, retired U.S. senator and diplomat, Danforth worships a humbler God and considers the right's certainty a sin. Legislating against gay marriage, for instance? "It's just cussedness." . . . Danforth is no squalling liberal. He is a lifelong Republican. And his own political history shows he is no milquetoast.

A man of God and the GOP, he is speaking out for moderation—in religion, politics, science and government. The lanky figure once dubbed "St. Jack," not always warmly, for the perch he seemed to occupy on Washington's moral high ground, expects people will sour on the assertive brand of Christianity so closely branded Republican.

"I'm counting on nausea," he says.[8]

When journalist Peter Slevin of the *Washington Post* asked me to comment on Danforth's remarks, I told him that votes reflect moral values, and the struggle for hearts and minds gets reflected in the ballot box. It sounded to me, I said, as if Danforth was sore that he lost the argument with a majority of the American people. Mr. Slevin quoted me on that, but he didn't include my response when he asked me about similar criticisms from President Jimmy Carter, my fellow Southern Baptist, criticizing people like me. I told him I guessed that President Carter liked democracy except in his own denomination, because the Southern Baptist Convention is a completely democratic institution. We have no hierarchy. We have no superstructure. Each church elects its own messengers, and they send them to the conventions where policy is made, budgets approved, and trustees elected. Those trustees elected by the church's messengers elected me to the presidency of the Ethics & Religious Liberty Commission. Apparently, the vast majority of people who call themselves Southern Baptist agree with the conservative positions rejected so dismissively by President Carter.

WHAT'S WRONG WITH BEING RIGHT?

It's a cheap shot to criticize the Right for narrowing the litmus test to abortion and gay marriage, because narrowing and prioritizing are two different things. Can there be a more compelling moral issue than three thousand six hundred babies dying every day? If a child is born poor, he at least has some chance of escaping poverty. If he is killed before he is born, he doesn't have a chance of escaping his mother's womb. And something no liberal wants to talk about is the statistic that black children are three times as likely to be aborted as white children. *That's* not an issue of grave moral concern? We lose more babies through abortion every year than the total fatalities in all of the wars in which we have ever participated, commencing with the French and Indian War and including the Revolutionary War, the War of 1812, the Civil War, the Spanish-American War, World War I, World War II, Korea, Vietnam, Gulf War I, and Gulf War II. What's wrong with religious people who are *not* making this their paramount issue?

Again, I would contend that supporting traditional marriage is not narrowing, but prioritizing. Marriage is the basic building block of human society.

A couple of years ago, I was lecturing at Harvard. During the question-and-answer period, a student asked me the following question concerning my opposition to same-sex marriage: "You seem like a nice guy. Why would you want to interfere in the personal, private relationship of two individuals?" I answered that marriage is anything but a personal, private relationship. That is one reason the state requires a license to get married. Marriage is a social and civic institution with profound social responsibilities, obligations, and impact. Every society in human history has severely regulated who may get married to whom, and under what circumstances they may dissolve the relationship, precisely because of this institution's enormous importance to the entire society. Same-sex marriage is a cultural and social issue with profound moral, social, and public policy implications.

I am stunned when someone *isn't* concerned about the threat of shattering the nation's social fiber by redefining marriage through judicial fiat against the will of the people. Even Supreme Court Justice Ruth Bader Ginsburg, probably the current Supreme Court's most liberal justice, has criticized *Roe v. Wade* as a misguided attempt to rewrite and liberalize the nation's abortion laws through judicial imposition rather than through a democratic movement to liberalize abortion through legislation.[9] Had such a popular movement succeeded, it would have built a more lasting consensus on social policy. Instead, the Supreme Court's rulings on abortion made the issue far more divisive than it otherwise would have been. If the courts try to force same-sex marriage on America, their judicial overreach will be equally destructive of the social fabric.

Just exactly what issue is it that Jack Danforth and his fellow critics would approve as suitably urgent for replacing abortion and same-sex marriage as top priorities?

Criticizing social conservatives for prioritizing opposition to abortion and same-sex marriage is like criticizing Martin Luther King Jr. for being "preoccupied" with racial reconciliation and social justice. Did Dr. King have other concerns? Yes. When he said his dream was a country in which people would be judged by the content of their character, not by the color of their skin, he wasn't exactly espousing a secular, relativist vision. What was his focus? He kept the main thing the main thing. The abolitionists in the nineteenth century kept the main thing the main thing. The twenty-first-century pro-lifers are keeping the main thing the main thing. What's wrong with the Danforths and the Carters for not keeping the main thing the main thing? The Bible specifically condemns the pagan practice of sacrificing children. I'm happy to be criticized for taking on the issue of abortion as a grave moral crisis.

It's funny how criticism that the Religious Right has been trying to take over the Republican Party usually comes from people who have lost power in it. Jack Danforth had no problem wielding the levers of power. Political parties are there to organize, to affect public policy, because elections have consequences. That is why the Republican Party was started—because neither of the two major parties would take a position against slavery.

The reason the Republican Party platform has a plank on abortion is that traditional Catholics and Protestant Evangelicals were increasingly anguished and outraged by the judicially-imposed declaration of open season on unborn babies. In America, we change public policy through a political vehicle called a political party. One party chose to be pro-life. The other party manifestly chose to be pro-abortion—so pro-abortion, in fact, that they wouldn't even let the pro-life governor of Pennsylvania, the late Bob Casey, speak at the 1992 Democratic National Convention in New York City. Casey was an indefatigable Democratic Party loyalist who was a natural choice to be a prominent speaker at the convention. Instead, he was denied a speaking role (one was given instead to a *Republican* woman from his home state who had campaigned against him), and he and his

Pennsylvania delegation were placed in a remote location in the Madison Square Garden arena.

Liberals can use loaded phrases such as "take over" and "wield the levers of power." I prefer the phrase "being salt and light." I prefer to speak of "seeking to change evil public policy," such as the policy of permitting and even subsidizing the wholesale taking of innocent human life. All the Democratic Party has to do to stop this tremendous electoral advantage for the Republicans is become pro-life. That's all. Then the two parties can compete over the best way to be pro-life in the same way that both parties are competing over the best way to bring about racial reconciliation. Both are committed to racial reconciliation. The only disagreement is over the best way to achieve it.

However, as long as one party remains a pro-life party and the other party remains a pro-choice or pro-abortion party, abortion will be a partisan issue. That's not the pro-lifers' fault. It's not the Republican Party's fault. It's the fault of people who want to deny an entire class of human beings (the unborn) Fundamental legal protections they rightly demand for themselves. It is the fault of people who, to protect abortion, have abandoned the Judeo-Christian and American belief in the profound, inherent, and equal dignity of each member of the human family. And it is the fault of the Democratic Party—and formerly pro-life politicians, such as Edward Kennedy, Jesse Jackson, Richard Gephardt, and Al Gore—for caving in to their pressure.

The Religious Left, such as Jimmy Carter, Jim Wallis, and Jack Danforth, like to refer to themselves as moderate Christians versus intolerant right-wingers. Are they more moderate in their theology? Yes. Are they more moderate in their behavior? I protest. When Jim Wallis writes a book called *God's Politics*, it would seem that he is proposing his own views as the answer to the question he raised in an earlier book, *Who Speaks for God?*[10]

Those who criticize the Religious Right for being intolerant sound distinctly intolerant while doing so. Noted legal scholar and author Stephen Carter has said that the one prejudice a person can safely get away with in America today is to stereotype, caricature, and be prejudiced against Evangelicals.

Liberals have been losing their grip on the levers of power. They have been challenged concerning the moral high ground in this society, and they are fiercely on the defensive. That is why they put up such a big fight over Samuel

Alito's Supreme Court nomination: they lost the Congress, they lost the presidency, and now they have lost their last refuge, the Supreme Court.

You can resist the will of the people for a while, but eventually the will of the people will prevail. Every two years President Carter, Senator Danforth, Jim Wallis, and their followers get an opportunity to make their arguments and convince the American people they're right. I'm perfectly content to leave the decision to the will of the people in every election cycle.

DOES ANYONE SPEAK FOR GOD?

With the end of the Civil War in sight, President Lincoln said that "with malice toward none, with charity for all, with firmness in the right as God gives us to see the right, let us strive on to finish the work we are in [i.e., the war]" (see appendix D).[11] He wasn't going to be paralyzed into inaction because he wasn't absolutely certain that God was on his side. He was going to do his very best to make sure that *he* was on *God's* side—then he was going to continue to move forward in the direction he felt God wanted him to go. Adopting such a posture is not assuming that God is on your side or that you are God's personal emissary.

However, it does assume that God has a side. God is not neutral about abortion. God is not neutral about marriage. God is not neutral about pornography. Conservatives believe that God has a side, that everything is not relative, that good and evil are real and it is possible to distinguish between them just as we distinguish between noonday and midnight. Moral issues cannot be neatly filed away under shades of gray. That is the big difference between liberals and conservatives.

Most conservatives do not automatically assume that God is on their side. They just assume that they have a right to bring their perspective to bear on public policy and to make their arguments—and if they can convince a majority of Americans that they're right, their view is going to prevail at least until the next election.

Former Senator Danforth says he hopes Republicans can run on what amounts to a liberal platform. Sure they can run, but they'll get clobbered.

Senator Arlen Specter ran for president as a "moderate" a few years ago and didn't even get out of the early primaries before he ran out of money and had to withdraw from the race from lack of support. What really upsets liberals is that 26 percent of the American people who voted in the last election identified themselves as Evangelicals, and 78 percent of them voted for George W. Bush. Liberals are irritated that the American people aren't listening to their supposed moral betters. Are liberals such as President Carter, Senator Danforth, and Jim Wallis arguing that God is on their side? Of course they are. They are doing everything they accuse the conservatives of doing.

Liberals like to accuse conservatives of imposing their religious moral values on others. Yet House Speaker Nancy Pelosi, then the House Democratic leader, mounted her moral Shetland pony and wagged an accusatory finger at the "immoral" Republican budget bill, urging a "no" vote as an act of worship.

> Mr. [David] Obey calls this "Scroogenomics." But really, associating Scrooge with this Republican budget gives Scrooge a bad name. The Scrooge saw the evil of his ways. The Republicans are so blinded by the greed of their special interest friends that they are stuck in their cruel ways. That is why leaders of every religious denomination have prayed in this rotunda, have prayed in churches across America, and as recently as a couple of days ago, more than 100 of them were arrested on the steps of the Cannon building to protest this budget. Religious denominations prayed and lobbied that Congress would do the right thing. They said that they were drawing a moral line in the sand against this budget. Democrats join them in drawing that line in the sand between a Republican government for the privileged few instead of a government for the many, which is the American way.

Having wrapped herself in the patriotic mantle by describing her position as the "American" way, implying that her opposition is "un-American," Minority Leader Pelosi tried to stake an exclusive claim to the moral high ground in a rather tit-for-tat reference to Christian values.

> Mr. Speaker, I associate myself with the gentlewoman from Florida, Ms. [Corrine] Brown, when she says, "shame." It is shameful that this Congress will

adjourn passing this immoral budget, meeting the greed of the special interest friends of the Republicans instead of the needs of the American people.

Mr. Speaker, as we leave for this Christmas recess, let us say, "God bless you" to the American people by voting against this Republican budget and statement of injustice and immorality, and let us not let the special interest goose get fat at the expense of America's children.

The gentleman from Washington, Mr. [Jim] McDermott, quoted the prophet Isaiah. And as the Bible teaches us, to minister to the needs of God's creation is an act of worship; to ignore those needs is to dishonor the God who made us. Let us vote no on this budget as an act of worship and for America's children.[12]

Presidential historian Paul Kengor points out that in the first three years of George W. Bush's presidency, President Bush invoked Jesus less than half as often in his public speeches as did President Clinton. In fact, Kengor notes, President Clinton's references to Jesus Christ always increased during election years. And Clinton felt free to invoke biblical passages in a kind of "How would Jesus vote?" encouragement to constituencies to vote for specific legislation.[13] Can you imagine if a Republican did that? The *Washington Post* would go into five-inch headlines.

I remember what my wife said to me when Bill Clinton became president: "The people who were sitting around in the sixties wearing peace symbols around their necks and smoking pot in psychedelically decorated VW vans are running the country now, aren't they?" I said to her, "Yes, dear, they are." Basically, the crux of the matter boils down to an enormous fault line: on one side are those with a traditional view of morality—some things are always right, and some things are always wrong—and on the other side are those who believe everything is relative, and therefore almost anything is permissible given the right circumstances in a world of peace and love. It's the difference between transcendent moral authority and subjective relativism.

This fault line is the frontline in the war of worldviews. One view posits that human nature is basically selfish and competitive as a consequence of what Christians call the sinful nature of fallen man. We have several millennia of evidence backing this up. The other view is still pushing the same tired old rhetoric: if only we could get back to the good old days of free love and world peace without all of these moralistic hate-mongers. And if people do bad things, it's because of their environment or emotional deprivation or deficient nurture during their formative years.

HAS GOD BLESSED AMERICA?

I was at a meeting with Jim Wallis when an audience member asked him to summarize the areas in which he and I agreed and disagreed.[14] Jim responded that we agree on the important role religion has to play in American society and culture—and together, we would disagree with the secularists in that respect. Then he responded that we disagree with each other on how that role is to be played out in American society and also in foreign policy. He did not believe in American exceptionalism, an American-imposed hegemony, or an American-imposed empire.

I responded that I did believe in American exceptionalism, but I didn't recognize it by Jim's definition. It is a doctrine of obligation, responsibility, sacrifice, and service in the cause of freedom, not a doctrine of pride, privilege, and empire. When Jim asked me what my scriptural reference for that was, I cited Luke 12:48: "From everyone who has been given much, much will be required; and to whom they entrusted much, of him they will ask all the more" (NASB).

I think most Americans—certainly significant majorities of traditional religious believers in Roman Catholicism and in both Evangelical and mainline Protestantism—would agree that America has been uniquely blessed. And if we say "blessed," then blessed by whom? If you believe in a Supreme Being, then you believe that God is the One who does the blessing. That makes it a providential blessing.

I believe God has providentially blessed the United States in unique ways, preserving us and protecting us, showering us with undeserved blessings. They are not merited, and we don't have the right to expect them. We didn't earn them. That's why they're called "blessings." Most of us live in houses we didn't build, drink from wells we didn't dig, eat from fields we didn't plant, and enjoy liberties we didn't risk our lives to defend.[15] All of these blessings have been poured out upon us as individuals and as a nation.

Many of us believe that this undeserved good fortune imposes upon America a special obligation and responsibility to be the friend of freedom, to be the friend of human rights in the world. We cannot have a foreign policy based solely on competing interests and shifting alliances, essentially amoral in nature. America must have a foreign policy. We are a nation with interests. It must never be forgotten, however, that we are also a cause, and that cause is freedom.

In her thoughtful and provocative book *The Mighty and the Almighty*, former secretary of state Madeleine Albright notes former president and founding father John Adams's distinction between liberty and democracy: "Liberty, at least in the sense of free will, is God's gift, not ours: it is also morally neutral. It may be used for any purpose, whether good or ill. Democracy, by contrast, is a human creation."[16] That distinction is an important one, because democracy can lead to mob rule or majority tyranny unless "its purpose is to see that liberty is directed into channels that respect the rights of all."[17]

Whenever the words *freedom* or *liberty* are referred to in this book, they are intended to be understood as a majority-determined government structure within each national society in the world that respects the rights of all, as defined by the Universal Declaration of Human Rights (see appendix E), and these rights are guaranteed by the rule of law, with full protection for individual and minority rights.

Liberals too often miss the rightness of basing a part of our foreign policy on the blessings that have been poured out upon us as a nation. And they fail to understand that this belief is not a doctrine of pride, privilege, and empire. It is not a belief that America is somehow God's chosen nation. Anybody can become an American. American exceptionalism is not based on ethnicity, race, or religion. It is a doctrine of obligation, responsibility, sacrifice, and service. And as former Secretary Albright has noted, "America has the right to share and support freedom, but must never assume the right to impose it on others."[18]

Liberals too often miss the fact that America has always been a profoundly religious country and that religion has always played a significant role in our history. When they ignore that reality, liberals too often go overboard in disavowing any kind of Christian heritage. The leftist magazine *Mother Jones* ran a special issue on the church-state controversy in which it warned of the dangers of those who are attempting to scale the wall of separation and plunder the pure secularism within.

"The government of the United States is not in any sense founded on the Christian Religion." Those words, penned in Article 11 of the 1797 Treaty of Tripoli, are as succinct a statement as we have from the Founding Fathers on the role of religion in our government. . . . It was debated in the U.S. Senate and signed into law by President Adams without a breath of controversy or complaint concerning its secular language, and so stands today as an official description of the founders' intent. . . . And it wouldn't stand a chance in the government of the country we've become. . . . [Some] among the faithful, uncomfortable with America from the start, saw secularism as the nation's fatal flaw, instead of its core strength, and have fought to transform the United States into an expressly Judeo-Christian nation. Recently, the inheritors of this viewpoint are prevailing. . . . It's been more than 200 years since the founders established the separation of church and state. The assault on that principle now under way promises to alter not only our form of government but our concept of religion as well.[19]

While it is true that America was not founded as a Christian nation, it was certainly founded by people who were operating out of a Judeo-Christian worldview, and the American government put in place by the Constitution was an attempt to wed Judeo-Christian values with Enlightenment ideas of self-government.

In his farewell address (1797), George Washington declared, "Of all the dispositions and habits which lead to political prosperity, religion and morality are indispensable supports. In vain would that man claim the tribute of patriotism who should labour to subvert these great pillars of human happiness."

Washington's successor, John Adams, reiterated the role of religion in our national life. In 1798 he explained, "We have no government armed in power capable of contending in human passions unbridled by morality and religion. . . . Our *Constitution* was made for a moral and a religious people. It is wholly inadequate for any other."[20]

President Kennedy once said, "The great enemy of truth is very often not the lie—deliberate, contrived, and dishonest, but the myth—persistent, persuasive, and unrealistic."[21] And one such persistent myth is that we cannot—or should not—legislate morality based on religious views, especially conservative Christian views. Yet a total separation of religiously informed morality and public policy debilitates moral values and public virtue as corrosively as a complete dominance of a church by the state or the state by a church diminishes personal and religious freedom.

Our forebears intended that the Constitution of the United States provide for a balance between religious morality and public virtue, and a separation of the "institution" of the church and the "institution" of the state. And that is what both sides are missing. Too many liberals are missing that separating religiously informed morality and public policy debilitates moral values and public virtue, and produces Richard John Neuhaus's "Naked Public Square."[22] It is important for conservatives not to miss the fact that allowing the state to dominate the church or the church to dominate the state can easily lead to the suppression of personal and religious freedom. This delicate constitutional balance, solidified and anchored by the First Amendment, is endangered at present, and it will not be put right unless people of faith insist upon it.

Quite a brouhaha resulted, by the way, when President George H. W. Bush said that with God's help America had prevailed in the Cold War. Most Americans believe that statement, yet the liberal intelligentsia went nuts. Too many liberals think even if God exists, He doesn't take sides in human conflicts. They would not want to attribute the fact that we won to God's having a preference.

We can't ever assume God is on our side just because we're America. We must do our best, as Lincoln said, to be on God's side. Most conservatives believe God had a side in the Cold War, and America was on it.

What's God got to do with America? Contrary to what many liberals think, quite a bit. Belief in God's special relationship with America is clearly part of our heritage and history, and we are all affected by heritage and history—both that of our families and that of our nation. It's part and parcel of who we are. We can't understand who we are, and who we are going to be, without understanding who we have been.

A significant majority of Americans say that religion is very important in their lives—and for a vast majority of those people, "religion" means either Catholic or Protestant Christianity. Upwards of 80 percent of Americans claim to believe in God. That's going to impact our society. The prevalence of religious belief seems to be increasing rather than decreasing. God matters to the vast majority of Americans. It is just wrong, factually and demonstrably, to deny that this has been, and is, the case.

Those of us who are Christians and believe that God has something to do with America need to assume that there are limits. We can't have a blurring of the distinction between America and Christianity. The blurring of national identity with Christian faith is what paved the way for National Socialism in Germany between 1933 and 1945. However, attempts to deny our heritage and to suppress religious belief are counterproductive and will lead to harsh reactions and bitter divisiveness, just as attempts to exclude people of no faith from participation in the public policy of the nation would be wrong and also would lead to serious repercussions.

Is it not better to respect each other's rights and to accommodate maximum plurality of religious expression in the public square, to foster public debate and discussion in which no one is discriminated against? The fact that people aren't discriminated against doesn't mean that decisions aren't made with which some people will be unhappy. Sometimes conservatives will be unhappy. Sometimes liberals will be unhappy. But when you have maximum accommodation of maximum expression and participation in the public square and the public policy debate, then even when you lose, you know that you have the right and the opportunity to live and fight another day and perhaps change the decision in the future.

This freedom for all views is by far the healthiest model we have yet discovered for maximizing protection of human rights. In other words, you are not discriminated against if you are defeated in a fair election. You are not being suppressed if you lose a fair election after an open, free, and spirited debate in the public square. The answer to losing is to make a more effective argument and convince more people, not attempt to get the government either to censor your opponents or to suppress their views.

However, this doesn't mean that God has *everything* to do with America, which some conservatives assume. Let's see what they're missing.

★ 3 ★

What Conservatives
Are Missing

To attack the [Confederate] flag is to deny the sovereignty, the majesty, and the might of the Lord Jesus Christ and his divine role in our history, culture, and life.
                                                                —JOHN WEAVER[1]

The phrase "God and country" means different things to different people, but when it is invoked to draw the color line between red and blue—while standing on the red side—it usually means something roughly like this: "God made this country great, and as long as we are a Christian nation, God is on our side." That's what the dude in the Dodge Ram pickup with the gun rack and the "God, Guns, 'n' Guts Made America Free!" bumper sticker would most likely say if we could ask him.

For a Christian, saying, "God is on our side," or "My country right or wrong," is idolatry, because that is making a god of one's nation. It is making patriotism one's god. As Jesus said, we must always render unto Caesar the things that are Caesar's and unto God the things that are God's.[2] Ultimate allegiance belongs to God. But God is not an American. He may choose to bless America or judge America, but He is not an American. Many Americans worship Him, but He is not an American. And America's purposes are not necessarily God's purposes. We must never presume that America's policies serve God's purposes.

The besetting sin of conservatives is to merge God and country as if they are virtually inseparable. A notable example of this error is proudly posted online by radio talk show host Chuck Baldwin, who quotes Pastor John Weaver of Georgia, a graduate in theology of Bob Jones University who has been preaching and teaching for thirty years. The following excerpt is from Pastor Weaver's sermon "The Truth about the Confederate Flag." Pastor Weaver is at pains to establish the justness of the South's cause as a revolt against the tyranny of the North—a battle of states' rights over a tyrannical and "unlimited" federal government.

When an uneducated man, one that could not write, needed to sign his name please tell me what letter he made? An "X," why? Because he was saying I am taking an oath under God. I am recognizing the sovereignty of God, the providence of God and I am pledging my faith. May I tell you the Confederate Flag is indeed a Christian flag because it has the cross of Saint Andrew, who was a Christian martyr, and the letter "X" has always been used to represent Christ, and to attack the flag is to deny the sovereignty, the majesty, and the might of the Lord Jesus Christ and his divine role in our history, culture, and life. . . . The Confederate Flag represents truth against error, freedom against tyranny, light against darkness and the Kingdom of Christ against the Kingdom of Governance.[3]

Notice how and with whom Weaver identifies the South as the "just" combatant in what he calls the "War of Northern Aggression," a term used by some Southerners in place of the Civil War or the War Between the States:

You see, we have forgotten the fact that the War of Northern Aggression was a cultural war. It was a religious war and the North was predominantly Unitarian and humanist, while the South was predominantly Christian. And in reality, the War was an attempt to crush Christianity and Christian culture. . . . What you and I need to do is this: we need to study our history. We need to study our heritage. We need to come back to the basics. We need to come back to our Christian roots. I want you to turn in your Bibles to Jeremiah 6. Let me close with this verse. Jeremiah Chapter 6:16, "Thus saith the Lord, Stand ye in the ways, and see, and ask for the old paths, where is the good way and walk therein and you shall find rest for your souls, but they (the wicked people) said, We will not walk (therein)." What did God say? God said, "Stand in the ways and see and ask for the old paths, wherein is the good way." Let me tell you something folks, I would trade the culture we have today in a heartbeat for the culture that the South had before the War of Northern Aggression.[4]

That's easy enough for Pastor Weaver to say, since he is white and would not be one of the three million African-Americans held in a horribly dehumanizing form of human bondage, and since he is a male and would not be a woman in a society where women couldn't vote and were second- or third-class citizens in virtually every important way anyone could imagine.

Weaver's views are the stuff of liberals' worst nightmares, and they have good reason to object to his prejudices. I and millions of my fellow Evangelical and Catholic social conservatives object to it because it is an egregious error to conflate the lordship of Jesus Christ and the authority of the Scriptures with the cause of fallen human beings—a grossly dubious cause, at that. The "old ways" to which the prophet Jeremiah was calling God's people were the ways of righteousness according to God's holy standards, not the days of white supremacy.

AMERICA'S GENETIC DEFECTS

During the Vietnam War era, the antiwar protests triggered a backlash reaction of "my country, right or wrong; love it or leave it." But loving America doesn't mean uncritically accepting everything this country does. It may mean that you don't leave it, but you do have both the right and the responsibility to criticize and to seek to reform it. There are times when you criticize those you truly love. If you "love" your country so much you never believe it to be wrong, you have fallen into idolatry.

For example, some Christians were on the wrong side of slavery, and some Christians were on the wrong side of segregation. They claimed erroneous interpretations of the Scriptures to support their views. Christians in the South claimed that slavery is in the Bible and God condones it in the God-blessed order of things. Some slavery advocates actually argued that slavery was a better system of labor management than the one that produced the industrial "wage slaves" of the North. As evidence to support their argument, they pointed to the desperately poor slums of New York and Chicago in the early Industrial Age.

In some cases, the proslavery advocates were accurate about the standard of living of some slaves versus that of some industrial workers in big-city slums, but that didn't make their argument right. Respected scholar Eugene Genovese, a cradle Catholic turned Marxist who returned to his Catholic faith later in life, provides a masterful analysis of how some Christians in the antebellum South mounted a defense of slavery on biblical grounds.[5] Anyone who thought that slavery would wither away of its own accord needs to read Genovese's *The Southern Front*, which profiles powerful and capable defenders of slavery whose erroneous understandings of the Bible led them to defend a status quo in which they were enmeshed.

When I was a boy growing up in Texas, I remember hearing segregation referred to as "our Southern way of life," and it was equated with godliness. It was wrong, and it needed to be denounced as wrong. I am forever grateful that I was taught by my godly Christian mother that racism is not only wrong, but sin, and contrary to true Christian faith.

I am not saying that there is always a clear right and wrong in every civil conflict. There were sincere Christians on opposite sides of the Revolutionary War. Many of those who argued against it landed in Canada after the war. But I think the clearest examples of wrongly conflating Christian faith with the American status quo are slavery and segregation. The first slaves came here in 1617. Slavery and racism have been defects in the American genetic code from our beginnings on this continent and led to our shameful treatment of Native Americans.

The racism of European whites against African- and Native Americans has been an enormous blind spot where Scripture was either not applied or hugely misapplied. Although hindsight is a tremendous advantage, I have to say our forefathers should have known better. Many of them did and spoke out against racism—men such as Roger Williams, Baptist pastor and founder of the Rhode Island colony, and David Brainerd, missionary to Native Americans. Williams treated the Native Americans with Christian compassion, and they took him in and treated him very differently than other whites of the colonial era. He was nearly sent back to England in chains when he insisted the colonists didn't own the land because they had obtained it by patent from the king and hadn't paid the Indians for it.[6]

So here we have Roger Williams, invoked today as someone who taught that religion has no place in politics, up to his colonial eyebrows in the most controversial social and public policy issue of early-seventeenth-century America: the colonists' shameful treatment of Native Americans. He also said that the Church of England was not a true church, so one shouldn't attend its churches or pay taxes to it. And he believed Church of England ministers were not true ministers, so one should not listen to them preach. But foremost in the Bill of Indictment against Roger Williams was his insistence that the colonists didn't own the land and hadn't paid the Indians for it. When he escaped into the bitter winter of the New England wilderness, the Indians took him in. They knew a friend when they saw one. Roger Williams believed in the separation of church and state—his metaphor was the garden of the church and the wilderness of the world,[7] but his actions indicate clearly that he didn't believe in the separation of Christian faith from public policy.

WATCHING THE BOUNDARIES

It is not heretical to display the Christian flag along with the American flag in a church auditorium—as long as the church members' primary allegiance is to the Christian flag and their secondary allegiance is to the American flag.

In my childhood, I attended Training Union (now called Discipleship Training) every Sunday night before church. We pledged allegiance to the Christian flag, to the Bible, and to the American flag. It was made very clear to whom ultimate allegiance belonged: first to the Bible and to the Christian flag, and then to America. And as long as that is the proper order and priority, there is no problem with flying the flags together.

In this country, we have never had an official relationship whereby the government has placed the flag in the churches. Here, if the U.S. flag is in a church, it is because the church members have chosen to place it there. That's very different than in European countries, where the flag was often placed in churches by the government because the government owned the church. Only one major country in Western Europe is purely secular—France. In England, Germany, Italy, Spain, and the Scandinavian countries, an official relationship exists between the church and the state.

Nevertheless, it is important for Christians to be reminded regularly and vigorously that their primary allegiance is to God, not country. Francis Schaeffer made this point forcefully to American Evangelicals in *The Church at the End of the Twentieth Century* (1970):

> In the United States many churches display the American flag. The Christian flag is usually put on one side and the American flag on the other. Does having the two flags in your church mean that Christianity and the American establishment

are equal? If it does, you are really in trouble. These are not two equal loyalties. . . . Caesar is second to God. This must be preached and taught in sermons, Sunday school classes, and young people's groups.

It must be taught that patriotic loyalty must *not* be identified with Christianity. As Christians we are responsible, under the Lordship of Christ in all of life, to carry the Christian principles into our relationship to the state. But we must not make our country and Christianity to be synonymous.[8]

For conservatives, watching the church-state boundaries means resisting the temptation to perceive Americans as God's chosen people and America as God's chosen nation. It means rejecting attempts to analogize God and Israel to God and America. Americans are not God's chosen people. America is not God's chosen nation. Although God may have a great deal to do with our history, and although God's involvement with America may put a special claim on America to stand for truth, righteousness, and liberty in the world, that does not in any way mean that America is somehow a privileged nation with a unique relationship to God. The argument that God has a special role for America to play in the world is a doctrine of obligation, responsibility, sacrifice, and service, not pride, privilege, and arrogance.

"God, guts, 'n' guns made this country free!" is national pride raised to the point of idolatry. It's as if I were born on third base and I thought I hit a triple. What did I have to do with being born American? What did any one of us have to do with being born American? We live in houses we didn't build. We drink from wells we didn't dig. As noted earlier, we eat from fields we didn't plant. I grew up in a working-class home, and I had more blessings and privileges poured out on me just by the providence of being born in the mid-twentieth-century United States than most human beings have had in the history of the human race. Those blessings impose responsibility and obligation.

God has had, and does have, something to do with America—and we have to assume that He will in the future because of the vast numbers of people of religious faith in this country. What many liberals are missing is the danger, the wrongness, the central unfairness of attempting to emasculate, eviscerate, censor, or suppress religious expression in the public square, particularly in an overwhelmingly religious country. What many conservatives are missing is that they too often tend to blur and merge the identity of Christianity and God with America—that's idolatry. Idolatry leads to worship of the state. It leads to suppression of minority viewpoints. Government shouldn't be discriminating either in favor of or against religion. Instead, government should be accommodating a maximum range of views in the public square.

Any attempt to restore government-sponsored religious observances, such as if the government were to mandate Christian prayer in schools, would inevitably lead to violations of individual freedom and freedom of conscience. That's the problem with saying, "We have to bring God back into the schools."

It may be true that we need to get God back into this country, or get this country back to God, but it's wrong to assume that the government is a legitimate or an effective means of accomplishing such a goal. The government shouldn't do it, and the government *can't* do it. To get God back into America, you need to get an acceptance of God back into individual Americans' hearts and minds, one at a time. If your goal is like mine—an American society that affirms and practices Judeo-Christian values rooted in biblical authority—then there is no substitute for getting a majority of Americans to affirm Judeo-Christian values rooted in biblical authority. You can't do that by mandating prayer and Bible reading in public schools. You can't get there by allowing the government to favor Christianity over other faiths. You can't do it by mandating government penalties for spiritual infractions of the Christian faith. You're going to have to have a significant majority of Americans who are seeking to lead lives that are pleasing to God and who are affirming Judeo-Christian values rooted in biblical authority.

Christian conservatives' first allegiance must be to God. And they must be very careful to avoid violating the rights of others who are not believers by getting government on the side of religion at the expense of nonreligion. I don't think it is constitutionally sound or preferable for America to say to its citizens, "Now we're going to say this prayer every morning." I grew up with that as a student in public schools that overtly embraced the Christian faith, and it was wrong. It was government affirmation of a majority religion—which meant necessarily there wasn't equal freedom for other religions. Every morning in the schoolroom, we started with the Pledge of Allegiance to the flag, and then we prayed the Lord's Prayer. In my case, this happened in junior high and senior high schools that were 30 percent Jewish. Nonetheless, each morning we prayed, "Our Father, who art in heaven . . . ," led by the principal, assistant principal, or the homeroom teacher. By doing so we violated the constitutional rights of all those Jewish students as well as the rights of all students of other faiths or no faith.

Unfortunately, the Supreme Court decisions abolishing these practices, along with mandatory Bible reading, didn't occur until the early 1960s.

WHEN GOD IS ON OUR SIDE

The concept that "God is on our side" has a unique history in the United States, but it is not unique to our country, nor is it unique to Christendom: just dip into the history of Catholicism during the Inquisition or Christians and Muslims in the Crusades or government persecution of Catholics and Jews by England's Protestants or persecution of religious minorities in Lutheran Europe and Calvin's Geneva, and you can see the historical tendency for a religious majority to dominate the public square in a way that eventually leads to a form of theocratic Fundamentalism.

The temptation to presume upon God to support a nationalistic agenda has plenty of historical precedents. Not many people are aware, however, of how self-professing Christians stepped into this trap in Nazi Germany. Gregory Paul points out that most people mistakenly think the Nazi movement was rooted primarily in paganism and the occult:

> During the same years neopagan and occult movements gained adherents and incubated their own form of Aryanism. Unlike Aryan Christians, neopagan Aryans acknowledged that Christ was a Jew—and for that reason rejected Christianity. They believed themselves descended from demigods whose divinity had degraded through centuries of interbreeding with lesser races. The Norse gods and even the Atlantis myth sometimes decorated Aryan mythology. Attempting to deny that Nazi anti-Semitism had a Christian component, Christian apologists exaggerate the influence of Aryan neopaganism. Actually, neopaganism never had a large following.
>
> German Aryanism, whether Christian or pagan, became known as "*Volkism.*" *Volkism* prophesied the emergence of a great God-chosen Aryan who would lead

the people (*Volk*) to their grand destiny through the conquest of *Lebensraum* (living space). A common motto was "God and *Volk*." Disregarding obvious theological contradictions, growing numbers of German nationalists managed to work Aryanism into their Protestant or Catholic confessions, much as contemporary adherents of *Voudoun* or *Santería* blend the occult with their Christian beliefs. Darwinian theory sometimes entered *Volkism* as a belief in the divinely intended survival of the fittest peoples. Democracy had no place, but Nietzschean philosophy had some influence—a point Christian apologists make much of. Yet Nietzsche's influence was modest, as *Volkists* found his skepticism toward religion unacceptable.[9]

A provocative film, *Theologians under Hitler*, based on a book by the same title by Robert P. Ericksen of Pacific Lutheran University, tells the story of how many in the German church not only capitulated to, but even supported, the Nazis.[10] It traces the careers of three of the most prominent Protestant scholars of the twentieth century who became enmeshed with the Nazi movement and to varying degrees became spokesmen for the Nazi cause: Paul Althaus (1888–1966), Emanuel Hirsch (1888–1972), and the renowned Gerhard Kittel (1888–1948), whose *Theological Dictionary of the New Testament* is still in use as one of the most important works of biblical scholarship of the twentieth century.

How is it that the very professors and theologians we would expect to see through the corrupt and unbiblical positions of Adolf Hitler and National Socialism were the ones corrupted and co-opted by them?

The complicity of large numbers of German church leaders and ordinary German church members in the horror of what transpired in Germany under National Socialism (Nazism) between 1933 and 1945 should serve as a sobering warning and a timeless cautionary tale of what can happen when Christians of any era, confession, or nationality lose their Christocentric focus of authority.

The dark tragedy of German Christianity under Hitler underscores dramatically what can happen when Christians allow their religious faith to be eviscerated by liberal theology and/or elevate their nationalism to the level of idolatry.

As *Theologians under Hitler* points out, the eighteenth-century Enlightenment, the so-called Age of Reason, enticed many Europeans to seek to "free humanity from superstition and religious dogma and draw humanity to a life built upon pure reason."[11] Nineteenth-century liberal theologians such as Friedrich Schleiermacher (1768–1834) and Albrecht Ritschl (1822–1889) "sought to make Christian theology palatable to those who pursued a reasonable faith."[12]

Under the tutelage of such liberal theologians, the church "began to wrestle with some of the peculiarities of its scriptures," since "teachings about a man who walked on water and raised the dead were perceived as embarrassments."[13] As *Theologians under Hitler* explains, "Throughout the nineteenth century teachers of the church went about the noble task of searching for a Christianity that could finally be embraced by rational, thinking people."[14]

As a result, significant segments of German and European Christianity, attempting "to address the concerns raised by the Enlightenment in Europe, created a portrait of Jesus as the ultimate moral guide and teacher."[15] Having compromised the miracles of Jesus and vitiated the authoritative nature of the Bible, European Christianity increasingly came to mean "to have faith in a mythological figure that represented the best and brightest of humanity."[16] This "mythological" Jesus often bore little, if any, resemblance to the promised Messiah and Savior of the New Testament who made compelling and exclusive truth claims rejected by the Enlightenment.

Such a weakened, fatally compromised faith was far more easily seduced by an idolatrous nationalism than the traditional, orthodox faith symbolized by the Confessing Church that produced the Barmen Declaration (see appendix B) in 1934 in response to Hitler and the Nazi-inspired German Christian (*Deutsche Christen*) movement. The Confessing Church supporters, who resisted the blandishments of Hitler and the Nazis, were "traditional in their religious beliefs."[17] In other words, they were the German Christians, led by Karl Barth, Dietrich Bonhoeffer, and Martin Niemöller, who believed that the foundation of the Christian church consisted of "the traditional teachings of the church and the reliance on the Bible and the Scriptures and the confessions of the church."[18]

Germany was arguably the most scientifically, culturally, educationally, and medically advanced society in the world in the 1930s, and yet it succumbed to the idolatry of an evil, twisted nationalism known as Nazism. How could this have happened?

Germany, like much of Western civilization, was struggling with the loss of traditional lifestyles and values precipitated by the rapid industrialization of the late nineteenth and early twentieth centuries. The average German in the early twentieth century "was searching for a solid foothold while the sands shifted beneath his feet."[19] Then came the horrific catastrophe of World War I (1914–1918)—a crushing military defeat (with two million dead German soldiers), a political revolution (November 1918) that forced the abdication of Kaiser Wilhelm II, and a humiliating and punitive peace treaty (Versailles) that crippled the nation. The only political system (the Hohenzollern dynasty) most Germans had ever known, or could have imagined, was gone with the wind.

Germany was in the midst of this profound national crisis. Living under a weak parliamentary democracy known as the Weimer Republic, which many Germans did not support and further viewed as an imposition of the victorious Allies, Germans of many segments of society, theologians prominent among them, searched for meaning, purpose, and hope for the future. Indeed, as Dr. Hartmut Lehmann of Goettingen University has explained, "Much of the theology of the 1920s was to explain to the German people that they were God's chosen people after all, that covenant had a meaning, and then prepare for a new revival, for a new reawakening, a rebirth of the Germans."[20]

The deadly combination of theological liberalism, German nationalism, abject military defeat, and massive cultural trauma proved to be a poisonous witch's brew, which bedazzled a nation and led them to the depths of degradation and ruin.

As one student of the period has observed:

Germany was the headquarters of classical theological liberalism, and . . . this movement was in the last stages of its ascendancy in Germany during the period. . . . This theological liberalism—with its loss of confidence in biblical authority, its loss of commitment to biblical fidelity, its faltering belief in the transcendent, holy God who took flesh in Jesus Christ the Jew, its weakened sense of the distinct identity and mission of the church, its openness to all manner of theological experimentation, and its lack of spiritual vitality—weakened the resistance of the German churches to Nazism. Such an accusation . . . emerged from within Germany itself, from such theological giants as Karl Barth and others who became involved in the Confessing Church movement during the years of the Nazi regime.[21]

This theological liberalism contributed significantly to a substantial conflation of traditional German culture and the Christian faith. As Ericksen observed, the German church's fatal flaw was "its failure to distinguish adequately between Christian values and German values, between inherently Christian concerns and inherently patriotic concerns."[22] When one considers a sampling of the statements from some of Germany's leading theologians, Ericksen's description is dramatically understated.

A substantial, if not total, identification of Christianity with the German *Volk* (and National Socialism) is seen in the response of Paul Althaus, a world-renowned Luther scholar, to the Nazi ascension to power in January 1933.[23] In October of that year, Althaus published *The German Hour of the Churches* (*Die deutsche Stunde der Kirche*), an enormously popular book "which went through three editions over the next year."[24]

In the book's opening sentence, Althaus declares (concerning Hitler's becoming chancellor), "Our Protestant churches have greeted the turning point of 1933 as a gift from God's own hand."[25] Althaus believed that the rise of National Socialism to power meant "that theology and nationalism and church and state should literally meld together in the service of national pride and renewal."[26] Incredibly, for Althaus in 1933, "faith in God also meant faith in Adolph Hitler."[27] As Dr. Hermann Lichtenberger of Tubingen University explained, "Althaus couldn't resist this seduction to find in Hitler and his adherents some sort of reformation of the German society and the German state."[28]

When the Confessing Church issued a clarion call to rally against such nationalistic seductions at Barmen in 1934, Althaus opposed them in written publications, denouncing the Barmen Declaration as "an attempt to stem the positive side . . . of patriotism, pride, and moral reform that had come to the *Volk* through the Nazi Party and Hitler."[29] In 1935 Althaus reiterated his support of National Socialism:

> We may express our thankfulness and joyful readiness for that which manifests a will for the genuine brotherhood of blood brothers in our new order of the *Volk*.
> . . . We Christians know ourselves bound by God's will to the promotion of National Socialism, so that all members and ranks of the *Volk* will be ready for service and sacrifice to one another.[30]

Althaus was hardly alone among German Christian leaders. As Dr. Hartmut Lehmann of Goettingen University explains, many German sermons and pamphlets appeared in which "Hitler was compared to Luther as the new big reformer of the Germans . . . You had Luther celebrations in 1933 in which Luther and Hitler were put into one basket as the great instruments of God through which God elevated the Germans in the right direction."[31]

An even more fervent supporter of National Socialism was Emanuel Hirsch, "the leading Kierkegaard expert of his generation in Germany."[32] In 1920 Hirsch wrote *Germany's Fate* (*Deutschlands Schicksal*), a popular book that went through several editions and printings over the decade. Hirsch's ardent nationalism permeates *Germany's Fate*:

> One describes Germany today most correctly as a colony of the Entente with sharply restricted self-government. . . . We were a world *Volk*, a noble *Volk*, perhaps the most flourishing and best of all. We now stand in danger of being humiliated or even destroyed as a *Volk*, so that only a formless mass of workers in the service of foreign interests remains.[33]

In 1933 Hirsch responded to Hitler's ascension to power by describing it "as a sunrise of divine goodness after endless dark years of wrath and misery." Hirsch officially joined the Nazi Party on May 1, 1937, and in 1939 reiterated his melding of being German and being Christian:

> There exists between German *Volkstum* and Christian belief absolutely no division or contradiction to make it difficult as a German to be a Christian, or as a Christian a German. . . . Whoever says differently, of him it means: either he misuses Christianity to anti-German purposes, or he has come to an incorrect judgment about Christianity through some other such misuse.[34]

A 1931 academic controversy in which Hirsch became involved reveals both his fatal susceptibility to excessive nationalism and the fact that there were German theology professors speaking out even before Hitler came to power. In 1928 a theologian and pastor, Günther Dehn (1882–1970), spoke out against glorification of nationalism and war and asked whether there should be monuments honoring the war dead in the churches. He was criticized by church authorities but still received a professorial appointment, first at Heidelberg and then at the University of Halle in 1931.[35]

Dehn was severely criticized by his more stridently nationalist colleagues and students. In December 1931 Dehn responded by launching a blistering attack on his opponents:

> It could be that the church of today stands on the threshold of a most difficult struggle with modern nationalism, in which her very existence will be endangered. . . . Here resistance must be given. . . . Distorted idealism is demonic. It is simply not true that this fanatical love of fatherland, which in my view is colored by religion, but actually dissociated from God, really helps the fatherland. On the contrary, it will lead the fatherland into destruction.[36]

How chillingly prophetic Dehn's words would prove in subsequent years! Hirsh, however, felt that Dehn's views disqualified Dehn from teaching German youth because such teachers must have

> the recognition that the nation and its freedom . . . remains for the Christian a good thing hallowed by God. It demands a complete devotion of the heart and the life. And from this recognition follows an endorsement of the passionate will to freedom of our *Volk*, which is being enslaved and violated by enemies hungry for power and possessions.[37]

And in 1933 Gerhard Kittel, a more prominent scholar than either Althaus or Hirsh, delivered a lecture titled "The Jewish Question" ("*Die Judenfrage*"), which was published and widely disseminated. Kittel argued that the "Jews represented a threat to the unity and strength of Germany" and that they must be reduced to "guest status" in Germany, segregated and ostracized from German society. Such views were codified in the 1935 Nuremberg Laws, and Kittel "became one of the most viscously anti-Semitic leaders within the Christian Church in support of the Nazi ideology."[38] Gerhard Kittel was found guilty of having assisted the Nazis in their "Final Solution," which resulted in the death of more than six million of Europe's Jews. He was imprisoned for seventeen months.[39]

As mentioned earlier, to counter these alarming developments, a group of church delegates known as the "Confessing Church pastors"—including Martin Niemöller, Karl Barth, and Dietrich Bonhoeffer—gathered in the Rhineland at Barmen on May 29, 1934, soon after the Nazis came to power. They formulated the Barmen Declaration, which served as the foundation for the Confessing Church movement (see appendix B). Its six-point statement of Evangelical confessions provides a marvelous description of the separation of church and state. Each of the statements begins with an anchoring Scripture passage, follows with a brief exposition, and concludes with an application. Its key themes include the following:

- The voice of Christ in the Word of God as the sole, final authority for the church: "We reject the false doctrine, as though the Church could and would have to acknowledge as a source of its proclamation, apart from and besides this one Word of God, still other events and powers, figures and truths, as God's revelation."
- The lordship of Jesus Christ over all of life: "We reject the false doctrine, as though there were areas of our life in which we would not belong to Jesus Christ, but to other lords—areas in which we would not need justification and sanctification through him."
- The separate functions of state and church: "We reject the false doctrine, as though the State, over and beyond its special commission, should and could become the single and totalitarian order of human life, thus fulfilling the Church's vocation as well. We reject the false doctrine, as though the Church, over and beyond its special commission, should and could appropriate the characteristics, the tasks, and the dignity of the State, thus itself becoming an organ of the State."[40]

What inoculated and protected the Confessing Church from the snare of German nationalism, from the egregious doctrine of Aryan racial superiority, and from supine subservience to Hitler? What protected the Confessing Church from the twin seductions of liberal, relativist theology and nationalist idolatry was that these "confessing" Christians embraced a doctrine of divine revelation and authority that affirmed the primacy of the truth claims of Jesus of Nazareth.

Dr. Hermann Lichtenberger's description of Karl Barth's "doctrine of revelation" is both an accurate summary of the Confessing Church's position and a vivid description of the Christocentric focus that protects loyal disciples of Jesus from idolatries of the left, the right, or the center:

> Jesus Christ is the only revelation and there is nothing else revealed: nothing—not the *Volk*, not the state, not anything like that is of divine order. It is human work, and is to be seen as human and Barth therefore could resist because of his theological concept of revelation.[41]

Unlike Dietrich Bonhoeffer, his fellow Barmen colleague who was imprisoned and executed for his complicity in the plot to assassinate Hitler, Barth, a German-speaking Swiss citizen, survived World War II to become one of the most influential theologians of the twentieth century. During the Nazi regime, he was stripped of his university professorship because of his refusal to swear a loyalty oath to Hitler.

What happens when Christians don't stand up and make a difference in the world? The conservative liability is to conflate nationalism with God's cause. The liberal liability is such weak belief in God that it slides into relativism. The answer is the Christocentric theology that Barth espoused and that Evangelical Christians are supposed to espouse—but many of them, perhaps without being aware of it, have shifted from a Christocentric to an America-centric theology. This is what conservatives too often miss in the God-and-country shouting match.

A RETURN TO "CHRISTIAN AMERICA"?

My friend Dr. D. James Kennedy, pastor of Coral Ridge Presbyterian Church in Fort Lauderdale, Florida, has scared liberals by deploring Jefferson's introduction of "the wall of separation between church and state" as a way of applying the First Amendment to the Constitution. He and other conservative leaders, such as Jerry Falwell and Pat Robertson, would argue for the notion of a "Christian America."

The principle established in 1947, when the U.S. Supreme Court announced, for the first time in American jurisprudence, that the "First Amendment has erected a wall between church and state" continues to work its mischief today. Millions are offended and troubled, and our nation's identity as a nation under God is assailed by yet another misdirected and frivolous attempt to purge the public square of any reference to God, no matter how slight.

It is increasingly clear that we are a nation at odds with ourselves and our history. On three separate occasions, the Supreme Court has ruled that America is a Christian nation. The Court's 1892 determination that "this is a Christian nation," was followed in 1931 by a subsequent ruling that Americans are a "Christian people" and, again in 1952, when Justice William O. Douglas, writing for the Court, said that "we are a religious people and our institutions presuppose a Supreme Being."[42]

I am absolutely certain that Dr. Kennedy does not envision an American version of the German Christian movement or anything remotely similar to it. Still, I am concerned that his vision could be manipulated by others to justify inappropriate governmental interference in matters of faith.

Although I would disagree with Dr. Kennedy that it would be theologically and politically accurate to call America a "Christian nation," he is hardly arguing for the hardcore theocracy of religious extremists in so-called dominion theology or Christian reconstructionism, such as the late R. J. Rushdoony and Gary North. This fringe movement, explicitly opposed to democratic means of government, has been largely responsible for the fantasy that if the Religious Right prevails, then the United States of America is headed into theocratic Fundamentalism. That idea is "nuts"—a bogeyman scenario cooked up by secularists who paint the opposition with one big brushstroke.

Stephen Carter points out the fallacy of lumping together all people of faith into one basket of fanaticism:

It is easy to paint people who put God first as dangerous fanatics, but, from the point of view of the believer, the fanatic is the one so certain that the state is right that he is willing to use the law to interfere with religious belief. To take a simple example, I am not sure why it is more "fanatical" for parents to tell their children that the creation story in Genesis is literally true than for the public schools to tell the same children, required by law to attend, that the religion of their parents is literally false. Or why it is more "fanatical" to criticize the culture for not reflecting a particular religious view on, say, the role of women than to criticize a religion for not reflecting the culture's views on the same thing. In short, the danger, if there is one, is mutual.[43]

One of the reasons I would not join Dr. Kennedy's call for a "Christian America" is that it can too easily lead to government establishment of religion. Not many people know that the rise of Catholic parochial schools in this country happened not because Catholics woke up one day and decided to create their own private schools, but because our government was using the public schools to try to Protestantize Catholic kids back in the nineteenth century.

In the 1850s there was a virulent form of anti-Catholic sentiment in a movement popularly called the "Know-Nothings," a semisecret society whose members committed themselves to reply, when asked about their movement, "I know nothing." This movement was fueled by suspicion that the political activity of Irish-Catholic immigrants was secretly machinated by the pope. Protestant fear of the "papists" conjured up the conspiracy theory that the pope was planning to take over America and destroy our democracy through his network of bishops, priests, and church followers whose allegiance lay not with the United States, it was supposed, but with the Vatican. (Of course, it didn't help that certain popes in church history had made a name for themselves by wielding worldly power with an otherworldly zeal.)

To protect against what they perceived to be a Catholic threat to American freedom, the Know-Nothings advocated policies such as placing Protestant-only teachers in public schools; restricting any political office to native-born Americans, not immigrants; making immigrants wait twenty-one years before they could become citizens; and instituting daily Bible readings in public schools from the Protestant version of the Bible only.

This push for Protestantization wasn't a desire for godly living so much as it was intolerance and bigotry: "This is a Protestant country, and we're going to keep it that way." It started as a backlash against the successive waves of Catholic immigration, mainly from Ireland and Italy. Many were deeply concerned that they were being invaded by Catholicism, so they wanted to use the public school systems to Protestantize Catholics.

This extreme Protestantization wasn't very prevalent in the South because there weren't very many Catholic immigrants in the South. It happened primarily in the Northeast, and it spilled over into violent riots in Philadelphia. In the 1850s it led to the rise and fall of a third political party, a burgeoning coalition of anti-immigrant, anti-Catholic hostility. We're still smarting from the wounds inflicted by this controversy, not only in the history of violating Catholics' civil rights, but in the resistance to any kind of religious expression in public schools lest it lead to this kind of trouble once more. Hence, what is known as the "avoidance" position on religion in the public square was spawned.

TRUE PLURALISM

When my Jewish classmates were expected to recite the Lord's Prayer in public school classrooms in the 1950s and 1960s, that was just plain wrong. It was an expression of the government-led "acknowledgment" (i.e., affirmation) position on church and state relations. What we need is "accommodation" (of individuals' right to public religious expression)—a middle way between "avoidance" (strict separation) and "acknowledgment" (government affirmation) (see appendix F).

At former President Clinton's Inaugural Global Initiative in New York,[44] I was asked to comment on models for separation of church and state. I explained that there are three main ways in which society tends to organize the religious impulse in human experience. The first is the theocratic impulse, exemplified by the Iranian mullahs who require women to wear Muslim headscarves. Next there is the secularist impulse, which idealizes secularism as the supreme virtue. This position is exemplified by France, which recently ruled that Muslim schoolgirls are prohibited from wearing headscarves—and Jewish boys are prohibited from wearing yarmulkes, and Christians may not wear crosses unless they are of a small, prescribed size—because any religious symbolism in personal attire is banned from public schools. Then there is the pluralist model, exemplified by the United States, where it was recently ruled in Muskogee, Oklahoma, about as deep in red-state America as you can get, that Muslim girls are free to choose whether or not they wear their headscarves to school. The theocratic model constitutes the acknowledgment position, the secularist model represents the avoidance position, and the pluralist model is based on the accommodation position.

That is what pluralism is all about—government accommodation of *all* people's rights to express, or to refrain from expressing, religious convictions and religious beliefs. The government doesn't require anyone to wear yarmulkes or crosses or say the Lord's Prayer, but neither does it forbid anyone to do so just because he or she happens to be on public school property. True pluralism celebrates the basis for Christmas in Christian faith, but it also celebrates Hanukkah if there are Jewish students in school and Ramadan if there are Muslim students. (See appendix A, "A Modest Proposal for Religious Accommodation.")

When John Kerry said in the 2004 presidential debates that he didn't have the right to impose his religious beliefs, to a certain degree he was right. Imposition of religious belief is certainly what we had when the government was requiring children to recite, "Our Father, who art in heaven . . ." An example of government imposition of religion would be if between downs of a public school football game a government-sponsored statue of the Virgin Mary was paraded on the field and/or government-promoted Billy Graham announcements were posted on the scoreboard. That would be imposing religious beliefs by declaring in effect that the pope and Billy Graham have a government-sponsored, privileged right to have their religious views promulgated.

However, Kerry's comments about not imposing his religious beliefs were in the context of a discussion about abortion, and in that respect he was wrong. It's one thing to agitate for the government to grant privileged status to one's faith, or to religion in general—that is seeking to have the government impose one's faith on others. It is an entirely different thing for a citizen, even an elected official, to have a religiously informed belief that abortion is the taking of an unborn human life and that no human being, not even a mother, should have an absolute right of life and death over another human being. Arguing that abortion should be severely restricted in America, and that society has a right to protect unborn children and to determine if and when their lives can be terminated, is not imposing one's religious beliefs on others, but bringing one's religiously informed moral values to public policy discussions. It could be argued, and it is argued by pro-life advocates, that the current abortion-on-demand legal regime in America has millions of mothers imposing their moral values on their unborn children—and it is always a fatal imposition, because the baby always dies.

AMERICA: MORE SECULAR OR MORE RELIGIOUS?

Interestingly, America *is* getting both more secular and more religious at the same time. Trends show that more and more Americans are taking religion very seriously in their lives, and the form of religion they are taking very seriously is, more often than not, a conservative Evangelical Christianity, a more traditional Catholicism, or a more traditional Judaism. At the same time, there has been a collapse of the Judeo-Christian consensus on social mores so that we no longer have constraints—neither government constraints nor informal social constraints—on living any way we desire. In consequence, the country is getting more and more devout, more and more traditional in its faith, but that trend is camouflaged by a significant measure of pagan behavior among people who have no internal reason to live by any religiously informed moral code.

For example, consider illegitimacy. When I was in high school in the 1960s, if a girl got pregnant, she just disappeared. I'm not suggesting that was the right course of action for the girl; I'm just commenting on the social sensitivity to the underlying issue. A girl pregnant out of wedlock was in school one day and out the next. She was sent either to a home or to a distant relative, and people suspected that something might be amiss because she just disappeared. Now public schools have nurseries for children of girls who have babies out of wedlock. I certainly prefer the presence of such nurseries if it encourages girls not to abort their babies; however, the loss of social stigma attached to out-of-wedlock pregnancies fosters a far greater incidence of illegitimacy and immorality—illegitimacy and immorality that are tragic for the babies, their parents, and the society at large.

It used to be that there were social—not legal—penalties for certain types of immoral behavior. Philanderers who cheated on their wives and then divorced them paid social and professional penalties. Now there are few penalties in the public square. In America prior to the 1960s, there was plenty of external pressure, as well as possible internal motivation, to live within certain social and moral boundaries. Those pressures have all but disappeared.

Sure, such pressures fostered some hypocrisy and sometimes caused people to do the right things for the wrong reasons, but was this country a better place for children? Yes. Virtually no research indicator would disagree. Most children had a mom and a dad who lived in the home and were married to each other. Were they always happily married? No. But then, nobody is claiming that no-fault divorce has led to more happiness—marital or otherwise. Was there a lot of hypocrisy? Sure. But there was also a lot more willingness to endure hardship with the attitude, "We're in this for the long haul; we'd better make it work." Today there is a terrible temptation to just cut and run. This should not be interpreted as an encouragement to spouses to endure physical or sexual abuse in the home. Wives exposed to such violence should immediately seek safety for themselves and their children.

Was pre-1960s America a more comfortable place for men who wanted to trade in their wives for a younger model with no penalties and no price? No. Was it a more accomodating place for people who wanted to break their promises and not fulfill their obligations and walk away from their responsibilities? No, it wasn't an accepting place for them.

Were the 1940s and '50s perfect? Of course not. In particular, they weren't perfect for ethnic minorities and women—but a strong case can be made that by and large, even if numerous wrongs were occurring unchecked, women and children were better off. Were women discriminated against? Yes. Were they patronized? Yes. Were they beaten up and abused and abandoned? Not with anywhere near the regularity they are today. Were they sexually exploited and abandoned? Not nearly as badly as they are today. Were girls sexually abused and molested with the regularity that they are today? Not nearly as much as they are today, and the perpetrators of such abuses were much more severely punished.

The answer is not an angry backlash by conservatives to force everyone to behave in Christian ways and try to make them think Christian thoughts. Neither is the answer to allow a secularized elite to divorce religious beliefs and values from the public square and public policy. Many people are living with an increasing sense of the centrality of personal devotion in their lives, yet they are being made to feel that they don't have the right to allow their religious beliefs to influence public life.

To get a better picture of where we are headed, it is important to understand where we have been. Let's take a look at the question of what God *has* had to do with America, as Americans themselves have understood it.

★ 4 ★

Where Has God Been in America?

We hold these truths to be self-evident, that all men are created equal, that they are endowed by their Creator with certain unalienable Rights, that among these are Life, Liberty and the pursuit of Happiness.

—THE DECLARATION OF INDEPENDENCE

The divisive issues of our time are shouted across emotional barricades in angry slogans and flashed across television and computer screens in simplistic sound bites. Ubiquitous video games reinforce hostile, adversarial combat as the imagery of human encounter. The downside of politics is that it may tend toward forfeiting healthy engagement for power struggles and manipulation tactics. If we reap what we sow, perhaps it is inevitable that in an entertainment-obsessed, self-centered society, healthy discourse will be dragged down into shallow shouting matches.

It is no great surprise, then, that the relationship of church and state gets reduced to a bumper-sticker war of simplistic, inflamed rhetoric. Either God has nothing to do with America, or God has everything to do with America. One side is trying to force God on everyone else, while the other side is attempting to marginalize God in our society. Dueling direct-mail campaigns alternately rouse the faithful and the faith-averse with sensational threats that the other side is taking over and disaster looms unless the recipients act now.

While we are busy swinging punches, perhaps we are overlooking a crucial reality that lies between the extremes of the God-and-country debate: *it is possible to affirm and practice belief in God while simultaneously practicing a rigorous separation of church and state.* We can embrace and encourage the role of religion in public life while ensuring that the state remains religiously neutral.

In fact, since our beginnings, the American experiment has intertwined the religious character of its citizens with the religious neutrality of the state. "Faith-based movements across our history have created some of the greatest progress in our history. The abolitionists in the nineteenth century and early twentieth century, the great fights for social welfare, child labor laws—all [were] led by faith-based groups," declares Senator Joseph Lieberman, a self-professed observant Jew, the Democratic vice-presidential nominee in 2000, and who now serves in the Senate as an independent. "And of course the Civil Rights Movement did the same. . . . You can't separate God from America. You go right back to the Declaration of Independence. We have to always remember that the Constitution . . . promises freedom of religion, not freedom from religion."[1]

Senator Lieberman's assertions suggest that by most indicators, belief in God has been a constant subtext of American history. Let's take a look.

SEARCHING FOR GOD IN AMERICA

C. S. Lewis recommended reading old books to open our mental windows to "the clean sea-breeze of the centuries."[2] Studying history should be an exercise in cleansing our senses of the stale, indoor air of the present. The past, Lewis said, can free us from the inevitable distortions of our own shortsighted vision.

> Not that the past has any magic about it, but because we cannot study the future, and yet need something to set against the present, it reminds us that the basic assumptions have been quite different in different periods and that much which seems certain to the uneducated is merely temporary fashion. A man who has lived in many places is not likely to be deceived by the local errors of his native village; the scholar has lived in many times and is therefore in some degree immune from the great cataract of nonsense that pours from the press and the microphone of his own age.[3]

What comes to us on the sea-breeze of the nearly four centuries since the first colonies of pilgrims began forming on the east coast of the continent?

We can pick up one central thread of the pilgrims' story in Elizabethan England. William Shakespeare is still writing plays and sonnets. Due in large part to the break with Rome of Henry VIII, there is great religious turbulence. England has an official state religion, and fines are assessed for refusing to attend its services. Catholics are not permitted to hold Mass, and Jews have been banned from England for some three hundred years. Protestant dissenters, who believe that the Queen (Elizabeth I) has been too accommodating toward the vestiges of Catholicism in Anglican ritual and theology, protest by separating themselves from the official Anglican Church.

A group of these Protestant dissenters is meeting at the manor house of William Brewster in the village of Scrooby, in the county of Nottinghamshire along the Great North Road stretching from London into the heart of Scotland. They have left the Church of England, believing it to be an idolatrous system attempting to usurp the divine covenant between God and His biblical people. Queen Elizabeth I has died, and James I has succeeded her to the throne. He is even less tolerant than she attempted to be, and these "separatists" annoy him greatly. He has threatened to punish them or expel them from the country. In 1607 the group flees the country for the more tolerant Netherlands. After a brief stint in worldly Amsterdam, they settle in the more suitable university town of Leiden, where they stay for twelve years before deciding to seek a new life in the New World.

In the summer of 1620, led by lay leaders William Bradford and William Brewster, three dozen people from the Leiden community sail back to England to board a ship for the New World colonies. On this voyage, Bradford dubs them "pilgrims," and the name takes. In September 1620, after several months of planning and false starts, they finally launch the *Mayflower* from the English town of Plymouth. With 102 people on board, financed by merchant investors, they set sail for a two-month voyage.

When the group drops anchor in a New England winter off the tip of Cape Cod, having failed to reach their destination of Virginia, where they had permission to land, they realize they need to have some kind of social agreement to govern their community once they go ashore. Before disembarking, they draw up a contract for their colony: New Plymouth, the first permanent European settlement in New England.[4]

Thus the Mayflower Compact was written, establishing the rules of their covenanted society. Signed by forty-one of the male passengers, it has sometimes been called the first constitution of what would later become the new country. Clearly, God was centrally located in their thoughts and purposes.

IN THE NAME OF GOD, AMEN. We, whose names are underwritten, the Loyal Subjects of our dread Sovereign Lord King *James*, by the Grace of God, of

Great Britain, France, and *Ireland,* King, *Defender of the Faith,* &c. **Having undertaken for the Glory of God, and Advancement of the Christian Faith,** and the Honour of our King and Country, a Voyage to plant the first Colony in the northern Parts of *Virginia;* Do by these Presents, solemnly and mutually, **in the Presence of God** and one another, covenant and combine ourselves together into a civil Body Politick, for our better Ordering and Preservation, and Furtherance of the Ends aforesaid: And by Virtue hereof do enact, constitute, and frame, such just and equal Laws, Ordinances, Acts, Constitutions, and Officers, from time to time, as shall be thought most meet and convenient for the general Good of the Colony; unto which we promise all due Submission and Obedience. IN WITNESS whereof we have hereunto subscribed our names at *Cape-Cod* the eleventh of November, in the Reign of our Sovereign Lord King *James,* of *England, France,* and *Ireland,* the eighteenth, and of *Scotland,* the fifty-fourth, *Anno Domini;* 1620. (boldface added for emphasis)

We can pick up the thread again in Philadelphia, one and a half centuries of turbulent history later, when the Continental Congress of the thirteen colonies formally declares their emancipation from British rule. Prior to detailing the "long train of abuses and usurpations" they have suffered under the tyranny of King George III, they appeal to natural law and God's divine provision to establish their right to live in a just society.

When in the Course of human events, it becomes necessary for one people to dissolve the political bands which have connected them with another, and to assume among the powers of the earth, the separate and equal station to which the Laws of Nature and of Nature's God entitle them, a decent respect to the opinions of mankind requires that they should declare the causes which impel them to the separation.

We hold these truths to be self-evident, that all Men are created equal, that they are endowed by their Creator with certain unalienable Rights, that among these are Life, Liberty and the pursuit of Happiness.—That to secure these rights, Governments are instituted among Men, deriving their just Powers from the consent of the governed.[5]

As Senator Joseph Lieberman observes, this cornerstone of American history shows that the new country was a "faith-based initiative."

> The mix of God and government, of religion and politics, is quintessentially American, and it was there at the beginning. The fact is that in the first American document, the Declaration of Independence, the founders of our country said that they were forming the new government to secure the rights to life, liberty and the pursuit of happiness that they saw as the endowment of our Creator. So this government, this country was not neutral about God right at the outset.[6]

Perhaps most astonishing in the American experiment has been the way that this affirmation of divinely ordained freedom has spread to include not only the original colonists, but also the multitudes of immigrants and peoples who formed this nation and shaped its history and growth in the centuries since then. Bradford and his Plymouth congregation may have been separatists breaking from the state church of England, but their convictions rooted in Christian truths of God's direct relationship with His covenanted people gave rise to a form of religious freedom the world had never before seen. So groundbreaking was this new development that Senator Lieberman, a member of a religious and ethnic people who have suffered unspeakable atrocities under so-called Christian governments, could exclaim:

> This is a country founded by Christians, a majority of whose citizens are Christians. But . . . those rights to life, liberty and a pursuit of happiness, which we have as the endowment of our Creator, have been given to everybody. So though this is a nation that—the majority of which is Christian, I will say to you as a Jewish American that I believe in the 5,765 years of Jewish history, there has never been a country, other than Israel during certain times of its history, which has given Jews more freedom. The same can now be said of Islam and Buddhism and Hindus, etc., etc., etc. That's the glory of this country and, frankly, the grace and gift of the Christians who founded the country and who continue to be the majority within it.[7]

Senator Lieberman could make this statement because the founders of our nation appealed to a divine foundation for human equality and freedom in the creation of the United States of America. They didn't say that only Protestants or only Americans got this endowment from the Creator. They made *a universal declaration of human rights.* That was possible only because as the basis for their extraordinary pronouncement they were able to appeal to a transcendent authority, a source of moral righteousness beyond human control to create or destroy. If we could get this truth to sweep a clean sea-breeze through the fetid air of our current stagnation, it would offer profound encouragement to all the peoples of the world that America is *not* out to "Americanize" or "Christianize" the rest of the world. Our nation's cause is freedom.

In 1831 a young Frenchman named Alexis de Tocqueville and his colleague Gustave de Beaumont received permission from their government to tour the United States, ostensibly to study the prison system, but in reality to satisfy Tocqueville's insatiable curiosity about America. For nine months they traveled from the wilderness of Michigan to the port of New Orleans and all over the eastern seaboard, observing America's political and social institutions and interviewing scores of people from all walks of life. Tocqueville later recorded his experiences and reflections in his influential work *Democracy in America,* a prescient analysis of American democracy and culture. He recognized the foundational importance of religion to the unique freedoms enjoyed by Americans.

> Religion in America takes no direct part in the government of society, but it must be regarded as the first of their political institutions; for if it does not impart a taste for freedom, it facilitates the use of it. Indeed, it is in this same point of view that the inhabitants of the United States themselves look upon religious belief. I do not know whether all Americans have a sincere faith in their religion—for who can search the human heart?—but I am certain that they hold it to be indispensable to the maintenance of republican institutions. This opinion is not peculiar to a class of citizens or to a party, but it belongs to the whole nation and to every rank of society.[8]

One of the most influential statements on what God has to do with America goes all the way back to John Winthrop, the Puritan governor of the

Massachusetts Bay Colony, who led a fleet of eleven vessels and seven hundred passengers to New England in the spring of 1630. Unlike Bradford's separatists, who completely broke with the Church of England, Winthrop's Puritan community hoped to reform the Church of England from within. They believed it had been corrupted by Catholic practices and rituals and was under God's judgment for heresy. In the New World, they felt, they would be sheltered from God's coming wrath upon the church and could start afresh to live in faithful covenant with God.

Winthrop's 1630 sermon "A Modell of Christian Charity" has since become well known as "The City upon a Hill," influencing America's self-understanding down through the centuries—for example, President Ronald Reagan alluded to it in his 1989 farewell address. Winthrop's message, based on the text of Matthew 5:14, in which Jesus told His followers that they were the light of the world, a city set upon a hill, challenged the Puritans to holy living. He compared their community to the Israelites moving into the Promised Land, cautioning them to remain faithful to God and warning them of the perils of idolatry.

Although Winthrop is no role model for civil leadership today (his Puritan vision of God's providence did not allow for the concept of democracy, which he despised), his Christian vision would later find common ground in the founding fathers' attribution of basic human rights to the God of Judeo-Christian heritage. As Robert Bellah points out:

> The Declaration of Independence points to the sovereignty of God over the collective political society itself when it refers in its opening lines to "the laws of nature and of nature's God" that stand above and judge the laws of men. It is often asserted that the God of nature is specifically not the God of the Bible. [But that] raises problems of the relation of natural religion to biblical religion in eighteenth-century thought. . . . Jefferson goes on to say, "We hold these truths to be self-evident, that all Men are created equal, that they are endowed by their Creator with certain unalienable Rights, that among these are Life, Liberty and the pursuit of Happiness.—That to secure these rights, Governments are instituted among Men, deriving their just Powers from the consent of the governed. — That whenever any Form of Government becomes destructive of these ends, it is the Right of the People to alter or abolish it." We

have here a distinctly biblical God who is much more than a first principle of nature, who creates individual human beings and endows them with equality and fundamental rights.[9]

Clearly, America was founded on a divine experiment rooted in Judeo-Christian worldviews. This does not mean that America was ever a "Christian nation," nor does it mean that we should pine for a return to some kind of "Christian" era in America's past. Years ago during the Reagan era, respected historians Mark Noll, Nathan Hatch, and George Marsden wrote a book titled *The Search for Christian America*, intended to temper what they saw as an overly romanticized view of America's Christian heritage. In a later edition, they reflected on the developments stemming from the resurgence of a conservative Christian political agenda: "It seems as though the proponents of restoring a Christian America are as adamant as ever in promoting that ideal. Although we have . . . seen occasional evidence of spokespersons for the Christian political right acknowledging that the United States never was or will be the Kingdom of God, we cannot claim that these views have often penetrated to the core of politically conservative Christian communities."[10]

I will go on record as a perceived spokesman for the conservative Christian political agenda that *the United States never was, nor will be, the kingdom of God, and any attempt to identify it as such is idolatrous.* What we need today is not a return to the past, but a turning to a future that has never been: a healthy pluralism in which all views are allowed, encouraged, and respected, and in which a healthy respect for the value of religion in America's past, present, and future permeates society.

WHEN GOD AND COUNTRY CLASH

But what of instances in which it appears that God and country are in conflict, when individuals feel they are being forced to choose between the divine dictates of their religious conscience and the mandates of the state?

First and foremost, it is critical to recognize that all Americans, regardless of their religious views, are expected to obey and uphold the laws of this country. If they feel the laws are wrong or unfairly constrain the free exercise of their religious rights, then they have recourse under the law to redress that legislation.

Again, thanks to our overheated God-and-country controversies, this boundary of the rule of law is sometimes overlooked. It is true that our forefathers defied British law by forming a new government and declaring their independence. They laid out in considerable detail their reasons for concluding that the British crown was no longer a legitimate government. I think they were right, and I applaud my ancestors for supporting that effort. I do not believe that rebellion is always wrong, but it should not take place until all legal redress of grievances have been exhausted.

This was clearly not the case in 2003 when Alabama Chief Justice Roy Moore took an impassioned, but utterly wrongheaded, stand by disobeying a federal court order to remove a display of the Ten Commandments from the state Supreme Court rotunda. This refusal placed him in contempt of court and forced his removal for breaking his oath of office—and it stirred up a hornet's nest of controversy and divided Evangelical Christians over two Fundamental issues.

The first issue was based on the expression of religious convictions in public buildings—specifically the Ten Commandments, and generally any acknowledgment of God. Judge Moore enjoyed consensus support among Evangelicals that such expression does not violate the separation of church and state. After all, American history is replete with public expressions of belief in God.

Judge Moore had good reason to be angry at attempts by the federal court to sweep the public square clean of any vestiges of religious belief. That is a form of secular Fundamentalism, as is the attempt to take "under God" out of the Pledge of Allegiance or to deny publicly funded scholarships to students who can study paganism and Eastern mysticism, but are not allowed to use their scholarship to study Christian religion or any field that is construed as preparation for Christian ministry. The inquisitorial impulse of secular Fundamentalism would also allow public school teachers to teach about Islam, but deny students the right to express their Christian faith at public school events. This, too, is wrong. We should protest such court rulings hostile to religious faith. Evangelical Christians should rise up and join the effort to reform this government and its courts when this kind of antireligious bigotry prevails.

Equally important in this Ten Commandments controversy is a second issue, which Judge Moore overlooked: we have a government committed to the rule of law. When Evangelical Christians by their actions proclaim that they are no longer obligated to obey the rule of law because they disagree with court rulings, in effect they are proclaiming that the United States government is no longer a legitimate government. This is at least moral insurrection.

If a Christian in public office believes in good conscience that he or she cannot uphold his or her sworn duty, then that official should resign rather than break his or her oath of office. If we disagree with a judicial interpretation of the law—as millions of Americans did in Judge Moore's Ten Commandments case—then we must change the judges and, if necessary, change the laws in the Congress or the legislatures and in the courtroom of public opinion. However, unless we are willing to abandon the rule of law or support rebellion against the government, we cannot support defiance of the law by officials sworn to uphold it.

The essential issue is the rule of law. The country cannot allow government officials to defy laws with which they disagree, whether they are the chief justice of the Alabama Supreme Court or the mayor of San Francisco.[11] To allow such moral defiance by government officials would subvert the rule of law and put the country on a steep and slippery slope either to anarchy or to personal rule by individual officials. Either consequence would be catastrophic for the country and for individual human rights.

If, as a private citizen, Judge Moore felt compelled by conscience to protest the removal of the Ten Commandments statue by engaging in a sit-in at the Alabama Supreme Court building, I would respect his freedom of conscience. If he were to be arrested for nonviolent protest of the court's action, I would contribute to his legal defense fund.

In his public comments after his eight fellow Alabama Supreme Court justices voted to comply with the federal court order, Judge Moore said, "I hear others talk of a rule of law. If the rule of law means to do everything a judge tells you to do, we would still have slavery in this country. If the rule of law means to do everything a judge tells you to do, the Declaration of Independence would be a meaningless document."[12]

Judge Moore was both right and wrong. He was right that on the slavery issue, the U.S. Supreme Court ruled in the 1857 *Dred Scott* decision that slaves were mere property, not human beings, and thus had no rights. He was wrong to imply that slavery was ended because the American people rose up in rebellion and disobeyed the law. In fact, three years after the *Dred Scott* decision, they elected a new president, Abraham Lincoln, who campaigned on a platform of no extension, and the eventual abolition, of slavery. So America did obey the rule of law, used the ballot box, and eventually eliminated slavery.

When the time comes that we feel compelled to examine whether the use of lethal force is justified in establishing a new government, then we must do so under Jesus' principle that we are to render unto Caesar what is Caesar's and unto God what is God's (see Matthew 22:15–22). If Caesar's demands are contrary to God's commands, we must obey God and, at a minimum, disobey Caesar nonviolently.

Of course, there is a limit to nonviolence. The freedom fighters in the American Revolution didn't practice nonviolence; they formed an army. But that was after a long history of patient endurance of injustices and attempts to rectify that injustice under the British system. In their bill of indictment, they listed twenty-seven devastating grievances against the king, pointing out that "in every stage of these Oppressions We have Petitioned for Redress in the most humble terms: Our repeated Petitions have been answered only by repeated injury. A Prince whose character is thus marked by every act which may define a Tyrant, is unfit to be the ruler of a free people." Since governments derive their power from the consent of the governed, and the British crown had forfeited its right to be the governor of the American people, they established a new government and raised up an army to protect that freedom.

Some of my Evangelical colleagues disagree with me at this point, arguing that the American revolutionaries did not have the moral right to declare their independence and that if our forefathers had just behaved themselves and continued to suffer, sooner or later we would have been given dominion status like Canada. But we have legal protections under our Bill of Rights that Canadian citizens don't have. I also think it's rather naïve to assume that if the United States of America hadn't given Britain a couple of black eyes and a broken nose, Canada would have obtained dominion status regardless.

When a government tramples on the people's rights, and the people have tried every redress and failed, and they are being persecuted and killed (the king was arming Native Americans to attack Americans on the frontier), then they have a right to establish a new government. The new American government was elected by the people and was authorized to use armed force in protecting their freedom by the creation of the Continental army.

Martin Luther King Jr. understood that there is a limit to nonviolent civil disobedience. He counseled that if your enemy has a conscience, follow Gandhi and the way of nonviolence. If your enemy is like Adolf Hitler and has no conscience, follow Bonhoeffer and the way of armed resistance. After much agonizing, Bonhoeffer finally concluded that not only did he have a responsibility to pray for the defeat of his own nation, but because it had become such an embodiment of evil, he had an obligation to take action in seeking its demise—therefore, he participated in the plot to assassinate Hitler.

TRANSFORMATION OF A SOCIETY'S CHARACTER

Some Christians wonder why Paul encouraged slaves to obey their masters rather than rise up against the injustice of slavery.[13] In New Testament times, the institution of slavery was different than in the United States. In the Roman Empire, slaves had rights under the law. They were really more like indentured servants. American slaves had no rights under the law. Also, possibly one-third of the population in the Roman Empire was made up of slaves. Paul addressed his admonitions not just to the slaves, but also to their masters. If Christian masters behaved the way Paul prescribed in his letter to Philemon, it would have transformed the institution of slavery—which it did, when Christianity became the dominant force in the Roman Empire and slavery ended along with gladiatorial combat and infanticide.

The situation is analogous with Paul's teaching on marriage. It is hard for us to get into the mind-set of the first century, when a woman had no rights. She was literally the property of her husband. When husbands of that day heard Paul's letter to the Ephesians, telling them to love their wives the way Christ loved the church and gave Himself for it, surely they fell off their seats. The New Testament is probably the most radical document in ancient history when it comes to assuming and recognizing women's rights as people. We look at it today in this egalitarian world and say, "What do you mean, 'Wives, submit to your husbands as to the Lord'?"[14] That wasn't controversial in the first century, because anything other than submission was not an option. As property, women had to be submissive to men. Christianity transforms all relationships. It transformed the marriage relationship. It transformed the role of women in society. Everywhere Christianity has gone, the role of women has improved drastically.

The history of Christendom is not without grievous sin, when the church wielded earthly power for earthly gain and disgraced the cause of Christ. But that behavior was a departure from Christian truth, not a result of belief in it. Neither is American history without stain. Under the banner of Manifest Destiny and soul-saving campaigns to the "savages," we committed great atrocities. However, I believe they are overshadowed by the great accomplishments of this country. In many cases, above all the dismantling of racial segregation and "Jim Crow," we have turned away from our national sins and toward the freedoms and equality that are the divinely ordained right of every human being. Again, that commitment to the universal worth of every human being, regardless of race or background, is rooted in belief in a transcendent God by whose grace we are all given the right to life, liberty, and the pursuit of happiness.

WHY GOD MATTERS

Someone outside Christian faith, unconcerned with the specific claims of Christ on individual and communal life, might question this effort in clarifying America's spiritual DNA. Why bother looking back to see where God has been in America? Why not simply move forward and let the course of our nation be directed by the will of the people?

Aside from the enormously important value of understanding history to inform present choices and shape future directions, perhaps the most important answer to this question is that America's understanding of the existence of God has helped preserve the very freedoms that all Americans enjoy, which they feel legitimately are their birthright. Whether people of faith, agnostics, or atheists, American citizens enjoy freedoms that were conceived and implemented in the context of a worldview that affirmed the centrality of divine providence to human affairs. Distinguished Catholic scholar Michael Novak points this out:

> Though both the conception of human liberty and the virtues necessary to its true exercise sprang from biblical teachings, the framers were careful not to endow biblical religion, or any religion, with state power. But their alternative to a society with an established religion was neither a society with no religion at all nor a secular society. . . . Given these peculiar circumstances, one cannot assume that the American experiment could be easily duplicated elsewhere. . . . Americans, for their part, should appreciate how much the Jewish and Christian traditions have provided the vision and context for creating and maintaining a society of ordered liberty. The belief that every human person possesses unalienable rights to liberty derives from a vision first introduced into history by Judaism and then taught to Christianity. Both Judaism and Christianity, despite historical sins and failures, cherish the religious liberty of even those who say No to their revelations. Both believe that true faith arises only in voluntary consent. Conscience can be neither feigned nor coerced.[15]

From its founding documents, American history has been seasoned with belief in a transcendent divine being. Where has belief in God been in America? Everywhere, imprinted in our national genetic code via Judeo-Christian belief, which is the foundation for the religious freedoms we enjoy. These freedoms are written into our founding documents, but as the turbulence of recent decades indicates, our ongoing understanding of, and respect for, those freedoms has radical implications for how we interpret and enforce them. Erosion of belief in God can lead to erosion of freedom if we pull the rug out from under it by exchanging a worldview that includes divine providence for a worldview that rejects any notion of transcendent authority. To put it plainly, if moral relativism is the prevailing truth, then it's all about me, and why should I care about you and your rights?

Belief in God is also embedded in American history through the sense of transcendent authority to which our lineage of U.S. presidents held themselves accountable. These men, who carried the burdens of the country—and sometimes the entire world, it seemed—on their shoulders, also turned to divine authority for guidance and support in carrying out their awesome responsibilities and leading the nation through harrowing trials. Their example is a ringing challenge to a thoroughly secularized culture. As the psalmist asked, "I lift up my eyes to the hills—where does my help come from?" And with the psalmist, these leaders found, "My help comes from the LORD, the Maker of heaven and earth" (Psalm 121:1).

★ 5 ★

All the Presidents' Faith

The Lord is always on the side of the right, but it is my constant anxiety and prayer that I and this nation should be on the Lord's side.

—ABRAHAM LINCOLN[1]

Religious language from the mouth of President George W. Bush tends to jar the ears of some of our citizens these days—but should it?

President Bush's religious faith has come under fire as critics have tried to paint it as a threat to his good judgment. Triggers for the criticism have included his willingness to take a stand against "evil," a word he has used repeatedly in reference to terrorism and to governments that commit tyranny against their citizens. Others claim to be uncomfortable with what is perceived to be his unprecedented frankness about his Christian faith.

"President George Bush uses religious language more than any president in U.S. history," Jim Wallis claims disapprovingly in his chapter on dangerous religion in *God's Politics*. Then he adds what he clearly perceives to be the disturbing news: "and some of his key speechwriters come right out of the Evangelical community."[2] Wallis makes these statements in building his case for what he sees as the Bush administration's misguided theology of empire.

Bush critic Kevin Phillips, author of *American Theocracy*,[3] supports his claim for an alleged Bush administration theocracy by calling in "expert witnesses" as a framework of explanation to interpret Bush's religious language. For example, Phillips cites research by Bruce Lincoln, professor of religion at the University of Chicago and author of *Holy Terrors*,[4] who deconstructed the president's post–9/11 speech and "found the president's rhetoric to be not unlike Osama bin Laden's own statements in that 'both men constructed a Manichean struggle.' . . . While the American chief executive's words were less overtly religious than bin Laden's, Lincoln described a 'double-coding' through which Bush signaled attentive Bible readers that he shared their private scriptural invocations." Perhaps someone has been reading too much of Dan Brown's *The Da Vinci Code*.

Phillips goes on to cite Bruce Lincoln's research, indicting Bush for using the phrase "I believe" twelve times in his 2004 acceptance speech, for using the term "resurrection" in reference to New York City's recovery from the fall of the World Trade Towers, and—the trump card—for saying, "I believe freedom is not America's gift to the world. It is the Almighty's gift to every man and woman." Ignoring the fact that such language is straight out of the Declaration of Independence, Phillips breathlessly concludes that "the man in the White House was becoming America's preacher in chief."

Has President Bush used more religious language than any president in U.S. history? Is his use of faith language really more dangerous and frequent than that of his predecessors? As noted earlier, presidential scholar Paul Kengor found that Bush used religious language far less than his immediate predecessor, former president Bill Clinton. What a difference a researcher makes. Kengor also pointed out that according to a 2003 Pew Research Center poll, the clear majority of Americans felt that Bush was striking the right balance in how often he mentioned his faith.[5]

Digging into critics' claims that President Bush and other Republicans used "God talk" more often than Democrats, Kengor tabulated references to "Jesus," "Jesus Christ," and "Christ" in official presidential documents to compare George W. Bush's speeches and Bill Clinton's speeches through 2003. Bush made 14 separate statements, compared to 41 by Clinton. Bush averaged 4.7 mentions per year to Clinton's average of 5.1 statements per year—in each year, Bush was always outdone by Clinton according to this measure of "God talk." Further, Clinton's references nearly doubled during election years. "Indeed, it is astonishing to note just how thoroughly President Clinton was given a pass by those who normally cry foul on separation of church and state," Kengor observed.[6]

Is President Bush really more religious than his predecessors?

Kengor's research also turned up an interesting contrast between Presidents Clinton and Bush in how often they visited churches. During the 2000 election campaign, Kengor found, the sitting president, vice president, and First Lady made more church appearances in one campaign week than George W. Bush did in his entire first term as president.[7]

If we do in fact have a rich tradition of American presidents using the language of faith, then which represents a departure from our history—President Bush's faith language, or the criticism of it? Who has changed?

RELIGION IN AMERICA IS
NO RESPECTER OF LEFT AND RIGHT

In a presidential election year, our two road warriors on America's cultural highway would be displaying bumper stickers for their party's candidates—predictably, one dismissive of, one heavy on, God talk.

When the Democrats stumbled badly over the faith issue in the 2004 presidential campaign in a misguided effort to speak to religious values voters, it reinforced the stereotypes of a religion-friendly Republican Party and a secular-friendly Democratic Party. Obviously this caricature is pasted over complex realities, to no small extent rooted in divisive issues involving deeply felt convictions and beliefs. However, it also suggests, erroneously, that the Religious Right's mix of religion and politics is a relatively new phenomenon.

In fact, it is not. Our country has a long lineage of religious faith informing politics, which is clear from any study of our nation's leaders. Although it may be instructive and illuminating to explore how "Christian" our presidents were or weren't, that doesn't diminish the reality that almost all of them affirmed the existence of a God who has a divine interest in the affairs of this country.

Any attempt to make an exhaustive, accurate listing of the formal religious affiliations of the presidents meets immediately with challenges: which researchers have done the best homework, which documents are reliable, which sources in reliable documents can be corroborated, to what extent a president actually observed the religious tradition with which he was affiliated or of which he was a member, whether he affirmed its doctrines or attended its church services. It is a fascinating topic, and many have written on it.

However, it is not necessary to conduct exhaustive research into the spiritual lives of U.S. presidents to establish that the vast majority of them affirmed repeatedly, in a variety of ways, their belief in a supreme deity. Depending on the president, this deity could be defined as the personal God who pursues intimate relationship with human beings, revealed in Jesus Christ; the covenantal God of the Judeo-Christian tradition; the supreme deity of natural theology, creator and sustainer of the world; the transcendent being whose power and timelessness supersede the frailty of human life; the God of self-help, who helps those who help themselves; or a deistic God, the great watchmaker in the sky, who wound up the universe and left it to run on its own.

What's God got to do with America? In the context of the religious faith of American presidents, belief in God has consistently imbued our leaders with a sense of accountability to divine authority, responsibility to seek divine guidance, and the hope of divine protection for the life of the nation. God has mattered to our presidents for several reasons. They have recognized that their decisions are answerable in a higher court of appeal than opinion polls. They have affirmed that the advice of advisers, cabinet staff, and joint chiefs, the opinions of spouses, and the dictates of personal conscience don't add up to enough guidance for the momentous decisions thrust upon them. And in times of crisis, they have admitted that even the very best human efforts and accomplishments are not enough to secure peace and safety for the country.

THE KING'S HEART IS IN THE
HANDS OF THE LORD (PROVERBS 21:1)

An interesting way to look at how various presidents viewed divine accountability, guidance, and protection is through their choice of the particular Bible passage on which they solemnly swore at their inauguration.[8] Not all presidents chose a passage each time, and sometimes they chose randomly: George Washington was in a hurry and flung open his Masonic Bible to the meaningless (in this context) Genesis 49:13—"Zebulun shall dwell at the haven of the sea; and he shall be for an haven of ships; and his border shall be unto Zidon" (KJV). Others who chose purposefully provide more revealing insights (in some cases ironically so, from the vantage point of hindsight).

The following examples are a sample of presidential inaugural texts (for a more complete list, see appendix C):

- Abraham Lincoln, 1865: "Judge not, that ye be not judged" (Matthew 7:1); "Woe unto the world because of offences! for it must needs be that offences come; but woe to that man by whom the offence cometh!" (Matthew 18:7); "And I heard another out of the altar say, Even so, Lord God Almighty, true and righteous are thy judgments" (Revelation 16:7).

- Andrew Johnson, 1865: "The king's heart is in the hand of the LORD, as the rivers of water: he turneth it whithersoever he will" (Proverbs 21:1).
- Ulysses S. Grant, 1873: "There shall come forth a rod out of the stem of Jesse, and a Branch shall grow out of his roots: and the spirit of the LORD shall rest upon him, the spirit of wisdom and understanding, the spirit of counsel and might, the spirit of knowledge and of the fear of the LORD; and shall make him of quick understanding in the fear of the LORD: and he shall not judge after the sight of his eyes, neither reprove after the hearing of his ears" (Isaiah 11:1–3).
- Benjamin Harrison, 1889: "I will lift up mine eyes unto the hills, from whence cometh my help. My help cometh from the LORD, which made heaven and earth. He will not suffer thy foot to be moved: he that keepeth thee will not slumber. Behold, he that keepeth Israel shall neither slumber nor sleep. The LORD is thy keeper: the LORD is thy shade upon thy right hand. The sun shall not smite thee by day, nor the moon by night" (Psalm 121:1–6).
- William McKinley, 1897: "Give me now wisdom and knowledge, that I may go out and come in before this people: for who can judge this thy people, that is so great?" (2 Chronicles 1:10).
- Theodore Roosevelt, 1905: "But be ye doers of the word, and not hearers only, deceiving your own selves. For if any be a hearer of the word, and not a doer, he is like unto a man beholding his natural face in a glass" (James 1:22–23).
- William Howard Taft, 1909: "Give therefore thy servant an understanding heart to judge thy people, that I may discern between good and bad: for who is able to judge this thy so great a people? And the speech pleased the LORD, that Solomon had asked this thing. And God said unto him, Because thou hast asked this thing, and hast not asked for thyself long life; neither hast asked riches for thyself, nor hast asked the life of thine enemies; but hast asked for thyself understanding to discern judgment" (1 Kings 3:9–11).
- Woodrow Wilson, 1917: "God is our refuge and strength, a helper who is always found in times of trouble. Therefore we will not be afraid, though the earth trembles and the mountains topple into the depths of

the seas, though its waters roar and foam and the mountains quake with its turmoil. . . ." (Psalm 46).

- Warren G. Harding, 1921: "He hath shewed thee, O man, what is good; and what doth the LORD require of thee, but to do justly, and to love mercy, and to walk humbly with thy God?" (Micah 6:8).

- Franklin D. Roosevelt, 1933, 1937, 1941, 1945: "Though I speak with the tongues of men and of angels, and have not charity, I am become as sounding brass, or a tinkling cymbal . . ." (1 Corinthians 13:1–13).

- Harry S. Truman, 1949: "Blessed are the poor in spirit, because the kingdom of heaven is theirs. Blessed are those who mourn, because they will be comforted. Blessed are the gentle, because they will inherit the earth. Blessed are those who hunger and thirst for righteousness, because they will be filled. Blessed are the merciful, because they will be shown mercy. Blessed are the pure in heart, because they will see God. Blessed are the peacemakers, because they will be called sons of God. Blessed are those who are persecuted for righteousness, because the kingdom of heaven is theirs. Blessed are you when they insult you and persecute you, and say every kind of evil against you falsely because of Me" (Matthew 5:3–11 HCSB; c.f. Exodus 20:3–17).

- Dwight D. Eisenhower, 1953: "Except the LORD build the house, they labour in vain that build it: except the LORD keep the city, the watchman waketh but in vain" (Psalm 127:1); "If my people, which are called by my name, shall humble themselves, and pray, and seek my face, and turn from their wicked ways; then will I hear from heaven, and will forgive their sin, and will heal their land" (2 Chronicles 7:14).

- Richard M. Nixon, 1969, 1973: "He shall judge among the nations, and shall rebuke many people: and they shall beat their swords into plowshares, and their spears into pruninghooks: nation shall not lift up sword against nation, neither shall they learn war any more" (Isaiah 2:4).

- Gerald R. Ford, 1974: "Trust in the LORD with all thine heart; and lean not unto thine own understanding. In all thy ways acknowledge him, and he shall direct thy paths" (Proverbs 3:5–6).

- James E. Carter, 1977: "He hath shewed thee, O man, what is good; and what doth the LORD require of thee, but to do justly, and to love mercy, and to walk humbly with thy God?" (Micah 6:8).

- Ronald W. Reagan, 1981, 1985: "If my people, which are called by my name, shall humble themselves, and pray, and seek my face, and turn from their wicked ways; then will I hear from heaven, and will forgive their sin, and will heal their land" (2 Chronicles 7:14).
- William J. Clinton, 1993: "For he that soweth to his flesh shall of the flesh reap corruption; but he that soweth to the Spirit shall of the Spirit reap life everlasting" (Galatians 6:8). In 1997: "And they that shall be of thee shall build the old waste places: thou shalt raise up the foundations of many generations; and thou shalt be called, The repairer of the breach, The restorer of paths to dwell in" (Isaiah 58:12).
- George W. Bush, 2005: "But they that wait upon the LORD shall renew their strength; they shall mount up with wings as eagles; they shall run, and not be weary; and they shall walk, and not faint" (Isaiah 40:31).[9]

All of these individuals were elected by the people of the United States. Almost all of them have been religious. What does that say about what God's got to do with America?

A few years ago, when those opposing U.S. and British intervention to liberate Iraq by deposing Saddam Hussein were taking potshots at the religious faith of President George W. Bush and British Prime Minister Tony Blair, Michael Gove of the *London Times* made a case for why secularists as well as people of faith could be glad when national leaders "took their cue from above."

> Christian faith . . . compels an examination of the conscience. As well as weighing the consequences of an action, the genuinely Christian politician will examine the sincerity of his intentions and be acutely aware of the fallibility of human reason. Far from encouraging rashness, Christian belief creates another hurdle a politician must clear before he acts. Subjecting decisions to extra moral tests that have nothing to do with strictly political calculation can only help to foster responsible leadership.[10]

It has become fashionable to criticize Evangelicals as wild-eyed fanatics who hear what they think is the voice of God in isolation of common sense and human reason, but that stone is too easy to hurl from one's own glass house. It is important and legitimate to question the depth and authenticity of a president's faith and to seek to understand how it informs his decision making. However, such criticism is usually one-sided, bereft of any credit where credit is due, as Gove points out. And it completely overlooks the reality that for the majority of people responsible for electing these individuals of faith to the highest office in the land, religious faith is perceived to be a benefit rather than a liability.

STATEMENTS OF FAITH

The archives of presidential papers, statements, and proclamations are rich with statements of faith. I quote just a sampling here of the most historically and theologically significant—some of them at length, because we need to become reacquainted with our own heritage. Too many Americans are ignorant of it, particularly in this day when it has become popular to dismiss the richness of our religious past.

George Washington

In 1893 an English instructor from Wellesley College, Massachusetts, spent her summer vacation out west. Struck by the natural beauty of the landscape, capped off by the view from the top of Pikes Peak in Colorado, she wrote a poem that has since become immortalized as the patriotic hymn "America the Beautiful." In the second verse, Katherine Lee Bates extolled the sacrifices of the earliest settlers of our land:

> O beautiful for pilgrim feet,
> Whose stern, impassion'd stress
> A thoroughfare for freedom beat
> Across the wilderness!
> America! America!
> God mend thine ev'ry flaw,

All the Presidents' Faith

> Confirm thy soul in self-control,
> Thy liberty in law!

Had this poem been around a century earlier, it might have served as a fitting epigraph for George Washington's eloquent decree establishing a national day of Thanksgiving on October 3, 1789.

> Whereas it is the duty of all nations to acknowledge the providence of Almighty God, to obey His will, to be grateful for His benefits, and humbly to implore His protection and favor; and Whereas both Houses of Congress have, by their joint committee, requested me "to recommend to the people of the United States a day of public thanksgiving and prayer, to be observed by acknowledging with grateful hearts the many and signal favors of Almighty God, especially by affording them an opportunity peaceably to establish a form of government for their safety and happiness."

Katherine Lee Bates's imagery echoes some of the same themes found in Washington's decree: profound gratitude for those whose sacrifices made the new nation possible, and a deep sense of God's gracious providence.

> Now, therefore, I do recommend and assign Thursday, the 26th day of November next, to be devoted by the people of these States to the service of that great and glorious Being who is the beneficent author of all the good that was, that is, or that will be; that we may then all unite in rendering unto Him our sincere and humble thanks for His kind care and protection of the people of this country previous to their becoming a nation; for the signal and manifold mercies and the favorable interpositions of His providence in the course and conclusion of the late war; for the great degree of tranquillity, union, and plenty which we have since enjoyed; for the peaceable and rational manner in which we have been enabled to establish constitutions of government for our safety and happiness, and particularly the national one now lately instituted; for the civil and religious liberty with which we are blessed, and the means we have of acquiring and diffusing useful knowledge; and, in general, for all the great and various favors which He has been pleased to confer upon us.

Finally, both share an emphasis on spiritual and moral character and humility before God.

> And also that we may then unite in most humbly offering our prayers and supplications to the great Lord and Ruler of Nations, and beseech Him to pardon our national and other transgressions . . . to promote the knowledge and practice of true religion and virtue, and the increase of science among them and us; and, generally, to grant unto all mankind such a degree of temporal prosperity as He alone knows to be best.

Abraham Lincoln

The theological depth of Abraham Lincoln's wisdom, the lyrical excellence of his oratory, and his penetrating insights into the nation's struggles and triumphs mark him as a giant in our religious landscape—a fitting image for a man who literally towered above others in physical stature.

Of all our presidents, Lincoln has perhaps the most to teach us about the relationship of God and country. One of the clearest statements of why the two must never be equated is his *Meditations on the Divine Will,* a private piece he wrote for himself that was not publicized until discovered posthumously among his papers. Lincoln's private secretary, John Hay, found it and titled it. Scholars estimate that it was written in 1862, at the height of the Civil War, when the issue of victory was very much in doubt and the unprecedented carnage and bloodshed had profoundly shocked the nation, North and South, to its core.

> The will of God prevails. In great contests each party claims to act in accordance with the will of God. Both *may* be, and one *must* be wrong. God can not [*sic*] be *for,* and *against* the same thing at the same time. In the present civil war, it is quite possible that God's purpose is something different from the purpose of either party—and yet the human instrumentalities, working just as they do, are of the best adaptation to effect His purpose. I am almost ready to say this is probably true —that God wills this contest, and wills that it shall not end yet. By his mere quiet power, on the minds of the now contestants, he could have either *saved* or *destroyed* the Union without a human contest. Yet the contest began. And having begun he could give the final victory to either side any day. Yet the contest proceeds.[11]

Three years later, in his second inaugural address, Lincoln was still wrestling with the same issue of how the opposing sides could both claim, simultaneously, that they had divine support. Even more, he struggled to understand what *God* thought of each side claiming His support.

Neither party expected for the war the magnitude or the duration which it has already attained. Neither anticipated that the cause of the conflict might cease with or even before the conflict itself should cease. Each looked for an easier triumph, and a result less fundamental and astounding. Both read the same Bible and pray to the same God, and each invokes His aid against the other. It may seem strange that any men should dare to ask a just God's assistance in wringing their bread from the sweat of other men's faces, but let us judge not, that we be not judged. The prayers of both could not be answered. That of neither has been answered fully. The Almighty has His own purposes.[12]

Lincoln knew that both sides couldn't be completely right and that this terrible war might be God's judgment on the nation for having profited from involuntary servitude. It wasn't just the South that profited from slavery; the whole nation did. Perhaps God would exact from them all of the wealth that had been produced by slavery before the end of this horrible conflict. Lincoln's position is a supreme example of not letting the perfect become the enemy of the good. Knowing that neither the North nor the country overall had a perfectly just cause, still, he determined, they would go forward seeking to do right as God gave them light to see it. Thus he continued:

If we shall suppose that American slavery is one of those offenses which, in the providence of God, must needs come, but which, having continued through His appointed time, He now wills to remove, and that He gives to both North and South this terrible war as the woe due to those by whom the offense came, shall we discern therein any departure from those divine attributes which the believers in a living God always ascribe to Him? Fondly do we hope, fervently do we pray, that this mighty scourge of war may speedily pass away. Yet, if God wills that it continue until all the wealth piled by the bondsman's two hundred and fifty years of unrequited toil shall be sunk, and until every drop of blood drawn with the lash shall be paid by another drawn with the sword, as was said three thousand years ago, so still it must be said "the judgments of the Lord are true and righteous altogether."

With malice toward none, with charity for all, with firmness in the right as God gives us to see the right, let us strive on to finish the work we are in, to bind up the nation's wounds, to care for him who shall have borne the battle and for his widow and his orphan, to do all which may achieve and cherish a just and lasting peace among ourselves and with all nations.[13]

During the Civil War, a preacher reportedly said to Lincoln that he hoped "the Lord was on our side." Lincoln is said to have replied, "The Lord is always on the side of the right, but it is my constant anxiety and prayer that I and this nation should be on the Lord's side."[14]

A classic criticism of conservatives is that they presume God is on their side. No, at their best, they hope, like Lincoln, that they are on God's side. The key difference is whether or not one believes God has a side. As noted earlier,[15] this contrasts with liberals, who too often don't believe God has a side in public policy issues. Conservatives believe in absolutes of right and wrong, and God is always the definition of right. As Lincoln's experience shows, in some conflicts it is no easy task to discern right from wrong in every respect. But we do have an obligation and a responsibility to seek to be on the side of right.

Moral relativism assumes that God doesn't have a side. Christian faith affirms that He is on the side of freedom against slavery. He is on the side of civilization as opposed to barbarism. He is on the side of innocent human life against the crimes of abortion and euthanasia. God is not neutral in human affairs. As Lincoln said during his debates with Stephen Douglas in the Illinois Senate race in 1858, "That is the issue that will continue in this country when these poor tongues of Judge Douglas and myself shall be silent. It is the eternal struggle between these two principles—right and wrong—throughout the world. They are the two principles that have stood face to face from the beginning of time, and will ever continue to struggle."[16]

Franklin D. Roosevelt

During the twelve years that FDR was president, he used the radio to connect regularly in an informal, conversational way with the American public through his famous *Fireside Chats*. There were twenty-seven in all, with topics ranging from an explanation of the banking system on March 12, 1933, to his plea on June 12, 1944, for Americans to buy war bonds. His final "chat" was the third time he had addressed the nation that month. On June 5, 1944, he had announced the fall of Rome to Allied forces. The very next night, he went on the radio again to tell the nation about the massive Allied assault on the beaches of Normandy, France.

On this D-day evening, June 6, 1944, the format of Roosevelt's *Fireside Chat* took a different turn. The event was so grave, the stakes so high, that information and encouragement alone would not do. Telling the nation that at the same moment he had announced the fall of Rome, Allied troops were crossing the English Channel to France, he implored, "In this poignant hour, I ask you to join with me in prayer."

President Roosevelt had written a prayer for this occasion, and with it he led the nation to the "throne of grace."[17]

And so, Almighty God: Our sons, pride of our Nation, this day have set upon a mighty endeavor, a struggle to preserve our Republic, our religion, and our civilization, and to set free a suffering humanity.

Lead them straight and true; give strength to their arms, stoutness to their hearts, steadfastness in their faith.

They will need Thy blessings. Their road will be long and hard. For the enemy is strong. He may hurl back our forces. Success may not come with rushing speed, but we shall return again and again; and we know that by Thy grace, and by the righteousness of our cause, our sons will triumph.

Remember that this radio address occurred before the advent of the television age, when for most Americans radio was still the primary means for connecting with the outside world. And although FDR himself was loved by many and hated by some, he had led the nation through some of its most agonizing trials, and the office of president still commanded a respect that would later be diminished by the turbulence of the Vietnam-era years and the Watergate scandal. As millions of Americans clustered around their radio sets for yet another critical interlude in the life of the nation, it is not too far a stretch to imagine most were praying along with their president:

And for us at home—fathers, mothers, children, wives, sisters, and brothers of brave men overseas—whose thoughts and prayers are ever with them—help us, Almighty God, to rededicate ourselves in renewed faith in Thee in this hour of great sacrifice.

And, O Lord, give us Faith. Give us Faith in Thee; Faith in our sons; Faith in each other; Faith in our united crusade. . . . With Thy blessing, we shall prevail over the unholy forces of our enemy. Help us to conquer the apostles of greed and racial arrogancies. Lead us to the saving of our country, and with our sister Nations into a world unity that will spell a sure peace, a peace invulnerable to the schemings of unworthy men. And a peace that will let all men live in freedom, reaping the just rewards of their honest toil. Thy will be done, Almighty God. Amen.

Did God have much to do with America on that fateful evening? Was this critical hour of America's history one that we should applaud or deplore, based on what we want for this country in the context of separation of church and state? You decide.

Dwight D. Eisenhower

President Eisenhower, the kindly, grandfatherly figure so warmly remembered by baby boomers like myself, we now know was a far more complex, knowledgeable, and capable political leader than he was previously thought to have been. Over the past few decades, "Ike" has undergone significant historical reassessment, and the general consensus is that President Eisenhower was "a canny knowledgeable leader who skillfully created the image of a bemused, inept, but kindly national grandfather because it served his political purposes."[18]

In the context of this revisionist history, Eisenhower's famous pronouncement about religion should be seen in a different light. As Ike prepared to assume the presidential mantle, he declared, "Our form of government has no sense unless it is founded in a deeply felt religious faith, and I don't care what it is."[19] Usually this statement has been seen as the trivialization of religion, a sort of "faith in faith," a fifties version of "May the force be with you."

However, in the context of the broader revision of Eisenhower, religion scholar Patrick Henry argued that this statement should be reassessed as well.[20]

He suggested that it deserved to be taken seriously because it "made in rather unpolished language, a point that many very sophisticated people would want to make: namely, that there are deep religious roots of democracy." The president-elect did indeed want to make this point. And he had a surprisingly well-developed understanding of the relation between religion and democracy.[21]

Could it be that rather than trivializing religion, the declaration "I don't care what it is" reflected Eisenhower's attempt to embrace pluralism by refraining from granting presidential imprimatur to any one faith tradition?

On January 20, 1953, the newly sworn-in President Eisenhower startled the nation, including even his brother Edgar, when he stepped to the podium to deliver his inaugural address and uttered these words: "My friends, before I begin the expression of those thoughts that I deem appropriate to this moment, would you permit me the privilege of uttering a little private prayer of my own. And I ask you to bow your heads."[22] Then President Eisenhower offered up the following prayer:

Almighty God, as we stand here at this moment my future associates in the executive branch of government join me in beseeching that Thou will make full and complete our dedication to the service of the people of this throng, and their fellow citizens everywhere.

Give us, we pray, the power to discern clearly right from wrong, and allow all our words and actions to be governed thereby, and by the laws of this land. Especially we pray that our concern shall be for all the people regardless of station, race, or calling.

May cooperation be permitted and be the mutual aim of those who, under the concepts of our Constitution, hold to differing political faiths; so that all may work for the good of our beloved country and Thy glory. Amen.[23]

In the midst of a surprisingly eloquent inaugural speech, President Eisenhower declared:

At such a time in history, we who are free must proclaim anew our faith. This faith is the abiding creed of our fathers. It is our faith in the deathless dignity of man, governed by eternal moral and natural laws.

This faith defines our full view of life. It establishes, beyond debate, those gifts of the Creator that are man's inalienable rights, and that make all men equal in His sight.[24]

John F. Kennedy

One of the ways in which John F. Kennedy's presidency broke new ground was the phenomenon of his Catholic faith. It revealed ugly anti-Catholic sentiments that had been simmering largely under the surface of public life since the public schools controversy of the mid-nineteenth century. Once again, fear of Vatican control fueled rampant speculation that a Catholic president would be a puppet for the pope, that U.S. policy would be dictated by Catholic teaching. During the 1960 presidential campaign, Kennedy found it necessary to address the issue head-on, and in a speech to the Greater Houston Ministerial Association (see appendix D), he did so in a marvelous description of what the separation of church and state ought to look like in American life:

[Because] I am a Catholic, and no Catholic has ever been elected President, the real issues in this campaign have been obscured—perhaps deliberately, in some quarters less responsible than this. So it is apparently necessary for me to state once again—not what kind of church I believe in—for that should be important only to me—but what kind of America I believe in.

I believe in an America where the separation of church and state is absolute—where no Catholic prelate would tell the President (should he be Catholic) how to act, and no Protestant ministers would tell their parishioners for whom to vote—where no church or church school is granted any public funds or political preference—and where no man is denied public office merely because his religion differs from the President who might appoint him or the people who might elect him.

Kennedy went on to clarify the importance of the state's neutrality in regard to specific religions to preserve the religious liberty on which the country was founded.

I believe in an America that is officially neither Catholic, Protestant, nor Jewish—where no public official either requests or accepts instruction on public policy from the Pope, the National Council of Churches or any other ecclesiastical source—where no religious body seeks to impose its will directly or indirectly on the general populace or the public acts of its officials—where religious liberty is so indivisible that an act against one church is treated as an act against all.

For while this year it may be a Catholic against whom the finger of suspicion is pointed, in other years it has been, and may someday be again, a Jew—or a Quaker—or a Unitarian—or a Baptist. It was Virginia's harassment of Baptist preachers, for example, that helped lead to Jefferson's Statute of Religious Freedom. Today, I may be the victim—but tomorrow it may be you—until the whole fabric of our harmonious society is ripped at a time of great National peril.

I believe in a President whose religious views are his own private affair, neither imposed by him upon the nation nor imposed by the nation upon him as a condition to holding that office. . . . I am not the Catholic candidate for President. I am the Democratic Party's candidate for President who happens also to be a Catholic. I do not speak for my church on public matters—and the church does not speak for me.[25]

Today there is debate about the degree to which a president's faith should or should not affect the way in which he fulfills his presidential responsibilities, as we have seen in the controversy surrounding President George W. Bush's Evangelical faith. However, Kennedy set a new tone for the nation in forcing it to come to terms with its assumptions regarding religious faith and the highest public office in the land.

In JFK's inaugural address (see appendix D), he challenged Americans to service with words that have echoed in our national consciousness ever since. His idea of responsible citizenship is a sacrificial, missional vision that we would do well to take to heart. After reminding the nation that the "beliefs for which our forebears fought are still at issue around the globe—the belief that the rights of man come not from the generosity of the state, but from the hand of God," President Kennedy inspired and challenged the nation:

And so, my fellow Americans, ask not what your country can do for you; ask what you can do for your country.

My fellow citizens of the world, ask not what America will do for you, but what together we can do for the freedom of man.

Finally, whether you are citizens of America or citizens of the world, ask of us here the same high standards of strength and sacrifice which we ask of you. With a good conscience our only sure reward, with history the final judge of our deeds, let us go forth to lead the land we love, asking His blessing and His help, but knowing that here on earth God's work must truly be our own.[26]

So began JFK's presidency. Tragically, President Kennedy's brief tenure in office was cut short by an assassin's bullet in Dallas on November 22, 1963. The speech the president was to deliver at the Trade Mart in Dallas (see appendix D) that sad, heartbreaking day would have concluded with this stirring reminder of the perils faced by free men and of America's dependence on divince providence:

We in this country, in this generation, are—by destiny rather than choice—the watchmen on the walls of world freedom. We ask, therefore, that we may be worthy of our power and responsibility, that we may exercise our strength with wisdom and restraint, and that we may achieve in our time and for all time the ancient vision of "peace on earth, good will toward men." That must always be our goal, and the righteousness of our cause must always underlie our strength. For as was written long ago: "except the Lord keep the city, the watchman waketh but in vain."

Lyndon B. Johnson

President Lyndon B. Johnson was called many things, and the appellations rarely concerned his piety. However, even he quoted Jesus and appealed to the favor of God on the nation's decisions when he asked Congress to pass a strong voting rights bill.

Rarely are we met with the challenge, not to our growth or abundance, or our welfare or our society—but rather to the values and the purposes and the meaning of our beloved nation.

The issue of equal rights for American Negroes is such an issue. And should we double our wealth and conquer the stars and still be unequal to this issue, then we will have failed as a people and as a nation.

For with a country as with a person, "What is a man profited, if he shall gain the whole world, and lose his own soul." . . . Above the pyramid on the great seal of the United States it says in Latin, "God has favored our undertaking." God will not favor everything that we do. It is rather our duty to divine his will. I cannot help but believe that He truly understands and that He really favors the undertaking that we begin here tonight.[27]

Ronald W. Reagan

Most Americans over thirty would not be surprised to hear that President Reagan was a man of religious faith and that his faith informed his approach to the presidency. Many Americans might be surprised, however, at just how serious a role Ronald Reagan's faith played in the years in which he pursued, then served, in the office of president.[28]

Even before he became president, Ronald Reagan had made it clear to anyone who was listening that his faith played a central role in his life. During his 1976 presidential campaign, Reagan wrote, "I have to realize that whatever I do has meaning only if I ask that it serves His purpose. . . . I believe that in my present undertaking, whatever the outcome, it will be His doing. I will pray for understanding of what it is He would have me do."[29] He then explained that if "the task I seek should be given me," then he "would pray only that I could perform it in a way that would serve God."[30]

When Reagan narrowly lost the 1976 Republican presidential nomination to President Ford, he seemed to be the only one in his entourage who was not devastated. As he told his sobbing daughter Maureen, "There's a reason for this. I don't know what it is. But there's a reason. . . . Everything happens for a reason. . . . If you just keep doing what you're doing, the path is going to open up and you'll see what it is you're supposed to do."[31]

Reagan, following his own advice, kept doing what he was doing and announced his candidacy for president in the 1980 election cycle with these words: "A troubled and afflicted mankind looks to us, pleading for us to keep our rendezvous with destiny; . . . that we will become that shining city on a hill. I believe that you and I, together, can keep this rendezvous with destiny."[32]

After winning his party's nomination in 1980, Reagan returned to this theme in his acceptance speech. In the closing moments of the speech, he said, "Can we doubt that only a Divine Providence placed this land, this island of freedom, here as a refuge for all those people in the world who yearn to breathe freely?"[33]

Reagan then closed the speech with "an extemporaneous moment" in which the real, unexpurgated Ronald Reagan spoke directly to America's heart: "I'll confess that I've been a little afraid to suggest what I'm going to suggest—I'm more afraid not to: that we begin our crusade joined together in a moment of silent prayer."[34]

A hushed convention center crowd bowed their heads in silence—then, after a dramatic pause, Reagan intoned, "God bless America."[35] As presidential historian Paul Kengor observed, "This was not the Reagan of the broad grin or cocked head, but a man of grave demeanor and spiritual conviction, choosing to link his personal religious vision with his party's political destiny."[36]

Many in the crowd and countless numbers watching on national television were deeply moved. The national press corps, however, had a very different reaction. "The crew of CBS Radio viewed the prayer as a display of 'almost inexpressible corniness,' according to one member who was present. It was a sign of things to come: even before his election, the divide between Reagan's solemn piety and the clucking of cynical elites had begun."[37] The national media didn't "get" Ronald Reagan, and many still don't—the culture gap is just too great.

When Reagan was grievously wounded in a foiled assassination attempt in 1981, he confided to Terence Cardinal Cooke, "I have decided that whatever time I have left is for Him. . . . Whatever happens now I owe my life to God and will try to serve him every way I can."[38]

On March 8, 1983, Reagan delivered a speech to the National Association of Evangelicals annual meeting in Orlando, Florida. Near the beginning of this speech, which in many ways came to define his presidency, President Reagan "commended the role of religious faith in American democracy. 'Freedom prospers only where the blessings of God are avidly sought and humbly accepted,' he mentioned. 'The American experiment in democracy rests on this insight,' he said; its discovery was the 'great triumph' of the Founders."[39]

Then Reagan asserted that "there was sin and evil in the world, and we're enjoined by Scripture and the Lord Jesus to oppose it with all our might."[40] He first applied the concept of evil to America, pointing to "a legacy of evil with which we must deal," referencing slavery, racism, and anti-Semitism.[41]

Then, and only then, did he refer to the Soviet Union as an "evil empire" and explain why:

> The real crisis we face today is a spiritual one; at root, it is a test of moral will and faith. Whittaker Chambers, the man whose own religious conversion made him a witness to one of the terrible traumas of our time, the Hiss-Chambers case, wrote that the crisis of the Western World exists to the degree in which the West is indifferent to God, the degree to which it collaborates in communism's attempt to make man stand alone without God. And then he said, for Marxism-Leninism is actually the second oldest faith, first proclaimed in the Garden of Eden with the words of temptation, "Ye shall be as gods."[42]

Is it any wonder that one of President Reagan's recurrent themes was "Freedom is the universal right of all God's children. . . . The cause of freedom is the cause of God. . . . I believe God intended for us to be free"?[43]

George W. Bush

President Bush has been forthright about his Evangelical faith, to the satisfaction of his supporters and the deep dismay of his critics. He pointed to one of his favorite hymns in recalling the church service he attended on the day he was inaugurated as governor of Texas.

> One of the hymns I selected is titled "A Charge to Keep I Have." Written by Charles Wesley, the words say:
>
> > A charge to keep I have,
> > A God to glorify,
> > A never dying soul to save,
> > And fit it for the sky.
> > To serve the present age,

> My calling to fulfill;
>
> O may it all my powers engage
>
> To do my Master's will!

[Hanging in my office is] a beautiful oil painting by W. H. D. Koerner entitled *A Charge to Keep*. The painting, inspired by the hymn, [pictures] a horseman determinedly charging up what appears to be a steep and rough trail. This is us. [The painting and] hymn have been an inspiration for me and for members of my staff. "A Charge to Keep" calls us to our highest and best. It speaks of purpose and direction. In many hymnals, it is associated with a Bible verse, 1 Corinthians 4:2: "Now it is required that those who have been given a trust must prove faithful."[44]

During a *Meet the Press* special on faith in America, NBC News host Tim Russert said to me, "Dr. Land, you were quoted in September of '04 as saying that George Bush said to you, 'I believe God wants me to be president.' Is that accurate?"[45]

I answered, yes, it was accurate, but it was also incomplete. The media has insisted on quoting that one sentence alone, which changes the entire context.[46] It is an example of the attempt to paint the president as a religious fanatic with delusions of providential grandeur. In actuality, the president made this statement after attending a worship service the morning he was inaugurated for his second term as Texas governor. The Methodist minister had delivered a very stirring sermon about "God has a purpose for your life and a plan for your life." Barbara Bush had reached over and said to her son, "George, he's talking to you."

When Governor Bush came back to the governor's mansion, he met with several of us and said, "I believe God wants me to be president, but if that doesn't happen, that's okay. I'm loved at home, and that's more important. I've seen the presidency up close and personal, and I know it's a sacrifice and not a reward, and I don't need it for personal validation."

I remember his remarks so clearly because I was so impressed by them at the time. I thought, *You know, that's about as healthy emotionally as you're going to find in someone who's willing to do all that you have to do and make all the personal sacrifices you have to make to run for the presidency in this society.* I think it shows President Bush's heart. I've known him since 1988, and I find him to be a man of spiritual humility who is going to do what he believes is right, as God gives him the light to understand the right. But I would also ask this question: How many of the men who have run for the presidency in the past quarter century did *not* think God wanted them to be president? Jimmy Carter didn't think that? Bill Clinton didn't think that? Al Gore didn't think that? These men were also open to the possibility that they might be wrong, as was George W. Bush.

Russert cited JFK's inaugural address and played a video clip of President Kennedy stating that "here on earth, God's work must truly be our own." That, Russert commented, was "politics and religion together in a very clearly stated way."

Few are quoting George W.'s inaugural addresses yet, but I think his second inaugural address was one of the best that has ever been delivered by an American president—one of the most eloquent and one of the most religious we've had in a long time. I find it interesting that neutral observers have said that they think it is the best since Kennedy's. It should hold up very well to the judgment of history. But it uses language that would be more familiar to Americans of an earlier time, and Evangelicals are more in touch with that earlier time.

President Bush is criticized for speaking of his sense of being led by God. The Left rears up in indignation, casting him as the chief priest of a cabal of theocrats. Yet in 1961 John F. Kennedy used explicitly religious language—read his inaugural address (see appendix D). Look up President Roosevelt's prayer for the D-day invasion (see appendix D), President Lincoln's sermonic second inaugural (see appendix D), and President Washington's Thanksgiving Day proclamation. Consider Paul Kengor's account of "God and Democrats" in *God and George W. Bush*.[47] Then ask yourself how well grounded the criticism is from a historical perspective.

Presidential candidate Al Gore wrote a best-selling book about his Christian faith and its relevance for every sphere of life, yet in the campaign leading up to the 2000 election, nobody made an issue of his use of religious language. His running mate, Joseph Lieberman, was even more proactive in discussing the centrality of his pious observance of the Jewish faith, yet there was nary a whisper about a Judeo-Christian ticket.

Could it be that there is a media double standard at play here, in which it is acceptable for liberal presidents and presidential candidates to speak the language of faith but it is verboten for conservative presidents and presidential candidates to do so? Is there a particular *kind* of religious expression that some have taken upon themselves to condemn over other kinds of religious expressions?

More broadly, how is it that we came to this point of assuming that separation of church and state means the exclusion of religious expression in the public arena? What has confused us into thinking it is inappropriate for an elected official to express his religious convictions in the natural course of explaining what personally motivates and informs the way he carries out his responsibilities? Perhaps it is time for a renewed understanding of the relationship of church and state as our founding fathers foresaw it and conceived it and as our leaders and people have practiced it in their lives over more than two centuries.

In the past, our leaders and people did not conceive that church-state separation required an eradication of religiously informed moral values from public policy discussions of what should and should not be done in society and law.

★ 6 ★

Why We're So Confused about Church and State

The traditional Evangelicals, those who come out of Billy Graham's mold, are not necessarily comfortable with the direction taken by the Dominionists, who now control most of America's major Evangelical organizations, from the NRB to the Southern Baptist Convention, and may already claim dominion over the Christian media outlets.

—CHRIS HEDGES[1]

A chronic annoyance in the media these days is the casual equation of religious conservatives with the Taliban.

—CLAUDIA WINKLER[2]

The logjam of extreme views on each side of the church-and-state debate was in full view during a PBS interview in 2005 with journalist Christopher Hedges and Judge Roy Moore, former chief justice of the Alabama Supreme Court. The interview took place in historic St. Paul's Chapel in New York, near the site where the World Trade Center once stood, where George Washington worshiped on his Inauguration Day. To address the question of what place religion should hold in the public square, host David Brancaccio had brought together two guests with radically different ideas on the subject, each of whom had recently authored a book on the Ten Commandments and also had been in the news for his high-profile position on religion in America.

Brancaccio first turned to Hedges, a Pulitzer prize-winning journalist and former war correspondent for the *New York Times*, who wrote one of two "Soldiers of Christ" articles published in *Harper's* magazine that were highly critical of Evangelical Christians. The first article, written by Jeff Sharlett, pilloried Ted Haggard, former senior pastor of New Life Church in Colorado Springs, along with many of those in his congregation. It depicted Colorado Springs as "home to the greatest concentration of Fundamentalist Christian activist groups in American history," populated by Christians who view it "both as a last stand and as a kind of utopia in the making."[3]

The second "Soldiers of Christ" article, authored by Hedges, was based on his attendance at an annual meeting of the National Religious Broadcasters. In the article, Hedges used a classic shouting-match tactic to discredit the entire gathering: he cited a fringe extreme (dominion theology) and then broad-brushed it across an entire mainstream movement of Evangelical Christianity in the twentieth century. His audacity was perhaps exceeded only by the ignorance of his statements, as anyone with a working familiarity of either the history of Christianity in America or its current expressions can attest.

> What the disparate sects of this movement, known as Dominionism, share is an obsession with political power. A decades-long refusal to engage in politics at all following the Scopes trial has been replaced by a call for Christian "dominion" over the nation and, eventually, over the earth itself. . . . America becomes, in this militant biblicism, an agent of God, and all political and intellectual opponents of America's Christian leaders are viewed, quite simply, as agents of Satan. Under Christian dominion, America will no longer be a sinful and fallen nation but one in which the Ten Commandments form the basis of our legal system, Creationism and "Christian values" form the basis of our educational system, and the media and the government proclaim the Good News to one and all. Aside from its proselytizing mandate, the federal government will be reduced to the protection of property rights and "homeland" security. . . . The only legitimate voices in this state will be Christian. All others will be silenced.

Equally astonishing are Hedges' unsupported—and indeed, unsupportable—flights of fancy regarding the Dominionists and mainstream Evangelical organizations. It is one thing for a journalist with a clear bias to commit such flagrant caricaturing. However, Hedges was also a visiting lecturer at Princeton University, teaching a course called "The Christian Right and the Open Society."[4] It is truly unfathomable that a premier institution would permit itself to be associated with such shallow and sloppy handling of important issues, as illustrated in the following statement by Hedges:

> The traditional Evangelicals, those who come out of Billy Graham's mold, are not necessarily comfortable with the direction taken by the Dominionists, who now control most of America's major Evangelical organizations, from the NRB to the Southern Baptist Convention, and may already claim dominion over the Christian media outlets. But Christians who challenge Dominionists, even if they are Fundamentalist or conservative or born-again, tend to be ruthlessly thrust aside. . . . Dobson is perhaps the most powerful figure in the Dominionist movement.[5]

This scandalously erroneous "description" of Evangelicals reveals Hedges to be either blinded by his own bias or shamefully dishonest. "Dominionists" control none of "America's major Evangelical organizations" and are considered a slightly "nutty" fringe group by most of them. I have been head of the Southern Baptist Convention's ethics and public policy entity for nearly two decades now, beginning in 1988, and I have met only about a dozen Southern Baptist "Dominionists." Virtually every Southern Baptist I know vehemently disavows both their theology and their public policy beliefs. The same is true of Evangelicals of other denominations. Dr. James Dobson of Focus on the Family, for example, would certainly be surprised to discover he is a "Dominionist."

In the PBS interview, Hedges explained that he had attended the NRB convention to study another instance of what he saw as the merging of religion and nationalism around the globe. David Brancaccio questioned Hedges about his condemnation of Christians in the *Harper's* article. Hedges' responses clearly show the slippery and contradictory nature of his criticism, which is filled with careless mistakes—strange errors for a career journalist. A skeptical listener might be tempted to wonder if he had an agenda involving scare tactics to sound his alarm.

BRANCACCIO: And as you looked around, as you talked to people you saw things that added up to quite a big word. I mean the headline to your piece in *Harper's* had the word "hate" . . .

CHRISTOPHER HEDGES: Because that's what the ideology is about. The final aesthetic of this movement is violence. This obsession with the apocalyptic end of the world with the rapture, which of course is not in the Bible, with you know, the torment that will befall unbelievers . . . the cult of masculinity, the notion of Christ the avenger. All of this has far more in common with despotic ideologies, even sort of fascist ideologies, than it does with the message of love, which I think is essentially certainly within the four Gospels the message that Jesus tries to bring.

BRANCACCIO: It's such a conundrum though. You use strong words to describe your fears about where some of these movements are headed. Totalitarian, seditious. . . . Like people are committing sedition. When you use [such] words in relation to people's religion or just deeply held convictions it does become difficult to have dialogue. I mean someone has to ratchet back the rhetoric. And the *National Review* didn't like your *Harper's* piece. . . . Stanley Kurtz writing in it said that your comments made in the name of opposing hatred license hatred. He's accusing you of what you're accusing them of.

CHRISTOPHER HEDGES: Well, I've never said that somebody doesn't have a right to believe that the Bible is the literal word of God. I've never said that somebody does not have a right to believe that abortion is murder. I believe that in an open society people have a right to those beliefs. What I'm saying is that when I'm faced with a movement who says not only where I'm coming from and who I am and what I represent is not legitimate but a force of evil, then at that point where does the dialogue begin?

What it is—what is it that we have to talk about?

BRANCACCIO: Help me understand something though. I mean who are you talking about? You're not talking about Christians, Evangelical Christians. Who specifically are the people that are worrying you?

CHRISTOPHER HEDGES: Yeah. I mean, David, that's a really good point. I'm not talking about Evangelical Christians. I'm talking about people we would classify as Dominionists . . . a term that they perhaps would not embrace themselves. I think they would call themselves Bible-believing Christians as a way to separate themselves.

BRANCACCIO: God's dominion over our civic life, over our government?

CHRISTOPHER HEDGES: Yes, very much so. And this comes out of a sort of theological or ideological movement begun roughly thirty years ago by J. Rousas Rushdoony [sic] with the Institutes of Biblical Law. And I think what a lot of people don't understand is that we're—when we talk about Evangelicals in America, we're no longer talking about the Billy Grahams or the Luis Palaus people who are concerned primarily with personal salvation. . . . We've had Christian revivals throughout this nation since our inception. But all of these revivals have called on followers to remove themselves from the contaminants of secular society to live a more Godly life. This movement is different. What it's calling on is for its followers to essentially take control of secular society and create a Christian, what they define as a Christian nation.

BRANCACCIO: And how would that live alongside people who may have different religious views in our republic?

CHRISTOPHER HEDGES: Well, what they would like to do is impose their—what they call as their moral agenda on the rest of us. You know, there's a real hostility to federal programs. Head Start, public education. I mean, you know, James Dobson, the head of Focus on the Family, has called for Christian followers to remove their children from public schools. And put them in schools that teach creationism. Put them in schools that teach them that they have been anointed as Christians to have dominion—dominion over the United States and dominion over the rest of the world.

There are very specific plans. I mean there's a book they use in the Christian schools as well as the home schooling movement called *America's Providential History*, and there's a chapter on Christian economics. And when you read through the book it's clear that what they want—the federal government essentially will be reduced to carrying out national defense and protecting property rights, and not much else.[6]

After interviewing Chris Hedges, David Brancaccio turned to Judge Roy Moore, whose book *So Help Me God: The Ten Commandments, Judicial Tyranny, and the Battle for Religious Freedom* addresses the question, "How did someone get to the highest judicial position in Alabama, only to be removed for upholding his solemn oath of office?"[7] Judge Moore contends that the separation of church and state has been so abused that God has been taken out of the public square. Therefore, Moore believes, in his refusal to obey a federal court order, he was obeying the rule of law by not following the unlawful dictates of man. Brancaccio asked Moore what he means by his message that judges need to answer to God.

ROY MOORE: The center of the message is judges need to answer to the Constitution. They need to answer to the law. And our law recognizes God. And today, we've divorced God from many things. So it's not answering directly to God. It's answering to our Constitution, which recognizes the sovereignty of God.

That's the whole purpose of the First Amendment. And the first thing that our forefathers did when they wrote the First Amendment was to acknowledge God. It was all about God. So when you say that God's not in the Constitution, it is because people don't understand what the Constitution is about.

Brancaccio then cited the Treaty of Tripoli, a treaty of "peace and friendship" signed in 1796 between the United States and the North African Muslim states of the Barbary Coast in order to protect the passage of American trade ships in the Mediterranean. Article 11 of the Treaty affirms that "the government of the United States of America is not in any sense founded on the Christian Religion, as it has in itself no character of enmity against the laws, religion or tranquility of Musselmen, and as the said States never have entered into any war or act of hostility against any Mehomitan nation, it is declared by the parties that no pretext arising from religious opinions shall ever produce an interruption of the harmony existing between the two countries." Because the Constitution grants to treaties the force of law, advocates for the wall of separation between church and state point to the Treaty of Tripoli as evidence of the founders' intent for religious neutrality. How did Judge Moore interpret this statement? Brancaccio wanted to know.

ROY MOORE: [The U.S. is not in any sense founded on the Christian religion.] As in no animosity towards the Muslim faith. Basically, what they were doing is casting away the fears of those people in North Africa that we were like the Crusaders. That we were going to force our religion upon them.

That is not what America was about. We were not a Christian nation in that sense. And that's what they were saying in that treaty. It's made—a matter of fact, the second Treaty of Tripoli took that out. But in no way does that forbid us to be a Christian nation, or a Christian people.

BRANCACCIO: What pushed you to take the step of wanting to bring the Ten Commandments into—really civil courtroom?

ROY MOORE: Well, because our civil justice system in Alabama, according to the Constitution, says that justice is established, and I quote, "invoking the favor and guidance of Almighty God." It's the same principle about which we're talking about. That that freedom to believe what you want comes from God, and can't be interfered with by civil courts.

Civil courts judge you on your actions. You're not judged on what you think. Because that relationship belongs to God. You're judged on what you do, on your actions. And that's why it's a predicate to recognize God. It was not about the Ten Commandments. It never was about the Ten Commandments. The judge himself said that he wasn't saying the Ten Commandments couldn't be displayed. But when you acknowledge the Judeo-Christian God, you've crossed the line between the permissible and the impermissible.

BRANCACCIO: And you don't think you crossed the line?

ROY MOORE: Absolutely not. It was a recognition of God. And government has no, the federal government has no right to interfere with the people of the state of Alabama, from recognizing this God.

Every constitution of every state, to include Maine, where you're from, recognizes God in the constitution. Every one of them. How can a federal judge come into a state and say, "You cannot acknowledge God if it's a particular God?" Of course it's a particular God. It's the God upon which this nation was founded. . . .

If you're uncomfortable with the recognition of the Judeo-Christian God, then you're uncomfortable with America. Because without a recognition of that God, America would not exist. America would have never been started. . . .

BRANCACCIO: If you are successful in persuading, for instance, maybe someday the U.S. Supreme Court that you're right in this matter, how does the country change? What follows from this idea?

ROY MOORE: Freedom, liberty, and that's exactly what it's been based upon for all these years. That's why we're—we have so many religions and faiths here, is because it comes from God. It's a recognition that things in the Constitution, for example, life, liberty and property under the Fifth and Fourteenth Amendment, came from a definition that those were God-given rights. Now, they're man-determined. . . . Without a recognition of the God of the Bible, we lose our national morality, and that's happening today, right under our noses. Nobody seems to understand it.[8]

What Judge Moore is missing is that no state-sponsored recognition of God or state sponsorship of religion will ever restore morality. The only thing that will restore morality in this country is the personal recognition of God in individual human hearts as Americans turn toward Him in repentance and belief in Jesus Christ. It is not the responsibility of the state to promote belief in God. This is in no way to suggest that there is anything inappropriate about our forebears' declaration that our Fundamental rights and obligations are rooted in a more than merely human source—a divine Creator, who endows us with unalienable rights.

What *did* the founders have in mind when they insisted that the state should take no role in establishing religion or interfering with its free exercise? Interestingly, one of the recent calls for moderation comes from Claudia Winkler, managing editor of *The Weekly Standard,* who takes liberals to task for comparing Christian conservatives to the Taliban.

> A chronic annoyance in the media these days is the casual equation of religious conservatives with the Taliban. One example from the left-wing British newspaper the *Guardian* is a doozy.
>
> In a January 15 [2002] editorial mocking a prominent conservative Southern Baptist on the occasion of his death at 92, the paper managed to refer to the Taliban in the second sentence, then went on to say of its subject (W. A. Criswell, warmly praised by President Bush and Billy Graham, a member of his Dallas congregation) that he "gave lip service to the constitutional separation of church and state."
>
> The generous explanation for this slur is ignorance: Maybe the *Guardian* really doesn't know the difference between an Evangelical and a theocrat. If it wanted to know, the antidote might be a series of new writings that highlight the religious roots—closely entwined with the Enlightenment roots—of that pivotal American invention, the separation of church and state.[9]

Winkler's cogent critique suggests the wisdom of a more thorough acquaintance with American history on church and state issues. Let's take a closer look at what both liberals and conservatives have been missing.

A LITTLE LESS TALK AND A LOT MORE HISTORY

The God-and-country shouting match tends to turn a deaf ear to history. Today the most vocal advocates of separation of church and state are typically found in the liberal secularists' camp: for example, the American Civil Liberties Union, People for the American Way, and the Freedom from Religion Foundation. Generally speaking, they consider themselves watchdogs of religious conservatives, whom they perceive to be busy trying to tear down the wall of separation between church and state.

What a stark irony: these liberals are missing the point that historically, the most vocal advocates of separation of church and state have been religious conservatives! Why? Because they have felt most keenly the dreadful consequences of state control of religion.

On the flip side of the coin, however, conservatives such as Judge Roy Moore err in celebrating our country's early and cozy familiarity between the government and the Christian religion. In fact, there was an all-too-cozy relationship between state governments and the Christian religion in the form of Episcopalianism, the U.S. version of the Anglican Church of England. Far from Christianizing the populace, this state-sponsored acknowledgment of religion tended to tyrannize the populace by punishing all who dared to differ from the state's mandated beliefs and practices.

Court records from the late eighteenth century contain the following descriptions of Baptist persecution under the state-established religion of Anglicanism in Virginia. Keep in mind that the offenses heinous enough to provoke such attacks comprised preaching the gospel without an Anglican state-church approved license (and it wasn't straight out of the *Book of Common Prayer*, either):

- "pelted with apples and stones"
- "ducked and nearly drowned by twenty men"
- "commanded to take a dram, or be whipped"
- "jailed for permitting a man to pray"
- "meeting broken up by a mob"

- "arrested as a vagabond and schismatic"
- "pulled down and hauled about by hair"
- "tried to suffocate him with smoke"
- "tried to blow him up with gun powder"
- "drunken rowdies put in same cell with him"
- "horses ridden over his hearers at jail"
- "dragged off stage, kicked, and cuffed about"
- "shot with a shot-gun"
- "ruffians armed with bludgeons beat him"
- "severely beaten with a whip"
- "whipped severely by the Sheriff"
- "hands slashed while preaching"[10]

A popular bumper sticker proclaims, "Freedom isn't free." Not many Americans today realize that their religious freedom was paid for by Baptists, among many others, who suffered decades of persecution and imprisonment in their refusal to bow to the king of the state instead of King Jesus in their religious beliefs and practices. These dissenting Baptists became a driving force behind the efforts of James Madison and Thomas Jefferson in securing a religious freedom provision first in Virginia and then at the federal level.

According to the First Amendment to the United States Constitution, "Congress shall make no law respecting an establishment of religion, or prohibiting the free exercise thereof." However, even after the First Amendment was ratified in 1791, religious conflict continued to simmer at the state level because the Bill of Rights restricted the actions of the U.S. Congress and the federal government, not individual state governments. It would not be until the twentieth century, when the Supreme Court began to incorporate selectively provisions of the Bill of Rights through the due process clause of the Fourteenth Amendment, that the religious freedom clause of the First Amendment would be applied to supersede state law.

Consequently, in 1801 a group of Baptists from Danbury, Connecticut, wrote their newly elected president, Thomas Jefferson, expressing their grave concerns about their state constitution, which permitted and endorsed a state establishment of religion (Congregationalist), and which granted "mere toleration," rather than full-fledged freedom, to minority faith adherents. As a minority faith, they were vulnerable to state, as opposed to federal, discrimination.

Our Sentiments are uniformly on the side of Religious Liberty — That Religion is at all times and places a matter between God and individuals — That no man ought to suffer in name, person, or effects on account of his religious Opinions — That the legitimate Power of civil government extends no further than to punish the man who works *ill to his neighbor*: But Sir our constitution of government is not specific. Our ancient charter together with the Laws made coincident therewith, were adopted on the Basis of our government, at the time of our revolution; and such had been our Laws & usages, and such still are; that Religion is considered as the first object of Legislation; and therefore what religious privileges we enjoy (as a minor part of the State) we enjoy as favors granted, and not as inalienable rights: and these favors we receive at the expense of such degrading acknowledgements, as are inconsistent with the rights of freemen.[11]

Jefferson's response to the Danbury Baptists affirmed freedom of conscience and introduced the metaphor of a wall between church and state:

Believing with you that religion is a matter which lies solely between Man & his God, that he owes account to none other for his faith or his worship, that the legitimate powers of government reach actions only, & not opinions, I contemplate with sovereign reverence that act of the whole American people which declared that their legislature should "make no law respecting an establishment of religion, or prohibiting the free exercise thereof," thus building a wall of separation between Church & State.[12]

This imagery for separation of church and state—even the very idea of church-state separation—didn't start with Thomas Jefferson, however. It originated with Roger Williams (an ordained Baptist minister later turned "seeker"), defender of soul liberty, who founded Providence, Rhode Island, in 1636 after being kicked out of Massachusetts for refusing to recognize the Puritan theocracy. As noted earlier, he insisted that the Church of England's ministers were not true ministers, the Church of England wasn't a true church, and nobody should be forced to attend its services or pay taxes to support its activities, since it represented an illegitimate union of church and state.

Williams narrowly escaped being sent back to England in chains when he disappeared into the wilderness, where he was befriended by Native Americans. The number one indictment against him, which they were going to pin on his neck for his return trip to England, was his insistence that the colonists didn't own the land because they had received it by patent from the king and didn't pay the Indians for it. In other words, Roger Williams, the supposed champion of church-state separation, was up to his colonial eyeballs in the number one moral and public policy issue of the era: the colonists' shameful treatment of Native Americans. Clearly, Roger Williams never understood separation of church and state to mean separation of religiously informed moral values from public policy.

When Williams cofounded Providence Plantations, which later became Rhode Island, he made sure that the colony's charter specifically established religious liberty and the separation of civil and ecclesiastical authorities. That charter founded the first government anywhere in the Western world in over a thousand years where people were free to worship as they pleased, or not worship at all, without any civil penalties whatsoever.

The separation of church and state, Williams maintained, was necessary to protect the garden of the church from the wilderness of the world. Jefferson's "wall" imagery came from Williams's idea that there needed to be a wall between the garden of the church and the wilderness of the world. The wall wasn't there to protect the wilderness; it was there to protect the garden. The metaphor did not depict a static situation, in which there were fixed areas of garden and wilderness, because the church would always be trying to expand the garden and retake the wilderness. Without a wall to separate them, however, the wilderness would encroach upon the garden and damage it.[13]

To understand what Jefferson meant when he wrote about the wall of separation between church and state, it is critical to recognize the context: he was writing to Baptist ministers in a state that had a tax-supported state church, which was discriminating against and persecuting Baptists. Nine of the original thirteen states, including Connecticut, had tax-supported state churches—and all of them discriminated against Baptists.

President Jefferson was writing to Baptists in a state (Connecticut) where there was no wall between church and state, but rather a union of the two institutions. Jefferson's affirmation that there ought to be a wall of separation between the institution of the state and the institution of the church *never* meant that religious values should be eliminated from public life. Jefferson would have been flabbergasted had anybody interpreted it to exclude religiously informed moral values from the democratic political process.

PRESIDENT JEFFERSON, THE "BIG CHEESE," AND AN EVENTFUL WEEKEND

Compelling evidence that Jefferson never intended by his wall-of-separation metaphor what modern jurists have done with it is found in the immediate context in which it was constructed. On January 1, 1802, sometime before 11:00 a.m., John Leland (1754–1841), prominent Baptist preacher, evangelist, and activist for religious disestablishment, first in Virginia and then in Massachusetts, arrived by appointment at the White House. Leland, serving as head of a delegation of Jefferson supporters from Cheshire, Massachusetts, brought a huge cheese to present to the president as a token of their admiration and regard. The cheese itself "measured more than four feet in diameter, thirteen in circumference and weighted 1,235 pounds."[14] "According to eyewitnesses, its crust was painted red and emblazoned with Jefferson's favorite motto: 'Rebellion to tyrants is obedience to God.'"[15]

This gargantuan cheese had been created under Leland's inspiration and leadership by the mostly Baptist residents of Cheshire in western Massachusetts to celebrate Jefferson's electoral victory. A special reinforced press had been constructed and over nine hundred cows milked. Baptists "turned out with pails and tubs of curds for a day of thanksgiving, hymn-singing, and cheese pressing," which produced the mammoth cheese.[16]

In late November 1801, Leland and Darius Brown commenced their journey to the Hudson River, transferred the cheese to a ship that brought it to New York, and then transferred it to Baltimore and finally to Washington by horse-drawn wagon. It caused an enormous stir among the press and the public, pro and con, and Leland stopped periodically along the route, preaching to gatherings of the faithful and the curious.[17]

President Jefferson stood waiting in the door of the White House, and the cheese was received "with an exchange of cordial expressions of mutual admiration and gratitude and exuberant cheese-tasting."[18] Leland read a proclamation of presentation "signed by fine citizens of Cheshire but undoubtedly composed by their revered Baptist elder," which said in part:

> Our attachment to the National Constitution in indissoluble. . . . Among its most beautiful features—the right to free suffrage, to correct abuses—the prohibition of religious tests, to prevent all hierarchy—and the means of amendment which it contains within itself, to remove defects as fast as they are discovered, appear the most prominent. . . . We believe the supreme Ruler of the Universe, who raises up men to achieve great events, has raised up a JEFFERSON at this critical day, to defend *Republicanism*, and to baffle the arts of *Aristocracy*.[19]

The Cheshire folk then assured the president, somewhat ironically given that the president was a slaveholder, that the cheese "was produced by the personal labor of *Freeborn Farmers*, with the voluntary and cheerful aid of their wives and daughters, without the assistance of a single slave."[20] President Jefferson made a gracious speech, accepting the cheese, and then returned to his presidential duties.

That very New Year's afternoon, Jefferson also sent the final form of a long-thought-out, carefully revised letter to the Baptists of Danbury, Connecticut.

> Jefferson drafted a response to the Danbury Baptists, which he circulated for comment from the key members of his cabinet. The surviving manuscripts reveal that Jefferson's reply to the Connecticut Baptists was written with meticulous care and planned effort. The fact that a rough draft of the letter, with scribbled amendments and a margin note explaining one major change, was retained in Jefferson's papers along with a copy of the final version indicates the significance the president attached to this statement.[21]

It is also clear from the surviving historical documentary evidence that President Jefferson "regarded his reply to the Danbury Baptists as a political letter, not as a dispassionate theoretical pronouncement on the relations between government and religion."[22]

It should also be noted that Jefferson *significantly* narrowed the scope of his wall metaphor when he used the term *church* in his "wall of separation." "The word *church* rather than *religion* in Jefferson's restatement of the First Amendment emphasized that the constitutional separation was between ecclesiastical *institutions* and the civil state. His choice of language, no doubt, appealed to pious, Evangelical Protestant dissenters who disapproved of established churches but believed religion played an indispensable role in public life."[23]

Let's review once again the time sequence of this eventful New Year's weekend. Friday morning, Baptist preacher and religious liberty activist John Leland delivered the "big cheese" to Thomas Jefferson. Later that day Jefferson sent his carefully crafted letter to the Danbury Baptists.

Then on Sunday, January 3, 1802, John Leland preached a sermon from the speaker's rostrum of the chamber of the U.S. House of Representatives to members of both houses of Congress and other assembled guests, including—quite surprisingly to regular attendees at such events—the president himself. One of the attendees, Rep. Manasseh Cutler of Massachusetts, a Federalist and a Congregational (the official state church) clergyman, was most disgusted with the entire spectacle.[24]

Congressman Cutler's description of Leland underscores the cavernous culture gap between the established church in Massachusetts and religious dissenters like Leland and their allies, such as Jefferson:

> Leland, the cheesemonger, a poor ignorant, illiterate, clownish creature . . . was introduced as the preacher to both Houses of Congress. . . . The President, contrary to all former practice, made one of his audience. . . . Such a farrago, bawled with stunning voice, horrid tone, frightful grimaces, and extravagant gestures, I believe, was never heard by any decent auditory before.[25]

The following day (Monday), Leland "paid his parting respects to the president."[26]

So from Friday morning to the following Monday, President Jefferson accepted the "big cheese" from a famous Baptist preacher, wrote a letter to the Danbury Baptists, attended a worship service in the Chamber of the House of Representatives, and received at the White House the same famous preacher who preached to Congress the day before. These hardly seem to be the actions of the ACLU type of strict separationist many modern interpreters make Jefferson out to be.

PURITANS, BAPTISTS, AND RELIGIOUS FREEDOM

The American model for religious freedom is the triumph of the Baptist concept of a church-state relationship. The impetus triggering the Reformation was an attempt to get back to the primitive New Testament pattern. After a thousand years of the church and the state being at best partners, at worst in a master-concubine relationship (with the church being the concubine), Luther and Calvin couldn't cut that umbilical cord to the state. Neither could the Anglicans, nor even the Puritans. The Baptists were the ones who finally cut the cord, declaring that there should be no official tie between church and state.

The Baptists espoused the view that the church was a gathered, visible body of saints, and the state owed full freedom to every church. Church members owed civil obedience and support to the state unless the state required them to do something clearly against God's mandates revealed in Scripture. If the state demanded such violation of their conscience, they had an obligation to obey God rather than men by passive civil disobedience, which included accepting the penalty imposed by the state for such disobedience.

The Puritans did not share the Baptists' vision for religious freedom. They wanted to further "purify" the Church of England from what they saw as the "vestiges of popery." Their understanding of church and state was a pure Presbyterian understanding of how the church should operate—supported by the power of the state behind it. When the British crown tried to force an Anglican establishment on the people of Britain, the Puritans went on a seventy- to eighty-year campaign to "purify" the Church of England—hence their name.

When those Puritans who gave up on Britain came to America, their desire was to build a New Jerusalem to show the Old World how it should be done. They came for religious freedom for themselves, not religious freedom for anyone else. In the new land, the Puritans severely persecuted Baptists and Quakers, targeting anyone who disagreed with them.

By the end of the American Revolution, as a result of the Great Awakenings, Baptists had grown from a small, persecuted minority to one of the two largest denominations in the country (the other was Methodism). They had completely swamped the Presbyterians and the Episcopalians and the small number of Catholics who were here.

One reason there was no official state church when the Constitution was formed was because there was no consensus about what the state church should be. New Englanders wanted a Congregational state church, Southerners wanted an Episcopal state church, and those in the middle colonies wanted a Presbyterian state church. The exceptions were Pennsylvania, founded by Quakers who didn't want a state church; Maryland, founded largely by Catholics who didn't want a state church; and Rhode Island, founded by Baptists. Across all thirteen states were significant numbers of Baptists who didn't want any state church.

The Baptist preacher of previously mentioned "big cheese" fame, John Leland, had planned to campaign against ratification of the Constitution. The Baptists living in Virginia, North Carolina, Massachusetts, and Connecticut feared a possible federal establishment of religion that would deny them their religious freedom in the same manner that the state governments with their established state churches were attempting to deny their religious freedom. They held the balance of power in these states despite their persecution (some would say because of it). At that time in early federal America, Virginia was the dominant state. Therefore, if Leland was successful in persuading the Virginia Baptists to vote against the Constitution, it would not be ratified in Virginia—and if Virginia didn't ratify the Constitution, there wasn't going to be a Constitution.

James Madison met with John Leland in Orange County, Virginia, and they cut a political deal. Madison gave Leland his word that in the first Congress, he would introduce an amendment reading, "Congress shall make no law affecting an establishment of religion, nor interfering with the free exercise thereof." In return, Leland gave Madison his word that in his candidacy for the

Constitutional Convention, he would reverse his position against ratification of the Constitution and work to deliver the Baptist vote in favor of it. Both Leland and Madison were true to their word, and that is how we got what is now known as the First Amendment.

However, the First Amendment to the Constitution did not prohibit a state from having a tax-supported state church. So when Jefferson wrote his letter to the Baptist ministers of Danbury, Connecticut, he was writing to separationists who lived in a state where they had to pay taxes to the Congregational state church—which discriminated against them, along with anybody else who wasn't Congregationalist, in myriad ways.

The same thing was true in Virginia, which had an Episcopal state church. Interestingly, the last two states to get rid of their tax-supported state churches were Massachusetts and Connecticut, in 1832. That was a long time after 1789, when the U.S. Constitution took effect.

For nearly a century, the Supreme Court has interpreted the Fourteenth Amendment to say that whatever the federal government is forbidden from doing in the First Amendment, local and state governments are forbidden from doing as well.

This has been an enormous protection to free exercise. I am not too worried about Baptists being persecuted in Tennessee by the Tennessee state government. Baptists are the majority faith in that state. I am worried, however, about Baptists and other religious minorities in states such as Oregon, California, and Connecticut because of several cases in recent years. For instance, a family in Connecticut was told they could not have a Bible study of more than ten people in their home and it could not meet more than once a week because the zoning commission said it caused parking problems. They lost in state court, but when they went to federal court, the judge found that the restrictions were a violation of their First Amendment guarantee of free exercise of their religion. The federal court overturned the state court and guaranteed their right to have a Bible study in their own home.

Similar situations in Oregon and California have occurred in which zoning commissions tried to tell local churches how big an auditorium they could build, when they could have services, what time they could offer them, and the maximum attendance for those services because of supposed parking and traffic congestion problems. Those churches routinely lost in local courts and in state courts, but won when they went into federal courts based on First Amendment provisions.

The First Amendment is essentially the codification of the Baptist understanding of a free church and a free state. Even the Roman Catholic Church has now substantially adopted it. In 1965 the Roman Catholic bishops of the entire world gathered in a council with the pope (known as the Second Vatican Council) and issued *Dignitatis Humanae*, a declaration on religious freedom, renouncing coercion in matters of religious faith. The Roman Catholic Church had long rejected officially the idea that faith could be coerced, though forced conversions had at various times been carried out in the name of the church, and church officials were sometimes complicit. *Dignitatis Humanae* broke new ground for Roman Catholicism in proclaiming the right of all to give public witness to their beliefs and to seek actively to persuade others to share them. Here is a key passage from the document:

> A sense of the dignity of the human person has been impressing itself more and more deeply on the consciousness of contemporary man, (1) and the demand is increasingly made that men should act on their own judgment, enjoying and making use of a responsible freedom, not driven by coercion but motivated by a sense of duty. The demand is likewise made that constitutional limits should be set to the powers of government, in order that there may be no encroachment on the rightful freedom of the person and of associations.[27]

Here, the Vatican Council is basically affirming the Baptist viewpoint that the state must not use its power on behalf of itself, religion, or any other authority to impose on individual religious conscience. God wants true worship from a willing heart, and neither state nor church should ever seek to use its power to enforce religious belief.

An individual's relationship to God is so sacred that any human attempt through government or church to coerce it or interfere with it constitutes a form of soul rape. In 1612 England, a Baptist minister named Thomas Helwys wrote a book called *The Mystery of Iniquity*, the first published plea in the English language for complete religious freedom. Helwys maintained that King

James was a mere man—a real shock to the king, when he finally received the autographed copy that Helwys had attempted to deliver to him personally. As such, the merely mortal king had no right to interfere with another human being's relationship to God. For this bold presumption, Helwys was locked up in the Tower of London for the rest of his life.

Christopher Hedges's contention that the Dominionists have gained control over the Southern Baptist Convention is ludicrous for any number of reasons, but chief among them is the fiercely held Baptist conviction that a theocracy is wrong—above all because it is unbiblical. The government should not be using coercive power to compel or to prohibit faith in general, or any particular faith, because that is not the government's role. Paul says in Romans 13:1–7 that the government is divinely ordained to punish evildoers and reward those who do right. He doesn't say anything about the government demanding or prohibiting faith or worship.

Second, Baptists are opposed to theocracies because they bear historical witness to the reality that whenever the government sponsors religion, it is like getting hugged by a python: it squeezes all the life out of you and you fall over dead. Just look at the official churches of Europe—they are all empty. They are empty in predominantly Catholic and Protestant countries alike. When government sponsors religion, they think they own it, and therefore they can tell you how to do it.

I was fascinated to hear a lucid explanation of why the state should not control religion and religion should not control the state from deep inside the Muslim culture. Leading up to the January 2005 elections in Iraq, National Public Radio reporter Peter Kenyon interviewed a woman named Amal Kashif al-Ghettah, who was running for a seat in the new Iraqi Parliament. She was a study in contrasts: an advocate for women's rights who wore the traditional dress of Muslim women, the black abaya. Now sixty years old, she had spent nearly two decades under house arrest, during which she wrote fifteen books, from religious nonfiction to novels. Liberal women looked askance at her for wearing traditional religious garb, but she enjoyed breaking the stereotype. The traditional dress was a major part of her identity. Her political views, however, were quite nontraditional: "One mistake the Islamists make is thinking religion should control the state," she commented. "And some liberals think that religion should be completely separated from the state. I disagree with both of them. There should be cooperation, not control."[28]

Third, Baptists would applaud Amal's censure of state control of religion because they believe that no human being has the right to use coercion in matters of faith toward another human being. Therefore, government owes to its citizens the protection of their soul freedom. Government can't grant that freedom, but it can recognize it, acknowledge it, and ensure its protection. That is why we have a long record of defending Jehovah's Witnesses making a nuisance of themselves on our doorsteps and Hari Krishnas making a nuisance of themselves in airports—first, because we believe in soul freedom, and second, if we allow the government to discriminate against these sects today, they can discriminate against Christians tomorrow. That is why Baptists have applauded the Supreme Court's decision that even radical Wiccan religious beliefs deserve protection. A pagan worshiper in a federal prison has the right to be protected in that worship—because a government's strategy is often to pick as a test case the most odious minority faith it can find. Then they will use that test case precedent to come after other religions later.

I disagreed with everything the atheist Madalyn Murray O'Hair believed, but I would defend to the death her right to believe it without government discrimination or persecution. I would defend to the death every atheist's right to be an atheist. I don't have the right to impose my Christian faith on an atheist, and an atheist doesn't have the right to impose his or her faith on me. Neither one of us has the right to use the government to discriminate against the other.

That is why we don't have a religious test for office in this country—it would be a form of religious discrimination, whether the test was pro or con for religious faith. You don't have to swear you believe in God to serve in office. Neither do you have to swear that your faith is not important to you to serve in office—that is what many required of John F. Kennedy in 1960, and it was wrong. Basically he was forced to say that his Catholicism would not have any impact on how he governed the country—that the pope didn't speak for him on political matters and that he didn't speak for the pope on religious matters.

During the course of the 2000 presidential campaign, Connecticut senator Joseph Lieberman was named Al Gore's running mate on the Democratic ticket. Lieberman was absolutely right when he said a person couldn't understand him as a candidate for vice president without understanding that he was an observant Jew. His faith would shape what kind of vice president he would be, and voters needed to have that information before they cast their ballots. As I applauded Senator Lieberman's proclamation of his faith in the face of severe criticism from major media such as the *New York Times*, I observed that it took a hard-line anti-Communist like President Nixon to make a state visit to Red China; it took a Democratic president like Bill Clinton to sign welfare reform; and it might take a Jewish vice-presidential candidate to make it "kosher" to speak about one's faith in public office.

THE THREE *A*s OF CHURCH-STATE SEPARATION

As noted earlier, there are three major ways in which societies around the world seem to be trying to regulate, control, or channel the religious impulse. The first is what I call theocratic sectarianism or Fundamentalism. Iran is a classic example. Iran says citizens will follow Muslim teachings, period. Women will wear Islamic clothing whether they are Muslim or not. In Afghanistan the Taliban sought to impose such rules in an even more extreme form.

A second way societies try to control the religious impulse is what I call supreme secularism. The example here is the French government's ruling that in the public schools Muslim girls may not wear their headscarves, Jewish boys their yarmulkes, and Christians their crosses—except for tiny crosses of a government-mandated length and width.

A third way is what I call principled pluralism, and the example is right here in the United States, as deep into Red America as you can possibly get—Muskogee, Oklahoma. A sixth-grade Muslim girl was banned by her school from wearing her religiously prescribed headscarf, and the U.S. Justice Department, under President Bush, intervened on her behalf. The courts found that the school's prohibition on headwear infringed on the girl's constitutional right to the free expression of her religious beliefs. They ruled that Muslim girls may or may not wear their headscarves in the public schools; it is their and their family's decision.

Principled pluralism is what our Constitution requires and what most Americans want, not theocratic Fundamentalism or supreme secularism. As described in chapter 3, I call these the three *As* of church-state separation: *acknowledgment*, *avoidance*, and *accommodation*. The *acknowledgment* position is expressed in Judge Roy Moore's view that tax-funded religious displays on government property are the rightful expression of America's founding, majority religion. The *avoidance* position, such as Christopher Hedges would take, argues that any display of religious expression should be banished from government property because it constitutes government sponsorship of religion and thus violates the separation of church and state. The *accommodation* position contends that the government should permit the free expression of religion so that if a particular religious group wants to purchase a display and place it on public property, it is their constitutional right to express their convictions in that way, regardless of religious affiliation.[29]

I am often asked about the role of Christians in the public square. One of my responses is a question: *Will* it be faith in practice? Maybe—if Christians are practicing their faith in the public square, it will not be through trying to create a religiously dominated public square, because that is not faith in practice. That is coercion. Neither will it be faith in practice if Christians withdraw from the public square, abandoning it to the secular Fundamentalists.

A *Meet the Press* debate engaged the former governor of New York, Mario Cuomo, a liberal Catholic, and conservative Catholic Douglas W. Kmiec, chair and professor of constitutional law at Pepperdine University, on the subject of whether it is appropriate to query Supreme Court nominees on their religious convictions. Professor Kmiec commented on the difference between illegitimately imposing one's religious views and legitimately sharing one's religious views in the public marketplace of ideas.

When Catholic politicians bring their faith to the legislative branch, they're not imposing. They're sharing. If their view is going to be adopted, it's because the consent of the governed has decided to accept their view. When judges bring their faith, covertly or overtly, to the bench, they're not accountable politically. They're given independence only for one reason, because they promise—and here the governor and I completely agree—they promise to observe the text of the Constitution, its history, its structure and the traditions and the Declaration of Independence that undergird it.[30]

People of faith *share* their faith. They don't assume that it should be accepted just because it is religious. They have the right to bring to the public arena the values that are informed by their faith, and to share with the public the insights they have gained through their faith. If the public agrees, then that becomes the public policy of the nation by consent of the people. We must always agree to government "of the people, by the people, and for the people"[31] and by consent of the governed. Even if the people make the wrong decision, we must abide by the will of the people and seek to change the will of the people in future elections. But there must be a commitment to having the will of the people be the final arbiter in human society. Otherwise there is a terrible tendency for it to become coercive, as vitiating of human freedom as a naked, purely secular public square devoid of religiously informed moral values is of the same freedom of conscience and belief. In either extreme, the rights of the minority and of the weak are not protected.

PUSHING THE HOT BUTTONS

Let's look at some hot-button examples of how the accommodation view can bring clarity to church-and-state arguments.

God, Mammon, and the Pledge

The acknowledgment position would force all citizens to recite the Pledge of Allegiance regardless of whether it violated their religious (or nonreligious) convictions. The avoidance position maintains that "under God" should come out of the pledge.

The legal argument for retaining the "under God" phrase in the pledge is that it does not promote any one religion. Because "God" is not specified as the Christian God or the Jewish God or the Muslim God, the phrase is not an establishment of religion.

"Aren't you splitting hairs?" the avoidance advocate might ask. "After all, 'God' is religious any way you want to look at the issue."

You can argue that point, but the Supreme Court has already said that having "In God We Trust" on our money and including the phrase "under God" in the Pledge of Allegiance do not constitute the establishment of a religion. Rather, the court said, these phrases are the recitation of the pledge an acknowledgment of the role that religion has played in American culture, in American history, in American life. And of course is not compulsory, another reason why it is not a violation of separation of church and state. That was settled back in 1943 (before "under God" was added to the pledge), when persecution of Jehovah's Witnesses who refused on religious grounds to recite the pledge led to the court's decision that the government has no right to compel public school students to say the pledge. If they wanted to remain silent or absent themselves during the pledge, that was their right.

Similarly, people aren't forced to read "In God We Trust" on their currency to get paid or spend their money. If the majority of the American people decide they don't want that phrase on their currency anymore, or if the majority decide they want to take "under God" out of the pledge, all they have to do is pass legislation to repeal it.

The debate has turned nasty because a secularist minority—expressing the avoidance position—wants to expunge all evidence of religion from America's public life. That is a difficult thing to do in a representative democracy that happens to be very religious. It is an attempt to impose an artificial secularism on America's public life—a secularism that the majority of Americans don't want because the overwhelming majority are religious and they want to be accommodated in expressing those religious convictions in their public life and in their institutional life. That is not a violation of separation of church and state, and it was never perceived to be such until the rise of the avoidance position in which a radical, secularist minority is attempting to impose its will on America through the courts. It is resorting to the courts because it knows it has a snowball's chance in the nether regions of doing so through the legislative process.

God at the Military Academy

There has been ongoing controversy at the Air Force Academy in Colorado Springs regarding what some perceive to be the undue influence of Evangelical Christians proselytizing at a government-supported institution.

The acknowledgment position would applaud activities such as use of e-mails by commanders to send messages with clearly Christian content to cadets.

Advocates of the avoidance position are currently suing the academy to stop any and all such religious activity at the academy. The accommodation position would say that it is wrong for commanders at a government institution to promote a particular religion, although chaplains are in a different category, because that is their purpose. As long as the various faiths that are represented in the student body of the Air Force Academy are represented in the chaplaincy—if you have a rabbi and a Catholic priest and a Protestant minister, and an imam if you have Muslim cadets—then chaplains ought to "chaplain" according to their faith tradition.

Cadets should certainly be free to share their faith with other cadets. However, when the football coach put up a banner in the locker room proclaiming, "I belong to Team Jesus Christ," that was inappropriate because the academy is a government school paid for by American taxpayers and not all of the football players are Christians. If an incident like that had happened at a private Mormon university such as Brigham Young or a Catholic university such as Notre Dame, it would have been entirely the school's own business. If the Air Force Academy football coach had been expressing his private religious views while out at dinner with friends rather than in an official capacity, that would have been different. However, as an Evangelical Christian, I would find it both inappropriate and offensive for the head football coach to say that the United States Air Force Academy's football team is "Team Jesus Christ." It is not the business of the United States government to be endorsing the Christian faith. America has a providential role in promoting freedom, not in promoting Christianity, internally or externally, domestically or in foreign policy.

Acknowledgment proponents would applaud if the coach prayed with his team before games; avoidance advocates would protest. Principled pluralism would suggest that it is okay for him to pray with the team before games if he chooses to do so, but it would probably be wiser for him, instead, to ask for volunteers from the team who wanted to pray. He could say, "I'm the coach, I'm a Christian, and my faith is part of what I do," or better yet, he could say, "We're going to have a moment of prayer," and he could ask the guys to let him know if they would like to volunteer to lead the team in prayer, and he would call on numerous volunteers of differing faiths in the course of the season. He could ask Roger Smith to pray this time and Abe Solomon to pray next time and Abdul Rahman to pray after that—that way, no one would need to feel necessarily excluded.

God on the High School Athletic Field

The God-and-country debate notched another round last year when a public high school football coach resigned his position after being informed by the school that he was no longer permitted to lead his team in pregame prayers. Some students had expressed discomfort with the prayers, and some parents had complained. The coach felt that he could no longer continue his job in good conscience because the pregame prayers were an expression of his identity as a person of faith.

This is a delicate area in which it is important to make distinctions between minors and adults and between a compulsory class and an extracurricular activity. Appropriate action for a college football coach is different from appropriate action for a high school coach because one works with adults and the other with minors. Also, in high school, football is an extracurricular activity; it's not like English class where one is required to attend.

In government institutions, the accommodation position would suggest that it is better for the government to accommodate the football players' right to pray together. Of course, it is much better if the Fellowship of Christian Athletes chapter on campus invites those who want to pray to join them in gathering on the twenty-yard line before or after the game. Those who don't want to gather, don't—they have an opt-in choice, not an opt-out choice. It is cleaner if the coach is not involved because in a state school, the coach is a symbol of the state. For a private school, it's a totally different ball game.

WHAT THE BIBLE SAYS ABOUT THE STATE

We are currently in the middle of a very heated debate over immigration. During my frequent visits to churches, the most consistent criticism I hear on current issues is the federal government's lack of a strong immigration policy. Millions of people are streaming across our borders in defiance of our laws. Some businesses are employing them at low wages and in exploitative conditions. There is also general consensus that our country has to have control of its borders.

By contrast, there is considerable division over what to do with the illegal immigrants who are already here. I find that in the churches I visit, there tends to be more support for refugees who are fleeing religious persecution and political oppression—Vietnamese and Haitians, for example—than those who are coming primarily for economic reasons. Consensus seems to gather around a three-pronged approach to the problem of illegal immigration:

1. The United States must get control of its borders so that it is in control of those who enter this country and the circumstances under which they enter.
2. A program is needed that gives illegal aliens protection under the law but does not reward illegal behavior by automatically granting citizenship. A program is needed that would allow people who came here illegally to work their way through a probationary status to some type of permanent resident status if they wish to stay here. Further, compassion should be expressed for the plight of illegal aliens and their families.
3. The United States should offer help to the government of Mexico, and then hold it accountable, for implementing social and economic reforms to improve the lives of its citizens.

Implicit in these views on immigration policy are assumptions about the roles of church and state. Churches may well choose to extend compassion and support for illegal aliens based on biblical commands to care for the poor and dispossessed, to show mercy to the least of these. However, Paul's teaching on the role of the state in Romans 13:1–7 declares that the civil magistrate is ordained by God to punish those who do wrong and reward those who do right:

Everyone must submit to the governing authorities, for there is no authority except from God, and those that exist are instituted by God. So then, the one who resists the authority is opposing God's command, and those who oppose it will bring judgment on themselves. For rulers are not a terror to good conduct, but to bad. Do you want to be unafraid of the authority? Do good and you will have its approval. For government is God's servant to you for good. But if you do wrong, be afraid, because it does not carry the sword for no reason. For government is God's servant, an avenger that brings wrath on the one who does wrong. Therefore, you must submit, not only because of wrath, but also because of your conscience. And for this reason you pay taxes, since the [authorities] are God's public servants, continually attending to these tasks. Pay your obligations to everyone: taxes to those you owe taxes, tolls to those you owe tolls, respect to those you owe respect, and honor to those you owe honor. (Romans 13:1–7 HCSB)

Unless state law specifically requires us to violate God's law, we are to be subject to civil authority as our moral responsibility, not just in fear of punishment. Paul was writing in the context of the Roman Empire. We have a far better government, which makes our obedience easier and more pleasant than what the apostle Paul's readers were facing.

Those who feel strongly that the United States needs to get control of its borders believe that the government's job is to enforce the law, not turn a blind eye to massive illegal activity. A provision that doesn't immediately lead to citizenship and requires people who have entered the country illegally to pay fines and undergo a probationary period means that the government is acting redemptively, giving wrongdoers a chance to right their wrongs instead of immediately throwing them into jail. They are still responsible for their former transgressions. God forgives and forgets, but governments can't. The government has an authority that individuals don't have. Liberals tend to confuse government's compassion and expenditures with their own. If they want to use their resources to exercise compassion toward all refugees and illegal aliens, that is commendable. But the church plays a different role in society than does the government.

There is a distinction between the compassion individuals ought to show and the compassion governments ought to show. Some Christians were delighted that infamous serial killer Ted Bundy apparently had a conversion experience, but those who support the death penalty felt he still deserved to die because of what he did to his victims.

Throughout the New Testament, distinctions are drawn between the individual's responsibility and the government's responsibility. For example, Jesus says to turn the other cheek. If someone murders my wife, I don't have the right to retaliate against her attacker, but I do have the right to expect the government to punish him. I don't have the right to use lethal violence personally against enemies of the state, but I do have the right to expect the government to authorize the use of lethal violence to protect the country. If we are attacked, I certainly don't expect the military to turn the other cheek.

Romans 13:1–7 is the most sustained passage in the New Testament dealing with the role of government, but liberal Protestant doctrine would not place as high a value on the Epistles as on the Gospels and so would be more likely to adapt Jesus' teachings for individuals to their views on church and state. Conservatives would view the Gospels and Epistles as equal in authority and therefore would have a higher view of the authority of the state based on Paul's epistle to the Romans. John's Gospel records that when Jesus was getting ready to leave His disciples, He indicated that He had more to say to them, but they weren't yet ready for it. They needed the Holy Spirit, who would lead them into all truth (John 16:7–16). Conservatives view the rest of the New Testament, Acts through Revelation, as the fulfillment of that promise, believing the liberal "Red Letter" distinction elevating the Gospels above the rest of the New Testament to be unbiblical and erroneous.

FREE-FOR-ALL IN THE PUBLIC SQUARE

During the confirmation hearings for Supreme Court Justice Samuel Alito, President George W. Bush's appointment to replace the retiring Sandra Day O'Connor, University of Notre Dame law professor Richard Garnett commended the departing justice for her legacy of welcoming the expression of religious faith in the public square. Judge Alito would prove to be a worthy successor, Garnett predicted, in his high value on freedom of religion.

> Like O'Connor, Alito understands that our Constitution does not regard religious faith with grudging suspicion, or as a bizarre quirk or quaint relic. They both appreciate that, in our traditions and laws, religious freedom is cherished as a basic human right and a non-negotiable aspect of human dignity. This is why both

jurists have occasionally come under fire from activists who misunderstand the "separation of church and state."

Our Constitution separates church and state not to confine religious belief or silence religious expression, but to curb the ambitions and reach of governments. The point of the First Amendment is not to "put religion in its place," but instead to protect religion by keeping the government "in its place." The Amendment's Establishment Clause is not a sword, driving private religious expression from the marketplace of ideas; rather, it is a shield that constrains government precisely to protect religiously motivated speech and action. . . .

At the heart of O'Connor's legacy is an insistence that our Constitution does not mandate a public square scrubbed clean of religious symbols and speech, and that equality and neutrality—not hostility or marginalization—are the watchwords of our First Amendment. With Judge Alito, that legacy is in good hands.[32]

Obviously, it is no easy task to interpret in every instance how to protect religious freedom and maintain the proper separation of church and state. In the American experiment of applying religious liberty to all aspects of public life and private conscience, our country has erred at various times in exacting religion penalties on specific groups. During the period of our founding, religion penalties were imposed on anyone—especially Baptists—who refused to comply with state-authorized churches. When Protestants were in control of public schools, religion penalties were imposed on Catholics. Today there is a huge difference of opinion among Americans who believe in traditional religious values and those who have a postmodern view of the world. Our confusion over the separation of church and state has led to such censure of traditional religion by those with a secularist mind-set that it raises the question of whether there is a new religion penalty in America.

★ 7 ★

Is There a New Religion
Penalty in America?

I would not want to be taken as suggesting that the moral arrogance of the Religious Left is greater than the arrogance of the Religious Right. That competition would, I suspect, be a very close and depressing one. . . . Still, the Religious Right's hopeless efforts to fiddle with the law pale beside the Religious Left's successful efforts to fiddle with the culture. The Religious Left is not necessarily better than the Religious Right, only smarter . . . and it has cooperated with elite efforts to fix the rules so that nobody else can win. Which is why clergy who endorse political candidates are condemned but clergy who destroy traditional values are lionized.

—STEPHEN L. CARTER[1]

A line often heard from the liberal Left is "You can't legislate morality." When activist Al Sharpton said that to me during a panel discussion in which we were participating, I replied that one of my personal heroes was Martin Luther King Jr., "and I sure am glad his morality was legislated on George Wallace and Lester Maddox."

Wallace and Maddox, governors of Alabama and Georgia, were staunch segregationists in the 1960s who resisted federal, court-ordered integration. George Wallace made headlines throughout his storied political career, including several runs for president, but one of his most memorable acts took place in June 1963 when he stood in the doorway of the University of Alabama to block the entrance of the first two black students to register for classes.

Before taking on the governorship of Georgia, Lester Maddox ran a restaurant in Atlanta near the Georgia Tech campus. He refused to serve African-Americans, and when three black customers tried to press the point, he barred the door wielding an ax handle, vowing that if they lived a hundred years they would never get a piece of fried chicken at his restaurant. Rather than obey the law and integrate his establishment, he sold it to his employees (and was praised by some of the local community for doing so).

The Civil Rights Movement represented the triumph of biblical moral values over the evils of racism. It is one of the greatest fallacies of our time that "moral values" can be kept off to the side as some kind of special interest category. Unless you want to live in a completely amoral society, *somebody's* moral values are going to be legislated.

Christian Left activist Jim Wallis identifies a bias against religious values among "new Fundamentalists in the land."

There are the "secular Fundamentalists," many of whom attack all political figures who dare to speak from their religious convictions. From the Anti-Defamation League, to Americans United for the Separation of Church and State, to the ACLU and some of the political Left's most religion-fearing publications, a cry of alarm has gone up in response to anyone who has the audacity to be religious in public. These secular skeptics often display an amazing lapse of historical memory when they suggest that religious language in politics is contrary to the "American idea." The truth is just the opposite.[2]

Somebody's moral values are going to get imposed. Wallis presents his in the context of biblical concerns for the poor and oppressed with economic prescriptions very much to the left of center politically. Those are indeed biblical concerns that we need to take to heart. However, I part company with him over *how* those values ought to be implemented and to what degree the government should be the agent of implementing them.

WHICH ECONOMIC MODEL WORKS?

Wallis points out that "for some time now, the U.S. government's annual budgets have shown record deficits. They reflect billions of dollars of tax cuts to the wealthiest Americans. They include huge increases for the costs of war, and they slash domestic spending."[3] This statement packs a load of assumptions, but the one I want to single out is the issue of tax cuts.

John F. Kennedy cut the top tax rate (Revenue Act of 1964, signed by Lyndon Johnson), and government tax revenues went up. Ronald Reagan cut the top rate on individual income from 50 percent to 28 percent, and government revenues went up. George W. Bush cut the capital gains tax in half, and capital gains tax collections by the government have gone up 22 percent.

Economist Bruce Bartlett, former senior fellow of the National Center for Policy Analysis and former deputy assistant secretary of economic policy at the U.S. Treasury Department, cites data released by the Internal Revenue Service (on tax year 2003) showing that during the same period when the tax rate of the wealthiest Americans (the top 1 percent) was cut in half, the percentage of federal income taxes they paid versus that paid by the rest of the population nearly doubled.[4] In 2004 the Internal Revenue Service calculated that when income and social security taxes were combined, "the top 1 percent paid 23.3 percent of combined payroll and income taxes, the top 10 percent paid 52.2 percent, and the top 20 percent paid 68.2 percent."[5] How does that square with Wallis's criticism that tax cuts give to the rich and take from the poor?

In a *USA Today* editorial, Senator Bill Frist (R-TN) cites the consistent rise in tax revenues in every year since 2003, when a major tax relief bill was passed. In fact, he points out, government tax revenues increased *more* after President Bush's tax cuts in 2003 than they did after President Clinton's tax *hikes* in 1994. "Many people in Washington have long known a dirty little secret about tax-cut measures," Senator Frist declares: "When done right, they actually result in more money for the government."[6]

A 2005 article in the *Wall Street Journal* observed the inverse relationship between falling tax rates and rising tax revenues, pointing out that "the mislabeled 'Bush tax cut for the rich' has in reality enormously benefited middle-income workers." President Bush's tax cuts were "narrowly enacted despite the usual indignant primal screams from the greed and envy lobby about 'tax cuts for the super rich.'" In the face of "overpowering confirming evidence" that lowering the tax rate leads to rising tax-revenue collections, *Wall Street Journal* editorial board member Stephen Moore raised the question of whether "Mr. Bush's critics' ideological blinders make them capable of being persuaded by facts and evidence."[7]

This is no longer a philosophical issue; it is an issue of numbers. It is a case of having your cake and eating it too. Government has actually collected more revenue under lower tax rates than had ever been collected under the previously higher tax rates.

Brilliant *New York Times* columnist David Brooks has made an observation that reverberates through all discussions of personal and corporate tax rates and government social policies.

Forgive me for making a blunt and obvious point, but events in Western Europe are slowly discrediting large swaths of American liberalism.

Most of the policy ideas advocated by American liberals have already been enacted in Europe: generous welfare measures, ample labor protections, highly progressive tax rates, single-payer health care systems, zoning restrictions to limit big retailers, and cradle-to-grave middle-class subsidies supporting everything from child care to pension security. And yet far from thriving, continental Europe has endured a lost decade of relative decline.[8]

How so?

Right now, Europeans seem to look to the future with more fear than hope. As Anatole Kaletsky noted in *The Times* of London, in continental Europe "unemployment has been stuck between 8 and 11 percent since 1991 and growth has reached 3 percent only once in those 14 years."

The Western European standard of living is about a third lower than the American standard of living, and it's sliding. European output per capita is less than that of 46 of the 50 American states and about on par with Arkansas. There is little prospect of robust growth returning any time soon.[9]

The neo-socialist economic and welfare state model advocated by Jim Wallis and his cohorts doesn't work, except in seeking to allocate more equally *smaller* and *smaller* slices of a stagnant and ever-diminishing economic pie. The malaise-ridden economies of Western Europe stand as eloquent testimony to this model's failure.

The free-market economic model does work. The transformed societies of South Korea, Taiwan, Malaysia, India, China, and Ireland, which are experiencing unprecedented prosperity, provide even more eloquent evidence of this essential truth.

Now, as increased wealth is being produced, society needs to have another discussion about how wealth is allocated in such economies. I am no laissez-faire "flat-taxer"—I believe there should be some progressivity in tax rates, with those who are able to pay more contributing a greater share of their income to help support those in need and those who are suffering. We have a shared social responsibility to make sure that those in need are dealt with adequately and compassionately, both through government programs and through nongovernment programs encouraged and subsidized by the tax-deductibility of charitable contributions. The trick is to hit the "sweet spot," where taxes are high enough to allow an able government to do its part in meeting the needs of those less fortunate in society, but not so high as to stifle productivity.

How do high taxes stifle productivity? A story from my time as a doctoral student in pre-Thatcherite socialist Britain, between 1972 and 1975, may help to illustrate. At that time I was also serving as pastor of a small Baptist church, and I discovered that it was virtually impossible to secure the services of a piano tuner. My numerous inquiries for help with our toneless instrument at the manse revealed that all piano tuners in Oxford were booked solid for the foreseeable future. No vacancies. Being an enterprising American, I waited for the regularly scheduled visit of the craftsman who maintained the piano at the church, took some freshly baked cookies to him, and struck up a conversation. When he was finished at the church, I asked if he would mind stopping at the manse to tune that piano as well. My wife would be serving refreshments, I added.

He was glad to come, and in the course of conversation, he revealed the reason why so few people plied his trade. He earned the equivalent of about twenty-five thousand dollars a year, and if he made any more than that in a given year, he had to pay 90 percent of it in taxes. Because he was unwilling to work for 10 percent on the pound sterling, he worked only until he reached the equivalent of twenty-five thousand dollars and spent the rest of the year at leisure with his family. This story illustrates why socialism never works.

The free-market system shouldn't elevate self-interest to a virtue, as does Ayn Rand libertarianism; it simply recognizes that this is the primary impetus driving productivity in fallen human nature. In other words, this may not be the way people ought to be, but it is the way people are. They are not going to work really hard and produce a lot of wealth unless they get to keep a good portion of it (the "sweet spot") for themselves and their families. However, since human nature is selfish and fallen, there has to be a system of checks and balances in the economy (trade unions to protect workers and government regulations); otherwise, unrestrained management and capital will exploit workers.

The question for people who take Wallis's position is, do they really want more government revenue to help alleviate injustice and poverty, or do they just want to stick it to rich people? If they want to help alleviate injustice and poverty, they ought to support the president's tax cuts. If they just want to stick it to rich people, they ought to oppose the president's tax cuts.

When government raises taxes to pay for government programs, it is not collecting donations. It is coercing payment under penalty of law. Helping the poor is a good thing. Increasing the tax burden on Americans as the best way to do so is another thing entirely. The average American already works more than half the year to pay his taxes (federal, state, and local) before keeping any of the money he earns. The average taxpayer works from Monday morning until sometime early Wednesday afternoon every week to pay his tax burden. Shortly after lunch on Wednesday afternoon, he gets to work the rest of the week for himself, his family, and the causes he wishes to support. Such a taxpayer might well feel that Jim Wallis is trying to impose Wallis's religious moral values on his earning power, rather than persuading him to make a donation.

BUT WHAT IF THE GAME IS FIXED?

Wallis is right that the secular Left would like to conduct public policy debates in which only secularly informed moral values are allowed on the playing field. They want to exclude religiously informed moral values from competing, from being part of the ball game. I call that an attempt to rig the game by fixing the outcome.

Secular Fundamentalists don't just want a secular state, they want a secular society. Most Americans want a secular state, free from religious control. A secular state is not devoid of moral values in decision making, however. Nothing could be falser than the persistent myth afflicting us that it is a violation of church and state to legislate morality. If only as a practical matter, all governments legislate morality. If we had no laws against murder, the violent death rate would explode. If we had no laws against theft, property losses would soar. If we had no laws against rape, sexual assaults would explode. If we had no laws against racial discrimination, segregation would still be the law of the land. Government *must* legislate morality in order to fulfill its purposes—what Christians understand to be its God-ordained purposes. The government is responsible to punish evil and protect its citizens (Romans 13:1–7). In doing so, the government doesn't impose morality on the murderer and the thief so much as it prevents them from imposing their immorality on their victims.

Let's look at the church-state issue through the metaphor of sports and the prism of the acknowledgment, accommodation, and avoidance church-state model. The American people are the participants, the competitors on the playing field seeking to advance their cause and score as many goals as possible for their side.

The acknowledgment position on the separation of church and state insists that religion always gets home-court advantage: majority religion gets primary consideration. There is a tremendous home-field advantage when playing in your own stadium in front of your own fans.

The avoidance position on the separation of church and state insists that *they* ought to get home-court advantage. In the name of separation of church and state, they see any attempt to give consideration to religion a violation of religious neutrality.

The accommodation position on the separation of church and state dictates that the game be located on a neutral site or played at each home field so it is balanced. Nobody gets special consideration, because everyone is on equal footing in a pluralistic democracy.

Team Acknowledgment wants the referees to give the benefit of the doubt to religion. Team Avoidance insists that the benefit of the doubt on any kind of judgment call goes to the secularists. Both want to fix the game so their side wins. Team Accommodation insists on objective, impartial referees who ensure that the American people win, in a competition as free and open and robust as possible. No position is disqualified from the competition.

When the Chicago White Sox won the World Series in October 2005, the celebrations were not only because it had been eighty-eight years since their last championship title, but because it seemed to wash away the stain of the 1919 Black Sox scandal, when professional gamblers enlisted a group of players to throw the series, intentionally losing to underdog Cincinnati. Evidently it wasn't the only series that was potentially "fixed"; there are several accounts from that time indicating that the early World Series were very much infected by gambling.

This is why there has been such a strict ban on gambling in baseball, and why Pete Rose got banished from the game when it transpired that he gambled on baseball games while he managed the Reds. Gambling corrupts the integrity of the game. If it hadn't been stopped, it would have destroyed professional baseball as the national pastime. The sport of boxing has never been able to rid itself entirely of rumors of fixed fights and gambling influence, and that is one reason why it still has a black eye in public opinion.

When the government doesn't allow free, fair, and neutral competition with neutral judges who make sure everybody plays fair and follows the rules, the outcome is not accepted by the American people. In fair competition, both sides are given an equal opportunity by playing by the same set of rules. When that is the case, one can truly hope that the best team wins.

The American ideal of fair play is another reason why baseball has lost a lot of its popularity—unlike football, basketball, and hockey, baseball has no effective salary caps. Therefore, the richest teams in the biggest markets can buy the best talent, thus skewing the competition. Some people love to hate the New York Yankees because owner George Steinbrenner opens his wallet to go shopping for the best players every year. Some people view this as buying his way into the playoffs. A team like the Pittsburgh Pirates starts off the season with the odds overwhelmingly against them because their whole payroll amounts to what the Yankees pay their top one or two players.

By contrast, because of revenue sharing in the National Football League, a small-market team like the Green Bay Packers can compete every year with just as much opportunity as the New York Giants or the Chicago Bears. There's a threshold of opportunity for everyone.

We strive for the same thing in the country economically, a certain minimal threshold of opportunity. Can we guarantee a completely level playing field? Of course not. When I turned twenty-one, I didn't inherit a $7.5 million trust fund the way the sons of Joseph Patrick Kennedy Sr. did. We don't write laws prohibiting such extra benefits, but we try to ensure a minimum threshold of opportunity. We just can't guarantee an equality of opportunity or outcome.

We do have a public school system that gave me, a welder's son, a good enough education to compete successfully for a full academic scholarship to Princeton. Did I start off with an opportunity equal to that of George W. Bush or Al Gore or John F. Kennedy? No, but I had a sufficient threshold of opportunity allowing people with ability and ambition to make their way in life.

I have heard it said that life is like hockey: skill counts, but what matters a whole lot more is whether you really want the puck. In a society without a minimum threshold of opportunity, it doesn't matter how much you want the puck.

America has success stories that are unheard of in other countries. When I was growing up in Houston, my father would stop after work to pick up tamales to bring home to us from a woman who sold them from a portable stand on Navigation Street. Her husband had died, and she was single-handedly supporting ten children. Her tamales were so good that by the time *she* died, her sons were running a corporate empire of Ninfa's Tex-Mex restaurants across the state of Texas. Her name was Maria Ninfa Rodriquez Laurenzo, and she became personal friends with President George H. W. Bush.

Only in America do things like that happen. Henry Kissinger has said there is no other country in the world where an eighteen-year-old Jewish refugee could immigrate from abroad and become the secretary of state. The country has recently been reminded of just what a unique and wonderful nation it is. Supreme Court Justice Samuel Alito's father, an Italian immigrant, arrived in this country speaking only his native tongue. He learned English, put himself through college, achieved a successful career as an educator, administrator, and civil servant, and empowered his son to get an education through scholarships at two of the most prestigious universities in America—Princeton and Yale. His son then went on to become a Supreme Court justice. In what other country could this kind of thing happen?

If we can't guarantee an absolutely level playing field, we can ensure a fair and competitive one that provides a minimum, but sufficient, threshold of opportunity—if everyone plays by the rules.

IS THERE A RELIGION PENALTY?

A democracy is governed by the will of the people. What do the American people want in respect to the role of religion in public life?

The Associated Press conducted a study of religious attitudes in industrialized countries and found that religion is more important in America than it is in any other economically advanced country in the world.[10] When asked if religion was important in their own lives (reply choices included "important," "not important," and "not sure"), responses varied from a low of 37 percent in France for whom religion was important to a high of 84 percent in the United States.

The poll also revealed that a higher percentage of Americans feel that religious leaders should try to influence public policy than in any other country—again, France was the lowest at 12 percent, and the United States was the highest at 37 percent. Of all the countries polled (Australia, Britain, Canada, France, Germany, Italy, Mexico, South Korea, Spain, and the United States), one of the few that has never had an official state religion is America. Americans are more comfortable with the influence of religious leaders because these leaders have the support of their constituencies. They are not named by the state and imposed on the people. They don't represent a record of abuse under an unholy alliance of church and state, which is the sad legacy in many of the other countries whose citizens were polled.

Despite the importance of religion to most Americans, the avoidance position would force off the field and disqualify any expression of religious faith. How pervasive is this position today?

I was interviewed on a national television show, and a Muslim guest said it was ridiculous to think that Christians are persecuted in America. America is full of Christians, he said. They aren't discriminated against in their own country. I commented on how interesting it is that the only people who think Evangelical Christians are free from discrimination are not Evangelical Christians. Evangelical Christians know when they are being discriminated against. They're not just paranoid; they know when people really are after them. Evangelicals are not persecuted in America—yet; but they are discriminated against.

In her book *The Criminalization of Christianity*, speaker, radio host, and pro-life activist Janet Folger documents appalling attacks on conservative Christians in the United States and abroad that would clearly never be tolerated by our society in reference to any other ethnic or religious group—such as radio host Howard Stern's 1999 outburst at a pro-life caller: "You're an idiot. I can't stand dumb people. If I was president, I would have you gassed. I would march you into the ovens."[11]

Folger carefully builds the evidence for a case of anti-Christian bigotry that extends across every spectrum of public life. When she turns attention to the judiciary, she lists case after case in which some judges have ruled against any reference in public to prayer, Jesus, the Bible, Christmas, and the Cross. For example, judges in some jurisdictions have made the following rulings:

- It is unconstitutional for a student to pray aloud over his lunch.
- It is unlawful to say the name *Jesus* during prayer at city council meetings (the prayer is allowed, however).
- It is unconstitutional for a classroom library to contain books that deal with Christianity or for a teacher to be seen in school with a personal copy of the Bible.
- School students are not allowed to bring holiday cookies to school in the shapes of stars or bells or colored red or green.
- It is unconstitutional for a war memorial in the shape of a cross to be erected. [12]

Fox News Channel's John Gibson, host of *The Big Story*, wrote an entire book documenting the attempts by multiple organizations, individuals, and groups of people to ban Christmas with the claim that any public expression of a Christian holiday is a violation of church and state. This ridiculous notion is perpetrated, Gibson says, by those "who are certain that the people who voted for George Bush want to install a Christian Taliban as custodians of the levers of power." [13]

I was in a same-sex marriage debate on a Nashville radio station with the executive director of the Tennessee chapter of the American Civil Liberties Union. She asked me if my opposition to same-sex marriage was based on my religious beliefs. "Yes, it is, absolutely," I answered. "God created marriage, and God gets to define it." Her response, with a patronizing smile, was that "here in America we can't base the laws on religious beliefs."

I told her that such thinking is dangerous nonsense. We do it all the time. What was Dr. King calling us to do when he was locked in a Birmingham jail? What were the abolitionists doing when they said that slavery was wrong? Should they have pretended to be schizophrenic in order to be nonreligious and secular whenever they discussed public policy? If people of faith are segregated and their religious perspectives on right and wrong are discriminated against whenever there is a debate on public policy, that is not fair play, is it?

Another incident I experienced that smacked of antireligious bias occurred during a BBC *World News* interview on ethical issues in the wake of the Terri Schiavo tragedy. The other interviewee was a lawyer from the Southern Poverty Law Center.

The BBC host confessed to us he was confused by the apparent contradictions in the positions we were taking. I was for capital punishment, against abortion, and for keeping Terri Schiavo's food and water tubes intact (absent a clearly written document from Terri Schiavo herself that she viewed hydration and nutrition as extraordinary medical means and opposed them if she became severely incapacitated). The lawyer was against capital punishment, for abortion, and for removing Terri Schiavo's tubes. When the host asked us to explain, I launched into the context for moral discussions about capital punishment, abortion, and end-of-life issues.

I started by explaining that I support capital punishment because I believe that human life is sacred, and anybody who wantonly and premeditatively takes another human being's life and is found guilty beyond a reasonable doubt by a jury of his or her peers has forfeited his or her right to life. It's the only way society can bear fitting tribute to the heinousness of murder. Further, I said, the Bible teaches in Romans 13 that one of the available options with which civil magistrates may punish evildoers is the lethal force of capital punishment.

This was more than the lawyer could stand, and I could hear him saying through clenched teeth, "But we don't live in a religious state."

"Careful, your antireligious bigotry is showing," I replied. It was fine to have a discussion about the moral rightness or wrongness of capital punishment, abortion, and Terri Schiavo's feeding tube *until* I started quoting my Christian reasons behind my positions. They were supposed to stay on the sidelines, off the field of our discussion. I'd call that a religion penalty, wouldn't you?

And then there was the time I was invited by a Baptist Student Union director to participate in a debate on a major university campus. It quickly became evident that I was the fall guy for the conservative position, but I was not especially interested in submitting to his take-down tactics.

This Christian organization leader scolded me for supporting a human life amendment to the Constitution that would grant personhood to unborn human beings under the law. I was denying my Baptist heritage as well as my

American heritage, he said, and I was attempting to subvert the Constitution by violating the separation of church and state in trying to impose my religious beliefs through legislation on other Americans who did not share my religious beliefs.

I happened to know that just weeks before this debate, he and several hundred other ministers had signed a manifesto committing themselves and a significant portion of the rest of their ministry to the abolition of nuclear weapons. This was back in the early 1980s, when debate was raging over whether or not to declare a freeze on all nuclear weapons.

"I want you to explain to this audience," I said to him, "why it is a violation of everything Baptist and everything American for me to bring my religious convictions and my religious beliefs to bear on the public policy of the issue of whether a mother ought to be able to kill her unborn child, but it is not a violation of the Constitution and not a violation of separation of church and state for you to bring your religious beliefs to bear on attempting to ban nuclear weapons from the globe. Why is that?" Of course he couldn't answer the question, because there is no difference. "What you need to admit here," I continued, "is that you don't like my position on abortion. Quit trying to disqualify me because my beliefs are religiously informed. Let's have a debate about abortion and nuclear weapons and quit all this nonsense about violating the separation of church and state."

Would you accept the results of a fixed game? In a game that was played fairly, on a level playing field, you accept the results. One team won, and one team lost. If you lost, you come back to play another game on another day. However, the secular Fundamentalists are trying to fix the game. They have appointed themselves the referees. At a Yale University debate on the use of embryonic stem cells for medical research, the late actor turned disabled activist Christopher Reeve declared, "When matters of public policy are debated, no religions should have a seat at the table."[14]

Religious beliefs shouldn't be treated any differently than any other beliefs. We accommodate everybody else's beliefs—why not religious belief?

We're not asking for special favors. We're just asking for an equal opportunity. Clearly I'm using sports as a metaphor, but this topic is not trivial. It is deadly serious.

THE THEOCRACY BOGEYMAN

One of the ways in which the other side is trying to fix the game is by setting up the bogeyman of theocracy—meaning that anyone who tries to bring religiously informed moral values to public issues is trying to set up a dictatorship of religion.

No one who is a leader of any significant or responsible part of the so-called Christian Right wants to see a government-sponsored religion. That's a fantasy of the secular Left. Do things get oversimplified in the heat of debate? Of course they do. The problem today is not conservative followers of religious faith trying to disqualify secularists from the debate, but secularists trying to disqualify Christians by claiming they are waging a religious war against democracy.

In December 2001, when Pat Robertson resigned the presidency of the Christian Coalition, the *Washington Post* ran a Christmas Eve article proclaiming that the baton of leadership of the Religious Right was now being passed to President George W. Bush. The article pasted together quotations and fragmented information from a variety of diverse sources in an effort to suggest that the Religious Right was an organized movement deliberately passing the baton of leadership to the White House. Further, it suggested, Robertson's resignation was the trigger, backed by the waning influence of other leaders, including Jerry Falwell, James Dobson, Billy Graham, and Franklin Graham, who were "no longer mobilized by their opposition to a president."[15]

This was quite a stretch, as anyone who has tried to coordinate efforts among these different ministries in pursuit of a common goal can attest. Dr. Dobson would no doubt be amused to hear that he has "retreated from political involvement." Billy Graham, receding from public involvement because of age and health, has carefully steered clear of political statements and would no doubt be surprised to hear that he is considered a former leader of the Religious Right.

This kind of straw-man stuffing has led to an entire industry of smear-and-scare tactics intended to conjure a theocratic bogeyman behind those with conservative religious values. Consider these cries of wolf:

- President George W. Bush is named the so-called First Prince of the Theocratic States of America in "The Despoiling of America: How

George W. Bush Became the Head of the New American Dominionist Church/State." According to the authors, "Within a period of twenty to thirty years beginning in the 1970s, Dominionism spread like wildfire throughout the Evangelical, Pentecostal and Fundamentalist religious communities in America."[16]

- An article titled "The Rise of the Theocratic States of America" provides information from a variety of sources documenting "the very real attempt by the radical Religious Right to take over the government and this nation and fashion it in their own image."[17]

- "What exactly does the Religious Right stand for? Its leaders have made some of the movement's values patently clear, such as destroying the First Amendment principle of church-state separation and privacy rights."[18]

- "This Republican Party of Lincoln has become a party of theocracy," according to Republican Representative Christopher Shays of Connecticut, who was commenting on federal intervention in the Terri Schiavo case.[19]

- "[What] is unique today is that the radical Religious Right has succeeded in taking over one of America's great political parties. The country is not yet a theocracy but the Republican Party is, and they are driving American politics, using God as a battering ram on almost every issue," says Bill Moyers.[20]

I represent members of the largest Protestant denomination in America, the Southern Baptist Convention, and I oppose a religious theocracy as vigorously as I do a secularist oligarchy. I don't think our position should be accepted because it is a Christian position. I'm not asking that it be accepted because it is a religious position. But I am insisting that it not be disqualified because it is based on religiously informed moral values. Everybody deserves an equal opportunity to compete for hearts and minds.

Judicial neutrality means that the referees are supposed to be impartial and interpret the rules. As Chief Justice John Roberts said during his confirmation hearings:

Judges and justices are servants of the law, not the other way around. Judges are like umpires. Umpires don't make the rules; they apply them.

The role of an umpire and a judge is critical. They make sure everybody plays by the rules. But it is a limited role. Nobody ever went to a ball game to see the umpire.

Judges have to have the humility to recognize that they operate within a system of precedent, shaped by other judges equally striving to live up to the judicial oath. . . .

It is what we mean when we say that we are a government of laws and not of men. It is that rule of law that protects the rights and liberties of all Americans. It is the envy of the world. Because without the rule of law, any rights are meaningless. . . .

I will decide every case based on the record, according to the rule of law, without fear or favor, to the best of my ability. And I will remember that it's my job to call balls and strikes and not to pitch or bat.[21]

If you don't like the rules, you work to change them. You don't let the refs change the rules on their own by dictating that this side is going to win over that side because this team gets eleven players but that team gets only three.

PLAYING FAIR

Liberals need reminding that people of religious faith must not be excluded from competition simply because their values are religiously informed. Conservatives need reminding that secular Fundamentalists must not be excluded from competition simply because this country was founded on Judeo-Christian principles. And neither should people of other religious faiths be excluded: Christians don't have an exclusive monopoly on religious expression just because Christianity has consistently been the majority religion in this country.

Playing without a religion penalty means that in the public square, we maximally accommodate the right of American citizens to express their religious (or nonreligious) convictions and beliefs as they choose, when they choose, if they choose to do so. If their expression of faith happens to offend advocates of some other faith, or those who dismiss faith, it is irrelevant. There is no constitutional guarantee against being offended. There *is* a constitutional guarantee of free exercise of religious faith, not to mention freedom of speech.

Is There a New Religion Penalty in America?

William Martin, professor of religion and public policy at Rice University, paints a clear picture of what "playing fair" looks like.

America has been remarkably favored—"blessed" if you prefer—by a wise and constitutional policy of non-preferential protection for the free and responsible exercise of religion. For the good of the entire community, religious and secular alike, we should protect that policy from encroachment from whatever corner. Each generation must redraw the lines of separation between the rights of religion and the rights of civil authority. If those we disagree with, whatever side they are on, cheat or lie or deceive, then we have every right to complain, to oppose, to expose, to embarrass them. If they play by the rules, however, we shouldn't cry foul when they organize themselves into an effective political force. Rather, we should play by the same rules and see if we can organize ourselves into an effective countergroup and see who can persuade the most people. If we are the ones who prevail, whether we are from the Left or the Right, who gain power, we should exercise it with humility and fear, recognizing always its tendency to corrupt its possessors and the causes they represent. . . . We cannot separate religion and politics. The question is how they are to be related in such a way as to maintain the pluralism that has served this country so well.[22]

If we allow a religion penalty to prevail, we deny the country the profound moral wisdom informed by Christianity, Judaism, Islam, and other religious traditions. We face problems as a nation with which human beings have never before had to wrestle: the technology for cloning and genetic manipulation, for example. Technology has propelled us to new frontiers, both expanding and blurring the borders of when life begins and ends and under what circumstances life should be perpetuated through technological means.

The attempt to rewrite history from a secular perspective by reading out of American history the enormous role that religion has played from the settlement of the country up to the present day deprives us of an enormous source of moral insight and moral truth at a time when we have never been more desperate for insight and truth.

Too often Americans have oscillated between the two extreme positions of acknowledgment and avoidance. The way to play fair is through an accommodation position, such that religion has no greater or lesser role in American public policy than it does in the lives of the American people. In this way, the government accommodates individual Americans' right to affirm religion and to bring religious values to public debate according to the dictates of their own consciences. So if 84 percent of Americans say that religion is important in their lives, then religiously informed moral values will play a much larger role than they would in a country such as France, where only 37 percent say that religion is important in their lives. And we will have an American society—not an American government—that affirms and, ideally, practices Judeo-Christian values rooted in biblical authority.

That seems to be what representative government is supposed to be about. To do otherwise is to discriminate against people of religious faith or to ask them to lobotomize themselves so they have one form of truth for home and hearth and another for the public square. That is totally unacceptable and discriminatory. When people of faith are candidates for office, they have every right as senators, congresspersons, governors, state legislators, city councilmembers, and public school board officials to bring their religiously informed moral convictions to moral debates about what's right and what's wrong and what should or should not be the public policy of the nation. They have a right to be on offense, not just on defense.

As former President Clinton observes in his introduction to Madeleine Albright's book *The Mighty and the Almighty*:

> Does this mean that policy makers should try to keep religion walled off from public life? As Madeleine Albright argues, the answer to that question is a resounding no. Not only shouldn't we do that; we couldn't succeed if we tried. Religious convictions can't be pulled on and off like a pair of boots. We walk with them wherever we go, the skeptics and atheists side by side with the devout. A president or secretary of state must make decisions with regard both to his or her own convictions and to the impact of those decisions on people of differing faiths.[23]

When, Catholic, Protestant, Muslim, or Jewish politicians bring their religious faith to bear on public policy issues, they aren't imposing their faith; they're sharing their faith convictions. They are saying, "This is the kind of senator I will be.

This is the kind of governor I will be. This is the kind of school board member I will be." The people they represent can then choose either to accept or reject the benefits of the insights of their faith.

The situation is utterly different for Catholic, Protestant, Muslim, or Jewish judges. Judges—and I would also include law enforcement officers here, and all those in a position of government authority who are to apply and enforce the law as opposed to writing the law—have the obligation and responsibility to be neutral umpires, to the best of their ability ascertaining what the law is, not what they would like it to be.

When Justice Samuel Alito was in confirmation hearings, I was asked if it would bother me that for the first time there would be a Catholic majority on the Supreme Court. I said that it didn't bother me at all—in fact, it was irrelevant. As with any judge, a Supreme Court justice needs to set aside his or her religious convictions and rule based only on the U.S. Constitution and laws. The Constitution, not his Judeo-Christian worldview, becomes his ultimate authority when he is serving in his role as a judge. If he wants his Judeo-Christian worldview to be part of his public service, then he needs to resign from the bench and become a senator or a congressman or work in an administration.

Describing how he allows his faith to influence his public service, Senator Lieberman explains:

My first obligation as a public servant is to the Constitution, the laws, the oath of office that I took, and the people of Connecticut. But many factors such as my religion have played a part in the development of my world view, my view of human nature. I believe that people have enormous potential for good, that we all are touched by the Divine. But we're all also imperfect, and we have the capacity to do great evil. And part of the answer to that evil, according to my religion, is the role of law as an attempt to create order, to establish standards for behavior, in some senses to express our best aspirations for ourselves and to deter our worst instincts. This is one reason I ended up wanting to be a lawmaker, and why I believe in the rule of law and order.[24]

That's playing fair! We need more such forthright expressions of religious faith in public life.

The law does make a difference. I think everyone would agree that the civil rights revolution was hugely successful. Have we eliminated prejudice? No. Have we reduced it about as far as the law can eliminate it? For the most part, yes. I think the rest of the heavy lifting that is to be done on racial issues in our society is not going to be done by the law. It's not going to be done by the government. It's going to be done in hearts and minds.

On another front, the revolution to legalize abortion has not been accepted; the majority of Americans oppose abortion on demand. Why hasn't abortion reached the acceptance level of the Civil Rights Movement? The reason is because Dr. King went out and won hearts and minds at virtually every major step in the civil rights revolution. The exception was *Brown v. the Board of Education* in 1954, which the Supreme Court was obligated to issue in order to rectify its egregious prior ruling that "separate but equal" was constitutional (*Plessy v. Ferguson*, 1896), thus sanctioning the rapidly spreading "Jim Crow" racial segregation in the South. That had to be reversed in order to move forward with integration. But apart from that, almost every other major step in the Civil Rights Movement was accomplished by legislation, through convincing a majority of the American people so that a majority of the people's elected representatives enacted laws that were then upheld by the federal judiciary.

In contrast, what the abortion revolution attempted to do—and what the homosexual rights revolution is attempting to do with same-sex marriage and the affirmation of the homosexual lifestyle—is to impose upon the American people against their will not a legislative revolution but a judicial revolution by imperial judicial fiat. The American people have never accepted abortion on demand the way they accepted civil rights legislation, and they have been rebelling against the attempt to impose it on them by a runaway judiciary.

To those who are advocating homosexual marriage, I say, if you think there ought to be same-sex marriage in the United States, then go out and convince a majority of the American people that is what should be done. Don't try to impose on them against their will something that the vast majority of them find morally repugnant. Which outcome do you want—a revolution as successful as Dr. King's or one as unsuccessful as abortion on demand?

HEALTHY PLURALISM

When a society practices healthy pluralism in respect to religion, you don't have to dumb down Christmas into some kind of "may the force be with you" generic holiday. That's just silly. People don't put up holiday trees in their homes; they put up Christmas trees. How ridiculous to try to ignore the fact that the vast majority of people in this country claim some kind of Christian heritage and have always celebrated Christmas, clearly a holiday with Christian origins. They ought to have a right to do that. Nobody should object to saying "Happy Hanukkah" to Jewish celebrants. It shouldn't be politically incorrect for merchants or others to say "Merry Christmas" to Christian celebrants.

The political correctness movement mouths words such as "understanding" and "respect for others' views," but the way to accomplish that is not by neutralizing everyone with some kind of politically correct stun gun. It is through pluralism that we get real understanding of, and respect for, faiths different from our own. The president has been severely criticized by some Christians, in my opinion unfairly, for having Muslim observances at the White House that coincide with Muslim holidays and for lighting a menorah at the White House to coincide with Hanukkah. In my view, doing these things is far more consistent with the pluralism we *say* we want than avoiding anything that might offend secularists. The government should participate in religious pluralism along with everyone else in society—although it would be best if the financial costs of such expressions were borne by private foundations.

Recently, the Ethics & Religious Liberty Commission of the Southern Baptist Convention sent out a Christmas card with a lovely photograph of the Supreme Court on the front—and inside, a Scripture verse and simple Christian greeting. In past years we had used pictures of the Capitol, and it seemed unwise to use a picture of the White House, as if we were staking some kind of claim to the president. We wanted to depict institutions representative of both Democrats and Republicans, of justices who had been nominated by both parties. We wanted to encourage people to be praying for the Supreme Court, especially at a time when new appointments were imminent.

Suddenly the Associated Press put out a story about our Christmas card—well, about the front of it, anyway—highlighting our use of the Supreme Court photo and quoting Americans United for the Separation of Church and State criticizing us for having a political agenda. "Control of the Supreme Court is at the top of Richard Land's Christmas list," they said.[25] Noticeably absent was any mention of the actual message inside, because that didn't serve their political agenda. It didn't matter what we *intended*; what mattered was another chance to cry foul because religious people dared to express their faith in the context of concern for our nation.

For the record, the greeting inside was, "May your Christmas be full of promise, joy, and blessing," accompanied by the following Scripture verse: "She will give birth to a son, and you are to name Him Jesus, because He will save His people from their sins" (Matthew 1:21 HCSB). What this has to do with "control of the Supreme Court" can only be understood by the fevered brains of those who write Americans United's press releases.

RELIGION-FREE ZONES?

What happens if we *don't* include religiously informed moral values in public policy debates? The alternative is allowing only those who have secularly informed moral values to make the decisions—or else we have a government that doesn't make decisions based on any moral values at all. We eliminate questions of right and wrong from the government's decision-making process. Do we really want a government like that? I don't think so. Moreover, as political philosophers have shown, the elimination of moral judgment from legislative deliberation is in many important cases literally impossible.

If you are a person who holds religiously informed moral values, you have a right to be on the field—but not only that, you have an *obligation* to be on the field. That is part of what it means to be salt and light in the world. Here is the answer to those who say you don't have a right to be on the field, and here is the answer to those who say you don't have an obligation to be on the field: the winning team is the one that can put the most able-bodied players on the field with the best game plan for victory. Moral values can carry an election because they are important to the majority of the American people.

The people with the best arguments will usually rally the support of the majority of the American people. Is this society better off because of Dr. King? Are we better off because we had a moral discussion in which people of religious values prevailed and we ended segregation? Of course we are. Is this country better off because we eliminated slavery? Of course it is. The best team won. Its moral arguments prevailed with the American people.

Founding father and second U.S. president John Adams cautioned that the United States has a government designed "only for a moral and a religious people." It is "wholly inadequate" for the government of an amoral or irreligious people.[26] The government's commitment to freedom is based on the assumption that the majority of the American people will voluntarily obey the law and voluntarily seek to do the right thing. If the majority are not moral and religious, there are not enough government constraints to ensure order, public decency, and freedom.

In other words, what we had in the formation of our country was an attempt to wed Judeo-Christian values with Enlightenment theories of self-government. Adams warned us that one won't work without the other. Without an underlying base of moral values, self-government will descend into a morass of self-seeking immorality and chaos. Without citizens who voluntarily march to the beat of their internal drummer, a morally informed conscience, we can't be sure the law will be obeyed voluntarily instead of under coercion and strong-arm tactics. If the law is not obeyed voluntarily, we will need a much larger and more intrusive government apparatus to ensure public order and safety.

On the other hand, without self-government, all of the moral values in the world will not add up to freedom and the rule of law instead of tyranny. Without self-government, moral values will be oligarchic impositions resented by the people and perceived as quenching the freedom that is the birthright of every divinely created human being. Government will present itself as a substitute for conscience, and we will end up with George Orwell's nightmare vision of Big Brother.

In a country as religious as America, if religious values are excluded from public policy, a significant number—if not the majority—of Americans are excluded from bringing their convictions to public life. In a country enduring a time of severe moral and spiritual crisis, as we are experiencing in America, excluding the rich mine of moral and spiritual wisdom that can be provided by people of religious faith is too high a price for insisting on a secular public square.

As noted earlier, a total separation of religiously informed morality and politics debilitates moral values and public virtue as corrosively as a complete dominance of a church by the state, or the state by a church, diminishes personal and religious freedom. Our forebears intended—and the Constitution of the United States provides for—a balance between religious morality and public virtue and a separation of the institution of the church and the institution of the state. This delicate constitutional balance, solidified and anchored by the First Amendment, is endangered at present, and it will not be put right unless people of faith insist on it.

Maybe it's not a bad idea, then, to mix religion and politics. Maybe it's not even an *unconstitutional* idea to mix God and country. What happens when you do? And just as important—what happens when you *don't*?

★ 8 ★

What Happens When You Mix God and Country—and What Happens When You Don't?

It is commonly said that stem cell research opponents are wrong to try to impose their theology—a "theology of the few"—on everyone else. That is true. What's more appalling is that so many of these people do not realize that they are being driven by their personal religious beliefs.

—RONALD M. GREEN[1]

That was exactly Ron Reagan Jr.'s disreputable strategy: blame it on religion, and it will go away; the health of the nation versus the "theology of the few."

—NIGEL CAMERON[2]

Some people say that when you mix God and country, that's where the trouble begins. Others would say that if you *don't* mix God and country, that's where the trouble begins.

Within ten years of the American Revolution, as the United States was settling into the new social and political order it had successfully created, France was overthrowing its centuries-long Old Order, the *Ancien Régime*, in a spasmodic and violent upheaval. The monarchy was brutally abolished, and a republic was declared, committed to *liberté, equalité,* and *fraternité*—the ideals of what was essentially a state-established, secularized religion complete with its own goddess, Reason. The new republic set about "unmixing" God and country with such ferocity that in one forty-eight-hour period, mobs brutally massacred three bishops and more than two hundred priests.

France ripped apart church and state, expunging religion from national life with draconian measures such as these:

- requiring priests to swear an oath of loyalty to the state, changing their status to that of civil employees;
- replacing the traditional Gregorian calendar with a newly created calendar of the French Republic, which abolished the Sabbath, saints' days, all references to the church, and even the very word *Sunday*;
- changing street and place names that had any religious connotations—St. Tropez became "Héraclée";
- banning religious holidays and replacing them with secular substitutes; and
- forbidding any displays of the Christian cross, silencing church bells, and banning religious processions.

Where did all that "liberty, equality, and fraternity" take the French people? Down into the darkness of a reign of terror.

The Russian Revolution of 1917 was another—and far more successful—attempt by the state to abolish the church. When the Bolsheviks seized power, they undertook a ruthless and thorough purging of religion:

- the Russian Orthodox Church was persecuted severely in the goal of replacing the deeply religious character of the Russian people with state-sponsored atheism;
- both Christmas and New Year's holidays were abolished;
- thousands of churches were destroyed, and monasteries were closed or converted into prison camps;
- priests were imprisoned and executed for various crimes against the state;
- an intense propaganda campaign was conducted throughout the history of the Soviet Union to discredit religion—Christianity in particular—and promote atheism.

This revolution, too, was heralded as a triumph of the people—and just as France's violent experiment resulted in the Reign of Terror, so did Russia's bloody experiment descend into the Red Terror.

In his influential work *The Roots of American Order*, conservative philosopher and prolific writer Russell Kirk illuminates the difference in worldviews underlying the revolutions in America and France:

> A conviction of man's sinfulness, and of the need for laws to restrain every man's will and appetite, influenced the legislators of the colonies and of the Republic. Thomas Jefferson, rationalist though he was, declared that in matters of political power, one must not trust in the alleged goodness of man, but "bind him down with the chains of the Constitution."
>
> A principal difference between the American Revolution and the French Revolution was this: the American revolutionaries in general held a biblical view of man and his bent toward sin, while the French revolutionaries in general attempted to substitute for the biblical understanding an optimistic doctrine of human goodness advanced by the philosophies of the rationalistic Enlightenment. The

American view led to the Constitution of 1787; the French view, to the Terror and to a new autocracy.[3]

If human rights and freedoms are God-given, then when one tries to separate God from them, all that is left are ugly power struggles—a Darwinian nightmare in which the survival of the fittest dictates the shape of human society and government.

Historically, our nation has not tried to wrest God away from the basis of human rights and freedoms. If we sought to rewrite history by removing God from our nation's identity, we would be draining the power from our founding documents. Secularists will argue that the Constitution itself nowhere mentions God, but that is a disingenuous attempt to assert that our founding fathers intended to leave God out of the experiment of American government. The Declaration of Independence, which is the founding document of the nation, says that all men are endowed by their "Creator" with unalienable rights.

The either-or deadlock of our public debate has thwarted our thinking and impoverished our imagination about God and country. Is it possible to mix them inappropriately? Yes. Do we have to keep the two apart, in separate realms? No—in fact, for the health of our nation, we must not.

The key to mixing God and country in a way that preserves the proper separation of church and state while allowing the religious character of the American people to flourish is through encouraging the robust, free exercise of individual conscience in the midst of a society-nourished and government-affirmed pluralism, rather than the sterile milieu of state coercion.

PLURALISM MEANS RELIGION IS PENALTY-FREE

A healthy, state-affirmed societal pluralism means no one is penalized for his or her views: neither those with religiously informed moral values, nor those with religion-free convictions.

However, I don't see Christians mounting a campaign to keep those with agnostic or atheistic views out of the public policy debate—although some of them do mix God and country indiscriminately. I *do* see secularists, in the name of separation of church and state, attempting to suppress the influence of religious convictions on public policy decisions.

The tendency to take God completely out of country runs counter to the convictions of the American people, as a major new national survey shows. Sponsored by the nonpartisan Public Agenda group, a study entitled *For Goodness' Sake: Why So Many Want Religion to Play a Greater Role in American Life*, reveals that religion is important to the lives of significant numbers of Americans.[4] Although they are wary of granting government the authority to determine which, if any, religious views receive preference, they believe that religious values can, and should be, a major factor for good in American society.

The survey found that approximately four out of five Americans believe that a more religious nation would mean improved parenting, increased volunteer and charity work, and less crime. In other words, most Americans believe that religion, in its diverse manifestations, has enormous potential to improve society's trouble spots through positive changes in behavior.

At the same time, results indicated that Americans are extremely uncomfortable with government imposition of religious views or bias toward one religious tradition over another. They don't want dominance of the majority religion in public schools, but neither do they want the secularized model dominant since the early 1960s in which the U.S. Supreme Court has consistently ruled against any forms of prayer and Bible reading in public. For example, when given a range of options concerning school prayer, 20 percent of the general public supported a nonsectarian prayer that mentioned God but not Jesus, and 53 percent preferred an organized moment of silence as the best public school prayer option. In other words, let us acknowledge the role religion plays in our lives, but let us each do so in a way of our own choosing with minimal intrusion upon others.

This clearly points to the middle way of accommodation, between avoidance and acknowledgment. This is a prescription for a healthy mix of God and country in what is clearly a religiously diverse, but hardly secular, society. It requires the government to protect the right of individuals to express their religious beliefs according to the dictates of their own consciences in the public square. On the other hand, it does not allow the government to take sides for or against one religion over another, or to attempt to silence all in deference to those who prefer no religious expression.

In his superb book *God's Name in Vain*, Stephen Carter observes that religion, by its very nature, addresses all of life, public as well as private:

> One of the things religion resists is our contemporary understanding of the separation of church and state. I do not mean that no religion teaches that a degree of separation of the two is important; in the American experience, most religions do. I mean that every serious religionist understands that complete separation is impossible. . . . As any serious student of religion knows, religion has no sphere. It possesses no natural bounds. It is not amenable to being pent up. It sneaks through cracks, creeps through half-open doors . . . and it flows over walls. The concept of *religion* is itself an idea that is necessary only if one plans to divide the world into multiple spheres, one of which is somehow related to the life led according to a narrative about God, and the other of which is somehow related to . . . well, to something else. Serious religions, however, do not conceive of the world in this way. In particular, the principal Western religious traditions, Judaism, Christianity, and Islam, all reject it. I do not mean that none of them preaches separation; I mean that none of them conceives of the world as divided into that which God created and therefore rules and that which God did not and does not.[5]

Too often in recent decades, Americans of religious conviction have been pressured by the state and the liberal cultural and media elites to segregate themselves and their views from the public sector. And if they don't, and their religious convictions are unacceptable to the gurus of political correctness, they are savaged publicly and often hounded by the legal system as well. A healthy pluralism that affirms separation as well as free expression will not tolerate a religion penalty.

RELIGIOUSLY INFORMED MORAL VALUES
ARE WELCOME HERE

Controversy over mixing God and country often arises over discussions of "moral values." Should the decisions and policies of our government be informed by moral values? If we say no, then we are saying that we want the public policies of our country to be amoral, devoid of moral content.

Had this view prevailed in our history, it would have meant perpetuation of slavery. After all, the institution of slavery was working economically and producing great wealth for a certain powerful segment of the population. But at some point a majority of Americans judged it to be immoral and embodied their moral judgment in the Fundamental law of the land in the form of the Thirteenth Amendment to the Constitution of the United States

In a new book, pollster Daniel Yankelovich identifies the decline of America's social morality in the wake of the "do your own thing" movement of the 1960s.

> The cultural issues roiling the nation are of a quite different character. Far from being a transitory move, they involve a long-term struggle over the direction of our future social morality. Traditionally, while the law marks the border between criminal and noncriminal behavior, social norms mark the border between right and wrong. In most societies, the layer of law is relatively thin, while the layer of social morality that sets the standards for how people and institutions should act is much thicker. This largely uncodified body of moral norms is essential to the healthy functioning of society.
>
> One unintended consequence of the American "cultural revolution" of the 1960s was that it caused this thick layer of social morality to erode. The emphasis on individualism—both culturally and economically—has led to the belief in a "live and let live" society bound only by legal requirements. People now unblushingly announce, "I didn't break the law—that proves I didn't do anything wrong." In earlier eras of American life, such a statement would have been met with incredulity. "What," people would ask, "does the law have to do with right and wrong?"[6]

Although I would disagree with Yankelovich's optimism about reconstructing a new social morality around a set of "core values" he perceives to be hidden underneath America's red-blue polarization, I agree with his diagnosis of our current moral crisis:

> Today there are numerous examples of wrong conduct being defined solely on the basis of their legality, and the most notorious of them are found in the business world (Enron, WorldCom, Tyco, HealthSouth, to name a few). But other

institutions have fared badly as well, including the American Red Cross and the highly venerated Roman Catholic Church. All of a sudden, what is called the "corporate culture" of any institution acts as if it can ignore social morality in favor of a self-serving code of conduct so long as it stays within legal boundaries.

But all is not lost. The majority of Americans have not become morally obtuse. In private life, most Americans maintain a strong sense of right and wrong for themselves and their families.[7]

So then the question becomes, whose moral values, and which moral values, are going to influence the public policies in the United States? If we're going to have a government "of the people, by the people, and for the people," then the answer must surely be the moral values of the American people.

To disqualify religiously informed moral values from public discussion is to ensure that the public policies of this country will be decided by a minority of Americans for whom religion is not important. Is that really a good long-term policy for determining the policies of the United States government? I think not.

How should we determine public policy? Do we believe that moral values, questions of right and wrong, should be part of the equation when the American people are deciding what the policies and laws of their government should be? I don't think very many Americans, aside from a handful of rigid secularists, are going to say no. Do we really think a majority of Americans are comfortable with government making policies in which religiously informed opinions about questions of right and wrong are deliberately excised? Once we eliminate distinctly religiously informed values (or values associated with the Judeo-Christian tradition) from debate about right and wrong, all that remains is a subjective moral relativism or utilitarianism, a system of thought and belief centered on the question, does it work?

Well then, how do you determine whether something is right or wrong? That is not a pragmatic question; that is a moral question. The Civil Rights Movement of the mid-twentieth century was about whether racial discrimination was right or wrong. When a majority of the American people concluded that it was wrong, the laws were changed. In earlier centuries, the slavery issue was a similar argument over right and wrong. It is true that many of the positions supporting slavery were based on utilitarianism. A surprising number of serious thinkers in the South argued that slavery was a better labor system than that of the North. It is true that some slaves were better housed and better fed than some factory workers in the slums of the industrializing North. So why did the country conclude slavery was wrong and must be illegal? Because it is always wrong for some people to own other people. That's a moral conviction, not a belief about utility or economic advantage, and it's not relative. It's the statement of a moral absolute: slavery is always wrong.

In a nation where only 37 percent of the people say that religion is important in their lives, such as France, it might be possible to claim that religion shouldn't play a role in public policy. But in the United States, 84 percent of Americans say that religion is very important in their lives. If we say that religiously informed moral values should not be part of the equation, then we are condemning ourselves to decisions made by a minority of the population for whom religion is not important.

Now, on the other side of the coin, no one has a right to say, "We have to do this because the Bible says so." Healthy pluralism means that not everyone claims the same source of moral authority for his or her values. Instead, we conduct debates about moral values and then vote our convictions.

A young woman at Harvard University said to me, "The Civil Rights Movement was inclusive, and your movement is exclusive." I said, "Really? So the Civil Rights Movement included George Wallace's views, did it? The Civil Rights Movement included the Ku Klux Klan? The Civil Rights Movement included the convictions of Lester Maddox?"

The Civil Rights Movement expressly excluded white supremacists from doing what they wanted to with their property and from organizing a society the way they wanted it organized. We didn't just leave this to moral persuasion. We passed laws against racial discrimination. We declared that healthy pluralism did not include allowing white racists to impose their moral values on the rest of us, because their moral values were wrong. Their moral values were depriving citizens of their guaranteed rights. But this is a democracy, so the white supremacists had the right and the opportunity to make their argument. We didn't deny them their First Amendment right to freedom of speech and freedom of expression. They simply lost the argument. A majority of the American people said, "You're wrong."

And guess what? Now one can advocate white supremacy, but one can't practice it by, for example, excluding blacks from a restaurant or hotel one owns. Some renegade Mormons may advocate polygamy, but they are not allowed legally to practice it—unless they can convince a majority of Americans they're right, in which case the laws would then be changed.

ANTIRELIGIOUS BIGOTRY MUST GO

A healthy mix of God and country leaves no room for antireligious bigotry. The claim that people of faith shouldn't get involved in politics and that religiously informed moral values shouldn't be part of the equation is demonstrably un-American. Religion and politics have been part of American life from the beginning, and this mix has produced tremendous freedom for religious people of all faiths as well as nonreligious people.

I'm not saying that people who aren't religious don't have moral values. Of course they do—most of them, at least. I doubt that very many of them are deliberately and consciously amoral. They have beliefs about what's right and what's wrong, and they have the right to bring those beliefs to the public square no matter what they're based on, religion or nonreligion. And then we have a debate.

It is a lot easier to win the discussion when you can simply disqualify the other side from participating, which is what the secular Fundamentalists want to do—a clever ploy because they are in the minority. Yet they will contend continually and erroneously that conservative religious views represent the fanaticism of the "few." Ronald M. Green, chair of religion at Dartmouth College, provides a blatant example when he condemns the role of religious views in the debate over embryonic stem-cell research: "It is commonly said that stem cell research opponents are wrong to try to impose their theology—a 'theology of the few'—on everyone else. That is true. What's more appalling is that so many of these people do not realize that they are being driven by their personal religious beliefs." Green goes on to condemn "the potent role of parochial religious views in our national debates."[8]

Nigel Cameron, research professor of bioethics at Chicago-Kent College of Law and president of the Institute on Biotechnology and the Human Future, accurately diagnoses Green's bigotry against religion as an attempt to silence opponents by disqualifying them from participating in public policy debates:

> I can't remember when I last saw such a vivid illustration of Peter Berger's brilliant epigram on America and its religion than in Ron Green's dismissal of religious views as "parochial." Berger, our most distinguished sociologist, has said that the most religious nation in the world is India; the most secular is Sweden, and America is a nation of Indians ruled by Swedes. Berger's point is that the assumptions of American public culture are secular and grossly out of step with the deep religiousness of most of the American people. But having dismissed religious views as parochial, Ron Green goes on to illustrate the role that religion is, as it were, *required* to play in this debate. It is evidently *necessary* to ascribe any and all opposition to mass-production cloning to parochial conservative religion. Why? Because if that can be done, there is then (given the assumptions of American public culture) no need to answer the arguments and address the moral force of those who see this as the first great global policy engagement of the "biotech century," and who have determined that the ethical health of biotechnology and the fundamental dignity of human beings require that it be won. That was exactly Ron Reagan Jr.'s disreputable strategy: blame it on religion, and it will go away; the health of the nation versus the "theology of the few."[9]

In *The Culture of Disbelief*, Stephen Carter demonstrates the extent to which the various elites in this culture have tried to disqualify religiously informed moral values from any participation in the public policy discussions and debates in this society.[10] That kind of antireligious bigotry is wrong. It is un-American. And it is a violation of the First Amendment rights of people with religiously informed moral values. It is also extremely counterproductive to successful government in America.

When a minority of the population are the only ones allowed to debate government policies, there will be an increasing disconnect in American society and an increasing disillusionment of the people with their government. That's dangerous for the government and for our society.

Jimmy Carter and John Kerry have said that although they are privately opposed to abortion on the basis of their Baptist and Catholic faiths, respectively, they don't have the right to impose their religious beliefs on any other American. Therefore, they keep their personal views private, separate from the positions they take in public.

I couldn't disagree more. There is a definitive difference between an elected official allowing his religious beliefs to inform his perspectives on public policy and the government imposing a particular religious belief on its citizens. Imposing religious beliefs means the government has children in public school saying, "Hail Mary, full of grace, the Lord is with thee. Blessed art thou among women . . ." every day. Imposing religious beliefs means the government is funding construction of Baptist churches or Catholic churches or Lutheran churches. Imposing religious beliefs means the government is teaching the Christian faith or some other religion in the public schools. Imposing religious beliefs means requiring those who are running for public office to take a religious test to determine whether they believe in God.

It is not imposing your religious beliefs on others to say as an American citizen, who also happens to be the president or a U.S. senator, that you believe abortion on demand is wrong. It is not imposing your religious beliefs to explain that you believe the wholesale killing of unborn American babies needs to stop. It is not imposing your religious beliefs on others to call for laws protecting embryonic human beings against being killed in experimental research designed hopefully to benefit others in the future. It is not imposing your religious beliefs on others to call for laws that restrict the times and the circumstances under which a mother can decide on her own to take the life of another human being, her child.

The fact that my religious beliefs inform my moral values does not disqualify me from bringing those moral values to bear on my views of what is happening in our society. To deny my right to do so is, in effect, to place a gag order on every American of religious faith. We are supposed to have a free church and a free state. The government doesn't sponsor religion. The government doesn't favor religion. The government doesn't penalize religion. The government doesn't silence religion. The government doesn't discriminate against religion. The people are free to share their faith and to propagate their faith with their own resources according to the dictates of their own consciences.

When religion makes a difference in people's lives, they have a right to bring their religious convictions to bear on public policy. This is called "the democratic process." And when they convince a majority of Americans they are right, they have a right to a government that reflects those moral values.

If you support same-sex marriage on moral grounds, religious or otherwise, come to the public square. Make your arguments. Let's debate and then let the people decide. Don't go running to the judicial system and try to impose on the American people what a clear majority of Americans do not believe is morally right and do not want. As noted earlier, if you want your social movement to succeed long term, you have to get the people behind it. You have to make your case to the people, which results in legislation, not to clever lawyers in courts that will impose upon the American people something that the vast majority of them find to be anathema.

BRING IT ON

It is immoral, imprudent, and destructive to the fabric of society to deny the majority the right to bring their moral values to bear on public policy. So I applaud Jim Wallis—let's have the debate about how to apply religious values. It will still be a lively debate, but it will be a healthier one for the country. The Democrats have been criticizing the Republicans for trying to become the party of religion. Nobody is keeping the Democrats from taking religious values seriously in public debates. If they did so, religious involvement in public policy would no longer be a partisan issue.

Today civil rights issues become partisan only at the point of application—for example, the justification for or against affirmative action—because both parties are committed to racial reconciliation, racial equality, and racial justice. The debate is over the best way to achieve these goals. Neither party is trying to repeal the civil rights laws. Neither party is the pro-racism party.

The same is true of the poverty issue. Jim Wallis accuses the conservatives of ignoring the issue, of being pro-rich. Neither party is pro-poverty. But the question is, how do we best eliminate poverty? The countries that are now emerging from poverty the most successfully and the most quickly are not those countries that have adopted the neo-socialist policies and confiscatory tax rates that Jim

Wallis seems to want the United States to enact. They are the ones that have rejected socialism and turned to free-market economies: South Korea, Taiwan, Malaysia, Singapore, and India.

When India was under the socialist economy they inherited from the British for forty years, it did very little to eliminate poverty. About fifteen years ago they adapted pro-Thatcher, pro-Reagan free-market economics, and now people are talking about India as the Asian miracle and saying that India may actually compete with the United States for economic supremacy in the twenty-first century. China had a horrific experiment with communism and socialism, which did nothing to eliminate poverty in the mainland of the country. And about twenty years ago they rejected Maoism and began experimenting with free-market reforms in their economy, but tragically not freedom in their political processes.

People are saying that America's prominence as the most influential country in the world for most of the twentieth century may actually give way in the twenty-first century to China or India. That wouldn't happen without free-market reforms.

Britain became a socialist country after World War II. It was heavily damaged by the war, but not as heavily as Germany. Germany was flattened. In the West, Germany adopted free-market reforms and a capitalist economy, and it rose from the ashes to become the economic miracle of Europe. Britain, meanwhile, was becoming the sick man of Europe. English girls were going to Italy and France to find work as domestic servants.

When Margaret Thatcher rose through the ranks and became prime minister in 1979, her mandate was to reverse Britain's decline and reduce the role of the state in the economy. She dropped the top tax rate from 83 percent to 60 percent, and finally to 40 percent, and the share of taxes paid by the top 1 percent of taxpayers rose during the same period from 11 percent to 21 percent.[11] She sold off the socialist industries that were losing money and let the people who were living in public housing buy their own residences. One could tell just by looking which flats (apartments or houses) were privately owned and which remained government property. When people owned their dwellings, they were impeccably maintained, as opposed to the often somewhat derelict appearance of government-owned property. Britain now has more personal computers per capita than any other country in the world. It has the healthiest economy in

Europe and has reduced poverty and raised the standard of living more than any other country in Europe.

By contrast, Germany has allowed socialism to creep in and a welfare economy to spread—the kind of economy that the Religious Left wants to establish in the United States. Germany has a 15 percent unemployment rate, and it is clear that they cannot continue to support their welfare system. They are in deep trouble economically. In November 2005 they elected their first female chancellor, Dr. Angela Merkel. She has been called the Margaret Thatcher of Germany. She was raised in East Germany, and she grew up under socialism. She knows firsthand how horrific it is, and she is committed to making Germany an economic miracle once more.

The Russians now have a flat tax, the lowest tax rate of any industrialized country in the world. They want to attract investment and build up an economy that has been horrendously damaged by nearly a century of socialism.

Noted columnist Thomas Friedman points out the widening gap between market-fueled economies in Poland, China, and India and Europe's "welfare states." Old-Europe values of government-subsidized shorter work weeks and longer vacations stand in stark contrast to Asian and new-Europe values of hard work, economic ambition, and business ownership. Friedman observes that India's hunger for opportunity "has been pent up like volcanic lava under four decades of socialism, and it's now just bursting out with India's young generation. . . . Next to India, Western Europe looks like an assisted-living facility with Turkish nurses."[12]

Questions about how to eliminate poverty in America and around the world are not questions of right and wrong as much as they are economic questions of prudence—what works and what doesn't. And we could have a moral debate about how to disperse the increased wealth being produced by a free-market economy, but that's a different question than which economic model "works" in producing wealth. That question, based on the world's experience in the last quarter century, is over and the free market model won.

The *Wall Street Journal's* editors sum this up nicely in "Reaganomics at 25":

Thus today, the top marginal personal and corporate tax rates are 35 percent, compared with 70 percent and 48 percent in 1981. In the late 1970s the tax on dividends was 70 percent and the capital gains rate was 50 percent; now they're both 15 percent. These reductions have increased the rate of return on capital, and hence some $3 trillion more was invested by foreigners in the U.S. between 1981 and 2005 than was invested by Americans abroad. One result: 40 million new jobs, more than the rest of the industrialized world combined.

The rest of the world, meanwhile, has followed the Gipper down the tax-cut curve. Daniel Mitchell of the Heritage Foundation finds that the average personal income tax rate in the industrialized world is now 43 percent, versus 67 percent in 1980. The average top corporate tax rate has fallen to 29 percent from 48 percent. This decline in global tax rates has been the economic counterpart to the fall of the Berlin Wall. Most of Eastern Europe has adopted flat tax rates of 25 percent or lower, and the Russians now have a flat income tax of 13 percent. In Old Europe, Ireland's corporate and personal income tax rate cuts have helped generate the swiftest economic growth in the EU.[13]

As the *Wall Street Journal* concludes, "In his 1989 farewell address, Reagan said that 'People say that I was the great communicator. It would be more accurate to say that I communicated great ideas.' He was right, and a remarkable global prosperity has followed in his wake."[14]

A young man at an Ivy League university asked me, in light of the fact that George W. Bush is a born-again Christian, as am I, and the Bible says it is more difficult for a rich man to get to heaven than it is for a camel to get through the eye of a needle, how we could defend giving a tax cut to the richest 1 percent of Americans.

I replied, "The president didn't give a tax cut to the richest 1 percent of Americans; he gave a tax cut to every American. Every American who paid taxes got a tax cut. Even those who don't pay taxes got a tax cut, because we have something in this country called the negative income tax for people who don't make enough money to pay an income tax. Even they got a refund from the government."

"Second," I said, "it sounds to me that you want President Bush to apply his religiously informed moral values on some issues, but not others. Why do you want him to impose his moral values on people who make money, but you don't want him to impose his moral values on women who are having abortions? That seems inconsistent. Religiously informed moral values are religiously informed moral values. My inconsistency meter is beeping. I want you to think long and hard about that, and then try to explain it to us."

And third, I explained that the budget is a moral document, but part of that budget is the tax code. In my opinion, it is immoral that the average American family has to work more than half the year to pay their tax burden before they can work for themselves and their families.

Somebody is going to be imposing somebody's moral values on somebody else. That's what public policy is all about. Telling people of religious faith to keep their moral values to themselves is like requiring them to take off their helmets before they step onto the playing field.

WHEN YOU DON'T MIX GOD AND COUNTRY

Fairness is not the only reason necessitating a principled pluralism in this country. Another reason is the disastrous consequences of chasing religion out of the public square in the name of keeping God and country separate.

One of the most serious consequences of eliminating religious insights from sources of moral values is that doing so abandons the field to the utilitarian philosophy that the government should do the greatest good for the greatest number of people. You decide whether or not to keep someone alive by calculating how much it costs. You ration health care to the sick and the elderly because it is too expensive to help those people, and the money can do so much more for younger people with better prospects for health. As former Democratic governor of Colorado Richard Lamm famously said in 1984 (interesting that it was the same year as George Orwell's nightmare vision of a utilitarian future), "Old people have a duty to die and get out of the way."[15]

By contrast, a sanctity-of-life view affirms that every human being is of inestimable value. Therefore, there are some things that must never be done to a human being. You must never take away another human being's right to life, no matter how many other people you can help through that person's death. You must never make judgments against, or separately from, the will of another human being about what is a sufficient quality of life for him or her. You don't presume to judge when that quality of life has fallen below a level that guarantees the absolute right to life that we have historically granted to human beings in this country.

In his speech at the Democratic National Convention in July 2004, Ron Reagan Jr. said that we can't allow religion to impede the progress of science: "We have a chance to take a giant stride forward for the good of all humanity. We can choose between the future and the past, between reason and ignorance, between true compassion and mere ideology. This is our moment, and we must not falter."[16]

That is the "anything that can be done, should be done" argument. The last time that argument prevailed, we got the Third Reich. "You may believe that embryos are human beings," Reagan Jr. was saying, "but I don't." Therefore, he asserted, we can do whatever we want with them. He tried to guarantee that his argument would win by declaring that anyone with a religiously informed opinion was an unenlightened, ideological ignoramus, obviously disqualified from participating in the debate. This is a new day, he was saying, and we can't let religion dictate science. (By the way, is not Ronald Reagan Jr. the best argument you've seen against hereditary monarchies?)

Do we really want a country that kills its tiniest human beings in order to seek cures for merely older and bigger human beings? I don't think I want to live in that kind of world.

How do we decide who makes the decisions when health-care funding is limited? In England today, if you're over fifty-nine and a half, you can't get a bypass operation in the National Health System because it's not considered cost-effective. You can't get a kidney transplant because it's not considered cost-effective. You're not a good return on the government's investment, so you are denied lifesaving care. I don't think I want to live in that kind of society.

Once you decide you're going to live in a society where nothing is unconditionally wrong, then you're going to live in a society where anything is possible under the right circumstances. That is where moral relativism (an absence of morally informed absolute standards and values) and utilitarianism lead. That is what is at stake here.

Education and scientific expertise are no inoculation against the darkness of the human heart. Germany was the most scientifically, technologically, educationally, and culturally advanced culture in the world—and all that did was make their barbarism more heinous once they severed themselves from Judeo-Christian absolutes and descended into Nazi tyranny. Robert Jay Lifton's book *The Nazi Doctors* profiles the German physicians who did the experiments and justified them based on utilitarianism.[17] Why isn't this scaring the daylights out of us when we debate embryonic stem-cell research and genetic engineering?

Using the same utilitarian argument, animal-rights extremist Peter Singer has descended down a twisted chain of logic to the conclusion that sexual relations between humans and animals are perfectly moral as long as they are consensual.[18] When you accept utilitarianism, you've given yourself a moral lobotomy.

I remember having discussions in high school about lifeboat scenarios: Who gets to stay in the lifeboat, and who has to be thrown overboard? What happens when you don't have enough supplies to sustain everyone and you start making decisions about which lives are worthier than other lives? I spoke up in class and said that we as fellow human beings don't have the right to say that somebody has less of a right to live than somebody else. The teacher countered, "Then everybody dies." And I replied, "Better that everyone dies than that we commit murder." This was considered quite a reactionary position by the teacher, even in the 1960s.

Understanding how to mix God and country, church and state, in a way that promotes healthy pluralism and avoids state interference with religion is critical; otherwise, confusion will prevail. That confusion will "fix" the game, and the game will be over before it has a chance to start, with dangerous consequences, particularly for the weak, the sick, the old, the infirm, and anyone who is considered "inferior."

ARE WE A NATION UNDER GOD OR NOT?

Another major area of confusion centers on whether it is right or wrong to say that we are "one nation under God" in the Pledge of Allegiance. That is a decision for the people to make. To date they have decided that they *do* want to be a people under God, a people who acknowledge the existence of God, a people who seek to put their trust in God. We have inscribed "In God We Trust" on our money—and money is serious business to Americans.

These references to God are being challenged now by the U.S. Court of Appeals for the Ninth Circuit. If the Supreme Court were to accept its silly arguments, it would trigger an uprising among the American people to over-rule the courts and retain references to God in the Pledge of Allegiance, on our currency, and in one of our national mottoes. Within eighteen months we would have the fastest-ever amendment to the Constitution.

Separation of church and state was never intended to mean that atheists and agnostics have a veto power over the majority of people in this country who have been, and are, believers in God as the source of our Fundamental rights and moral obligations. America is one of the most religious nations on earth. The government is not sponsoring religion. The government is not penalizing people who don't believe. However, if the majority of the American people want to have "In God We Trust" on our money or "one nation under God" in our pledge, they have the right to do so. That's not discriminating against peo-ple of no faith. No one is required to read "In God We Trust" on his money when he receives it or spends it. No one is required to recite the Pledge of Allegiance to the flag.

The final verse of the "Star-Spangled Banner," our national anthem, reads:

> O thus be it ever, when free men shall stand,
> Between their lov'd homes, and the war's desolation!
> Blest with vict'ry and peace, may the heav'n rescued land,
> Praise the Pow'r that hath made and preserved us a nation!
> Then conquer we must, when our cause it is just;
> And this be our motto: "In God is our trust!"
> And the star-spangled banner, in triumph shall wave
> O'er the land of the free and the home of the brave!

That's the national anthem! If it's wrong, then our forefathers have been wrong from the beginning. Either we are the luckiest people in the world or we are the most blessed people in the world. I don't believe that history is happen-stance. I believe there is a God, and He is in control, and He exercises divine providence in all of human life. God has been doing a providential work in history and, yes, in American history.

God has blessed the United States of America in unique and wondrous ways, and that is a doctrine of obligation, responsibility, sacrifice, and service, not a doctrine of pride and privilege. Should we not give from the spiritual and philosophical wealth we have received? This raises the fundamental question of whether America has a special role in the world.

★ 9 ★

Does America Have a Special Role in the World?

American exceptionalism is the delusion that the United States is different.

—KEVIN PHILLIPS[1]

My own inclination is to say "Bunk" to those who argue that America is not an exceptional country.

—MADELEINE ALBRIGHT[2]

In his book *American Theocracy*, Kevin Phillips calls the school of thought known as exceptionalism "the delusion that the United States is different."[3] He supports this statement by charting patterns characteristic of theocratic empire building, which he suggests the United States shares with ancient Rome, Hapsburg, Spain (1516–1700), the Dutch Republic (1581–1795), and Britain (from the mid-nineteenth century through World War I). For Phillips, the presumption that America is somehow special is a dangerous development driven by a rabid and irrational Christian Fundamentalism that dominates both the Oval Office[4] and the GOP, "the first religious party" in American history.

The concept of American "exceptionalism" was first popularized by Alexis de Tocqueville, although the idea was hardly invented by him. The roots of this view go back to the beginnings of Puritan settlements—how else do you explain the Puritan understanding of a "shining city on a hill" to light the way for the Old World? Or Francis Scott Key's imagery of "the heav'n rescued land" in our national anthem, which he wrote in 1814 after he saw the American flag over Fort McHenry survive a night of fierce bombardment from British ships? American exceptionalism is the understanding that America is a unique nation with a unique sense of purpose that started with the nation's settlement and has since morphed through various meanings, all of them centered on the observation that America is distinct from other countries in the world—in its founding, in its government, in its social and economic structures, and in its religious and cultural character. American exceptionalism is often invoked by liberals to disparage what they see as American imperialism and unilateralism, and by conservatives to hail what they see as America's strength as the guardian of freedom and liberty both at home and abroad.

In contrast to Phillips's "delusion," a different view of American exceptionalism was espoused by U.S. Secretary of Labor Elaine L. Chao, the first Asian-American woman to be appointed to a presidential cabinet in American history, in a speech she gave to newly naturalized citizens on New York's historic Ellis Island. She recalled arriving in the United States when she was eight years old aboard a freighter with her mother and two sisters. As they chugged into New York Harbor, she caught sight of the Statue of Liberty, which "symbolized all of the hopes and dreams of our young family. I will never forget that day as long as I live." After summarizing the amazing benefits of living in this country—the freedom to realize dreams; the acceptance of people from diverse backgrounds and cultures who become part of the country's mosaic of diversity; a level playing field for people of all races and creeds because of the unique combinations of free markets, transparent and accountable institutions, and the rule of law—she urged her audience to become part of the legacy that America bequeaths to each generation.

> America is special not only because of what it gives us, but because of what it asks of us. To guarantee your freedom, America asks not only for your allegiance, but also for your involvement in community and civic life. The philosophers who formed the ideas upon which our republic is based made that very clear. A republic is only as good as the character of each and every one of its citizens. Each of us has rights. But as Americans, we also have responsibilities. And the future of our country depends upon the active involvement of each and every one of us in our democracy. Each generation of citizens is a steward responsible for the care and preservation of our democracy. As new citizens, I welcome you into this historic fellowship. America's values of liberty and justice are a heritage passed on to us by those who came before us. In turn, our country is depending upon us to pass these values on to our children and grandchildren. Freedom, opportunity, transparency and the rule of law can never be taken for granted.[5]

Chao's ringing challenge suggests that America is fundamentally distinct from all other countries in its founding, in its national life, and in the values and privileges it confers upon its citizens. In other words, America is *exceptional*. And if it is exceptional in its domestic character, in what it offers to immigrants in search of a better life, then it would follow that America is exceptional in what it has to offer to the global community.

America is not an ethnicity or mere geography, but a creed, a set of first principles to which we pledge allegiance—freedom, human dignity, self-government, and equality. Anyone who pledges allegiance to these values can consider himself or herself an "American."

One of the most heated arguments in our public life today is over this very question: Does America have a special role in the world, or is America simply one of the 193 countries on the United Nations' membership list? Are we just a country, with interests and friends and allies and opponents and adversaries, or are we also a cause?

This controversy takes a particular form in Christian circles, and it has everything to do with what God has to do (or not to do) with America. At one extreme, Christian liberals are scandalized by the notion that God has something particular to do with America, because they see it as a dangerous confusion of the kingdom of God with misguided, even rabid, patriotism. In their view, singling out America as a special nation is unbiblical, prideful, and sinful. It is nationalistic jingoism to think of our own nation more highly than we ought.

At the other extreme, some conservative Christians see the notion as evidence of America's birthright as a "Christian nation" and denounce the "myth" of separation of church and state for stealing that birthright. The loony fringes at the edge of this extreme are the ones who want to institute Old Testament laws in a so-called Christian dominion over all aspects of life. That actually has very little to do with Christian faith. The historic, biblical Christian faith is based on the New Testament message of redemption and grace in Jesus Christ. It does not teach a return to Old Testament law; it teaches the fulfillment of it in Christ's law of grace.

Dominionism (Kevin Phillips's conspiracy theory of choice) is an appalling totalitarianism that virtually no one takes seriously except liberals who are more interested in propping up a bogeyman of the Religious Right than taking the time and effort to understand Evangelicalism, Fundamentalism, and Pentecostalism in all their theological, historical, and cultural fullness and diversity. But that would mean having to take conservative religious people seriously instead of writing them off as fanatics—clearly too much to ask of many liberals, judging from their statements.

What liberals and conservatives both are missing is that America has been blessed by God in unique ways—we are not just another country, but neither are we God's special people. I do not believe that America is God's chosen nation. God established one chosen nation and people: the Jews. We are not the new Israel. We do not have "God on our side." We are not God's gift to the world.

America does not have a special claim on God. Millions of Americans do, however, believe God has a special claim on them—and their country.

America has been blessed in manifold ways. When you look at our resources, our protection by two oceans, our standard of living, can you argue that America has not been uniquely and providentially blessed? The natural resources that lie within the confines of our borders are without parallel anywhere in the world: not just rich, arable land, but vast resources of iron, coal, and oil under the ground. We didn't put them there; we were just led to the place where they were. We have had the opportunity to enjoy them and to benefit people around the world with them. Perhaps the most fertile land on the planet is our Great Plains. We have become the breadbasket for the world. We feed much of the world's population, in part because we are good farmers, but also because we believe in private ownership of land and property. Can you name a nation that in any way can claim to have been the recipient of God's unearned blessings to the measure that we have been?

The blessings are not just material, however. It is remarkable that the one generation that produced our founding fathers emerged and put together the Constitution that has served us so well for more than two centuries and has brought unparalleled freedom for an unparalleled number of people—unequaled by any other country in the world.

We enjoy freedoms that most of us have not risked our lives to establish, protect, or preserve. All of us, unless we are immigrants to this country, have by the providence of birth been bequeathed an incredible legacy. Over the last two and a half centuries, there has been no other country in the world within which such a high percentage of the population has had the guaranteed freedoms we possess: freedom of speech, freedom of worship, freedom of assembly. We have guaranteed freedoms in our Constitution that even Canadians and Britons don't have.

There was either a fortuitous or a providential set of circumstances in the development and rise of this nation. Since I'm a Christian, I believe in providence more than fortune. I believe that it was a uniquely providential set of circumstances that allowed the flourishing of this triumph of freedom and the dignity of human beings. It certainly didn't happen that way in the French Revolution, and I believe it is no coincidence that the philosophy and convictions fueling that revolution were not based on a transcendent divine authority. They were based in human reason (or what the revolutionaries mistook for reason) alone, and the upheaval quickly degenerated into a maelstrom of chaos, violence, and power struggles.

The founding fathers of the American Revolution, by contrast, affirmed that human rights are not mere human constructions, but are unalienable rights conferred by God. Government could not create those rights; all it could do was recognize them and support them. This idea of divinely ordained rights had not taken root anywhere else in the world. It was a new and unique concept. Because it has been around our whole life as a nation, we tend to take it for granted.

From the richness of our undeserved legacy comes obligation. If we have been given much, we are obligated to give much to others. If we love our neighbors as ourselves, we will seek not only to preserve and protect our liberties, but to assist others in their efforts to attain these same liberties.

I think one reason George W. Bush won the 2004 election is that a majority of American Evangelicals and a majority of traditional Catholics believe that America is not just a nation; America is also a cause. Nations have self-centered interests. Causes are purposes larger than ourselves. I think most Americans believe that we are all bound up in a purpose that stretches farther than our territorial borders, that is bigger than our self-interests. Most Americans, I believe, share a sense of responsibility to stand for freedom, democracy, and human rights.

As President Bush said in closing his first inaugural address (see appendix D):

After the Declaration of Independence was signed, Virginia statesman John Page wrote to Thomas Jefferson: "We know the race is not to the swift nor the battle to the strong. Do you not think an angel rides in the whirlwind and directs this storm?"

Much time has passed since Jefferson arrived for his inauguration. The years and changes accumulate. But the themes of this day he would know: our nation's grand story of courage and its simple dream of dignity.

We are not this story's author, who fills time and eternity with his purpose. Yet his purpose is achieved in our duty, and our duty is fulfilled in service to one another.

Never tiring, never yielding, never finishing, we renew that purpose today, to make our country more just and generous, to affirm the dignity of our lives and every life.

This work continues. This story goes on. And an angel still rides in the whirlwind and directs this storm.

God bless you all, and God bless America.

Madeleine Albright, who immigrated to the United States from Eastern Europe and eventually became secretary of state under the Clinton administration, affirms the necessity of American leadership abroad. "Why wouldn't I?" she exclaims. "When I was a little girl, U.S. soldiers crossed the ocean to help save Europe from the menace of Adolf Hitler. When I was barely in my teens, the American people welcomed my family after the communists had seized power in my native Czechoslovakia. . . . I love to think of America as an inspiration to people everywhere—especially to those who have been denied freedom in their own lands."[6]

Dr. Albright's views, seasoned by her years in high office as a shaper of America's role abroad during the 1980s, contrast sharply with Kevin Phillips's assessment that American exceptionalism is a delusion.

My own inclination is to say "Bunk" to those who argue that America is not an exceptional country. I can point to the Declaration of Independence, the Constitution, the Bill of Rights, the Gettysburg Address, the role of the United States in two world wars, and the example of America's multiracial, multiethnic democracy and ask: what country can compare? A few are as big, some are as free, many have admirable qualities, but none has had the same overall positive influence on world history and none has been as clearly associated with opportunity and freedom.[7]

I agree with Dr. Albright that the exceptional history of the United States does not constitute a "divine mission to spread liberty across the globe." However, I would point out that while she is uncomfortable with the idea of some outside force—"God, providence, nature, or history"—defining our nation's history, she does affirm what Christians know to be the biblical principle that "much is expected from those to whom much has been given."[8] From her Catholic upbringing, Dr. Albright would understand the biblical origin of this concept as well.[9]

I would ask that if much has been given to us, then who has been doing the giving? From where has the "much" been bestowed upon us? While I agree that America does not have a divine mission, I would contend that we have a *sacred obligation and responsibility* that is the direct consequence of God's providential and unique blessings. American exceptionalism means that we hold ourselves to a higher standard, and we expect others to hold us to a higher standard. For Evangelicals, this principle has a theological basis.

AS SPECIAL AS APPLE PIE

Kevin Phillips is wrong—American exceptionalism is not a delusion of national grandiosity. Jim Wallis is wrong—American exceptionalism is not a doctrine of pride and privilege. It is a belief that God has blessed this nation in amazing ways, and those blessings invoke a reciprocal obligation and responsibility to seek to share, but not impose, the blessings of freedom and democracy with others.

No matter what your views are on the question of whether God has a special purpose in mind for America, you live in a country that believed that very thing throughout its entire history, generation upon generation, until the 1960s. This understanding of America is not new. It goes all the way back to John Winthrop's imagery of a "shining city on a hill" to light the way for the Old World. It has been under severe challenge, but it is as American as apple pie. For most of our history, a significant number of Americans have believed that America does have a special role to play in the world.

Some liberals don't want the Declaration of Independence to be included as one of our founding documents because it refers to God. Because the Constitution does not mention God, they claim that is the test of our founding fathers' intent. We have already clearly seen that it is not true that our founding fathers wanted to create a governing structure bereft of any reference to God. Regardless of whether our founding fathers were Christians, deists, civil religionists, or churchgoing or church-skipping nominal members of their religious tradition, they were clearly saturated with the idea that God created the human race and holds all humans accountable to His judgments. (See President Lincoln's second inaugural address, appendix D.)

I attended a 2000 conference of the American Assembly in which a supposedly equal number of liberal and conservative leaders were gathered to hammer out a statement of common ground on the role of religion and society. We spent at least fifteen minutes arguing over the phrase "founding documents." Liberals argued that it should be singular—"founding document," referring only to the Constitution. Conservatives insisted that it be plural—"founding documents," referring to both the Declaration of Independence and the Constitution. They saw the Declaration of Independence as the founding document and the Constitution as the document of implementation.

I helped win the argument with math by citing the opening of Abraham Lincoln's Gettysburg Address: "Fourscore and seven years ago our fathers brought forth on this continent a new nation, conceived in liberty and dedicated to the proposition that all men are created equal" (see appendix D).[10] When you start with the date of the address—November 19, 1863—and go back four score and seven years, you come up with 1776, the date of the Declaration of Independence. The Constitution wasn't ratified until 1788. Clearly Lincoln believed the Declaration of Independence to be the founding document of the American nation, and I proposed that we agree with his judgment on the matter.

President Lincoln also clearly believed that America had been preserved by divine providence: "Now we are engaged in a great civil war, testing whether that nation or any nation so conceived and so dedicated can long endure," he went on. The nation would resolve that those who died in the Civil War did not do so in vain: "that this nation under God shall have a new birth of freedom, and that government of the people, by the people, for the people shall not perish from the earth." His vision was a nation in which self-governing human beings could acknowledge and protect their divinely granted right to freedom.

Eight decades later, President Franklin Delano Roosevelt closed his State of the Union address to Congress on January 6, 1941, with an articulation of the "four freedoms," a universal foundation of human rights. The United States, he believed, had a duty to uphold these freedoms not only at home, but also in the face of tyranny abroad (see appendix D).

> In the future days, which we seek to make secure, we look forward to a world founded upon four essential human freedoms.
>
> The first is freedom of speech and expression—everywhere in the world.
>
> The second is freedom of every person to worship God in his own way—everywhere in the world.
>
> The third is freedom from want—which, translated into world terms, means economic understandings which will secure to every nation a healthy peacetime life for its inhabitants—everywhere in the world.
>
> The fourth is freedom from fear—which, translated into world terms, means a world-wide reduction of armaments to such a point and in such a thorough fashion that no nation will be in a position to commit an act of physical aggression against any neighbor—anywhere in the world.[11]

Still convinced that American exceptionalism is the invention of the Bush administration to justify its ambition to engage in "empire building"? Read this excerpt from John F. Kennedy's inaugural address:

> The world is very different now. For man holds in his mortal hands the power to abolish all forms of human poverty and all forms of human life. And yet the same revolutionary beliefs for which our forebears fought are still at issue around the globe—the belief that the rights of man come not from the generosity of the state, but from the hand of God.
>
> We dare not forget today that we are the heirs of that first revolution. Let the word go forth from this time and place, to friend and foe alike, that the torch has been passed to a new generation of Americans—born in this century, tempered by war, disciplined by a hard and bitter peace, proud of our ancient heritage, and

unwilling to witness or permit the slow undoing of those human rights to which this nation has always been committed, and to which we are committed today at home and around the world.

Let every nation know, whether it wishes us well or ill, that we shall pay any price, bear any burden, meet any hardship, support any friend, oppose any foe, to assure the survival and the success of liberty.[12]

And it sounds as though President Kennedy believed that his was a "chosen" generation:

This much we pledge—and more. . . . In the long history of the world, only a few generations have been granted the role of defending freedom in its hour of maximum danger. I do not shrink from this responsibility—I welcome it. I do not believe that any of us would exchange places with any other people or any other generation. The energy, the faith, the devotion which we bring to this endeavor will light our country and all who serve it. And the glow from that fire can truly light the world.

And so, my fellow Americans, ask not what your country can do for you; ask what you can do for your country.

My fellow citizens of the world, ask not what America will do for you, but what together we can do for the freedom of man.

Finally, whether you are citizens of America or citizens of the world, ask of us here the same high standards of strength and sacrifice which we ask of you. With a good conscience our only sure reward, with history the final judge of our deeds, let us go forth to lead the land we love, asking His blessing and His help, but knowing that here on earth God's work must truly be our own.[13]

"Here on earth God's work must truly be our own": clearly, President Kennedy's eloquent words represent a belief that America was at a special moment and a special place, and America had a special obligation to be the defender of freedom and liberty in the world.

I don't believe America is perfect, but I do believe that God has blessed our nation in providential ways and that we have a special obligation in the world to be the defender and propagator of freedom—not by imposing American ideals on the world, but by supporting universal ideals. As President Bush said in his first inaugural address (see appendix D):

> We have a place, all of us, in a long story, a story we continue but whose end we will not see. It is the story of a new world that became a friend and liberator of the old, a story of a slave-holding society that became a servant of freedom, the story of a power that went into the world to protect, but not possess, to defend, but not to conquer.
>
> It is the American story—a story of a flawed and fallible people, united across the generations by grand and enduring ideals. The grandest of these ideals is an unfolding American promise that everyone belongs, that everyone deserves a chance, and that no insignificant person was ever born. Americans are called to enact this promise in our lives and in our laws. And though our nation has sometimes halted and sometimes delayed, we must follow no other course.
>
> Through much of the last century, America's faith in freedom and democracy was a rock in a raging sea. Now it is a seed upon the wind taking root in many nations.
>
> Our democratic faith is more than the creed of our country, it is the inborn hope of humanity, an ideal we carry but do not own, a trust we bear and pass along. And even after nearly 225 years, we have a long way yet to travel. It is a trust we bear, an ideal we carry.[14]

If those words sound strange, as in "too religious," the strangeness is in the ears of the hearer, not in the words of George W. Bush. He is continuing an American tradition that has been transmitted in a nearly unbroken line from generation to generation since the founding of our great nation.

EXCEPTIONALISM EQUALS ARROGANT EMPIRE?

Critics of American exceptionalism dismiss it as dangerous, nationalistic arrogance, pointing to unilateralism as evidence of a defiant refusal to play by the global rules. Jim Wallis warns of the Bush administration's "theology of empire."[15] Kevin Phillips denounces "hubris-driven national strategic and military overreach" fueled by blind faith and religious excesses in the American empire's illusory, crippling belief in its own exceptionalism.[16]

A different perspective, from a European observer who has experienced first-hand the benefits of American power and influence abroad, points out that one man's "American imperial hegemony" is another man's "guarantor of a particular international order." Dr. Jan Winiecki, an economics scholar in Germany who was economic adviser to the leadership of the underground Polish Solidarity movement from 1985 to 1989 and a member of Polish President Lech Walesa's Political Advisory Council in 1991, points out that the term *empire* has historically included positive connotations of stability, order, and relative economic prosperity. "Americans intervene, usually in the enlightened self-interest, but also mostly at the request of local states, threatened by external force or externally supported insurgency," he observes. He quotes eminent philosopher Karl Popper, who commended the United States for its liberation of Kuwait from Iraq in 1991. In the influential German weekly *Der Spiegel*, Popper said, "We should not be afraid to wage war in the pursuit of peace. . . . We should try to actively support Pax Americana in order to make it Pax Civilitatis [the peace extending to all civilization]."[17]

Pax Americana (an echo of the ancient *Pax Romana*) refers to the relatively stable global peace since the end of World War II, in which the United States has been the dominant superpower. This term is used positively and negatively by those on the right and left of American foreign policy. Which side has the better argument?

History shows that the United States has handled the obligation and responsibility thrust upon it since the Second World War more altruistically than not. In 1945 we stood astride the globe a colossus, the only atomic power. We were the lone superpower. Russia was exhausted and bled dry by the war, having lost twenty million of its own people. We were the only nation that came out of World War II richer than when the war started. We could easily have exerted American hegemony on the world at that point. So what did we do? Did we attempt to impose a *Pax Americana* on the world?

No, we spent billions and billions of our own treasure to rebuild our defeated enemies, Germany and Japan, to put into place the Marshall Plan, to resist Soviet aggression, and to contain the emerging tyranny of Communism.

What did we ask in return? As Colin Powell so eloquently put it, all we ever asked for when we went to Europe's defense in World War I and in World War II was the ground to bury our dead.[18]

Nowhere else in the world do you see the awesome economic and social engine of freedom the United States of America has been since its founding. The British were a civilizing influence, but they kept the colonies they took and only grudgingly granted them freedom. When we inherited colonies after the Spanish American War, we immediately set about bringing freedom to the Philippines, and they were en route to becoming a free and independent country when the Japanese attacked them in 1941. We offered independence to Puerto Rico, but they wouldn't take it! Rather than become a free country, they wanted to remain a commonwealth protected by the United States.

Have we always been perfect? Of course not. But on the whole, we have a proven track record of extending to others the freedom and prosperity we have established and continue to enjoy. American influence has been a civilizing influence, a benign influence, a freedom-enhancing influence in the world.

This does not mean we have license to act unilaterally at our whim. Most of the multilateral alliances defending freedom in the world today were built by the United States. It is no accident that the headquarters of the United Nations is in New York City, because the UN was brought into being by the leadership of the United States. The North Atlantic Treaty Organization (NATO) also was brought into being by the leadership of the United States.

Sadly, sometimes these multilateral strategies don't work. The organizations become paralyzed by competing internal interests. In the case of NATO, they often become paralyzed by their own members' discordant views; in the case of the UN, by potential enemies such as Russia and China, which share veto power. When these multilateral remedies are emasculated, the United States has an obligation to do what it can. That is not arrogant empire building. That is exceptionalism in the service of moral goals for global peace and security.

We are not omnipotent, and our resources are not limitless, but they are great. With those great resources and that great strength comes a particular responsibility to act multilaterally when we can, but unilaterally when we must, to fulfill what we believe is our destiny as a nation: to be the friend and defender of freedom at home and abroad.

Consider the genocide in Bosnia and Herzegovina that took place in the early 1990s while the world stood by and watched. The European NATO allies could not manage to bestir themselves when this kind of atrocious ethnic cleansing was going on in their own backyard. The ultimate futility of the multilateral, internationalist strategy was in full view in the pathetic photos of Dutch—UN peacekeepers handcuffed around trees outside Srebrenica. Meanwhile, Serbian thugs went in, separated men and boys fourteen and over, took them out into the woods, and systematically slaughtered them—in the thousands.

At that point, once multilateralism had been tried and failed, we should have taken unilateral action by declaring to our NATO allies that what was going on in Bosnia-Herzegovina was unacceptable. We should have said, "This is a crime against humanity committed by one ethnic group against another, and we have the ability to stop it. We invite you, our allies, to come with us. We want you to come with us. But if you will not, we are going to take action and stop it." Had we done that, the British and the Germans and the French probably would have gone with us. They did join us when we finally initiated action in Kosovo in 1999.

Another example is Rwanda, where the world allowed between five hundred thousand and seven hundred fifty thousand people to be systematically killed with machetes, burned alive, and otherwise horribly slaughtered. Two or three battalions of U.S. Marines could have stopped it. But we didn't send them because we couldn't get our allies to go with us.

Without a sense of America's special role in the world, we are reduced to multilateral cooperation under global values created by multilateral committees. That was certainly not the position of the United States in the cataclysmic world wars of the twentieth century—and millions of people have reason to thank God that it wasn't. Is American exceptionalism the "delusion" that we are different? Or is it the conviction that when we can do something to prevent horrible evils, and others won't act, we have an obligation to do so, based on the blessings God has poured out on us and the ability God has given us to do something about such evils?

I believe that if we do not act in such circumstances, we become morally culpable. Now, there are times when terrible things are happening, but the consequences of our intervention would be as horrible or even more horrible than what we're trying to stop: North Korea is a good example. Probably no country in the world is routinely committing more atrocities against its own people and crushing more human rights on a daily basis than the North Korean government. If we were to attempt to intervene militarily either unilaterally or multilaterally, in the first week or two alone, the intervention likely would cause the deaths of between five hundred thousand and a million North and South Koreans and several thousand Americans. The only institution that functions in North Korea is their military, and they would respond to any attempt by us to intervene with massive attacks on South Korean and American facilities. The disproportionate death toll among Koreans as well as Americans seeking to intervene would outweigh the intended good of such action.

The same thing would be true of any intervention in China. We know there is systematic abuse of human rights in China, but once again unilateral intervention by the United States must always be a last resort. Short of that, whenever people are having their rights or their lives trodden down, we have an obligation to express our concern, to do what we can to alleviate their suffering, and to help bring about their freedom.

One of the criteria for just war is the question of proportionality: Will the suffering caused outweigh the human benefits of success, and will the cost of success therefore be too high? If Christianity at its outset had said we oppose slavery and we call upon slaves to rebel against their masters, Christianity would have been even more viciously persecuted and driven even further underground. So Paul said that if both masters and slaves were Christians, the relationship and the institution would be transformed. When a sufficient number of both masters and slaves became Christians, slavery ended in the Roman Empire.

During the Reagan years, although the United States didn't militarily intervene in the Soviet Union, we made it a part of every one of our diplomatic negotiations with them to express our concern for the plight of the Refuseniks: Jews who were being systematically discriminated against and persecuted. Eventually we were able to help achieve their right to leave the Soviet Union and emigrate to Israel. Hundreds of thousands of them did so.

Kevin R. den Dulk, a scholar of the role of religion in public life, cites research from the Pew Center showing that the vast majority of Evangelicals believe that moral principles ought to guide American foreign policy.[19] Professor den Dulk points to this as part of his assessment of a significant shift among American Evangelicals in support of America's global engagement in the cause of liberty and justice. He rightly observes that although "Evangelical elites" have theological disagreements over specific issues, they are increasingly united in their attention to a global vision for American influence: "Many Evangelical opinion leaders are not motivated solely or even principally by missions-oriented purposes, though that remains important. Rather, they insist that Evangelicals have *civic* (in addition to Evangelistic) obligations to internationalize their worldview and to understand, as United States citizens, what their faith means for foreign policy."[20]

From this perspective, it becomes clear that when we can act to fight great injustices, we have an obligation and a responsibility to do so. Genocide is taking place in Sudan. We could stop what's going on in the Darfur region, and I believe we should—not necessarily with American troops, but at minimum with American logistics and American leadership saying, "We must do this. This is not the kind of thing that human beings should allow to happen to other human beings in the twenty-first century. We as an international community must act to stop it."

WAR AND PEACE AND PICKING OUR BATTLES

America's special role in the world is currently under hot debate because of our liberation and subsequent occupation of Iraq. So what does belief in God have to do with America's role in Iraq?

After 9/11 President Bush declared that for the last fifty years, under both Democratic and Republican presidents, the United States had been pursuing a wrongheaded Middle East policy. We had been supporting fascistic and oligarchical regimes, first in the name of anticommunism, and then in the name of stable oil supplies—but these repressive and terrible regimes were the breeding ground for terrorism. The only long-term strategy for combating radical

Islamic jihadism, he maintained, was to help build stable democracies in the Middle East.

Critics say that we are inappropriately trying to impose our own way of life on a different culture. In my opinion, the suggestion that Arabs don't want stable democracies is at root a racist belief. I think human beings anywhere, given the choice, will choose governments that are accountable to them and not governments that feed the ambitions of megalomaniacal dictators.

We didn't go into Iraq to conquer and subjugate, but to liberate people. We turned over sovereignty to a provisional government, and now an elected government under a voter-approved constitution is functioning. We are there as guests of the Iraqi government. If the Iraqi government asked us to leave, we would leave. But the last thing the Iraqi government wants is for us to leave. They want us to leave when they are able to defend themselves and their society. We are helping them do that, and when the task is done, we will leave.

With the benefit of hindsight, could we have done things differently? Sure—but that's always the case once armed conflict begins. We probably should have sent more troops in the immediate aftermath of the initial fighting to present overwhelming force, as we did in Germany and Japan after World War II, to keep looting from taking place in Baghdad. We lost a lot of confidence with individual Iraqis at the very beginning that we were going to be able to provide security. I profoundly wish that the Abu Ghraib atrocities had not taken place, and I am grateful that our government has prosecuted the people responsible to the fullest extent of the law. Some of them are in prison now, as they deserve to be, for having dishonored their uniform and their country by committing egregious human rights abuses. Let's remember, however, that such atrocities and far worse occurred every day in that prison under Saddam Hussein. Torture, rape, and death were the rule rather than the exception under Saddam, and the perpetrators were rewarded, not punished.

I wish we had invested earlier in more training of the military and police forces in the way that we're training them now. However, one doesn't have the benefit of hindsight when making decisions in a war zone.

If the situation in Iraq were to devolve into sectarian civil war, we would have a moral responsibility to help bring it to an end. The consequences of failure in Iraq are horrific for the security of the United States, for the security of the Iraqi people, for the security of moderate Islamic regimes, and for the security of moderate followers of Islam around the world.

The Religious Left says that the Religious Right is pro-war. But sometimes war is the least bad alternative—does that make you pro-war? Were those who wanted to depose Hitler pro-war?

I believe that freedom is a universal longing of the human heart, and that as a country we have to act on what we believe. Under certain conditions, war is justified as a least-bad alternative. The first condition is that there is a just cause. Our cause in Iraq is just; it may be one of the nobler things we have done in recent history. We went to liberate a country that was in the grip of a terrible dictator who had perpetrated horrible atrocities and crimes against humanity, against his own people, and against his neighbors. We removed him, and we are giving the Iraqis the ability to defend themselves and to build a stable democracy. We have a responsibility and an obligation based on the blessings that have been showered upon us to help others when we can.

FACTS, FICTION, AND THE END TIMES

Former president Jimmy Carter has said:

> One of the most bizarre admixtures of religion and government, is the strong influence of some Christian Fundamentalists on U.S. policy in the Middle East. Almost everyone in America has heard of the *Left Behind* series, by Tim LaHaye and Jerry B. Jenkins. . . . It is the injection of these beliefs into America's governmental policies that is a cause for concern. . . . Based on these premises, some top Christian leaders have been in the forefront of promoting the Iraqi war, and make frequent trips to Israel, to support it with funding, and lobby in Washington for the colonization of Palestinian territory.[21]

Carter is only one in a chorus of voices on the Left who is using the Left Behind novels to accuse Evangelical Christians en masse of (mis)reading the signs of the times through apocalyptic lenses, eager to welcome the onset of the world's death throes. Such caricaturing presumes that all Evangelicals read this fiction as fact. On top of that leap of imagination, they construct conspiracy theories about Christian theocrats driving American foreign policy based on these novels.

Regardless of how Christians do, and don't, interpret the timing of the specific events predicted in the Bible and imaginatively portrayed in the Left Behind novels, the fact is that these biblical events are prophecies regarding the end times. Nobody knows when they will occur, what the world will be like when they do, and whether they will involve the nation we know as the United States. The apocalypse could be soon; it could be a millennium or two from now—the emphasis is on *could*. We have the words of Jesus Himself that "no one knows about that day or hour, not even the angels in heaven, nor the Son, but only the Father. . . . The Son of Man will come at an hour when you do not expect him" (Matthew 24:36, 44).

We don't know when the Lord will return. We do know that we have been given a Great Commission (Matthew 28:19–20), and that we have been commanded to be salt and light. It could be that before Jesus returns, another Great Awakening will occur—perhaps another Reformation—that will shake America for the cause of Christ as profoundly as Calvin and Luther shook Europe, Wesley and Whitefield shook Britain, and Whitefield and Edwards shook colonial America.

I have little, if any, disagreement with Dr. LaHaye and Mr. Jenkins about the sequence of the eschatological events they portray. However, I would also point out that many Christians before us have been convinced that they lived in the end times. As the world turned the corner from the eighteenth century to the nineteenth, many believed that Napoleon Bonaparte was the Antichrist. In the twentieth century, many believed that Mussolini or Hitler was the Antichrist. History is replete with supposedly suitable nominees for the Antichrist.

I would argue that the special role America has to play in the world is not to hasten the second coming of Jesus Christ. That is in the Lord's timetable, and there is nothing America can, or should, do either to hasten or to retard His coming. I have indicated elsewhere that preoccupation with the end times distracts too many Christians from taking the gospel into our culture, keeping them huddled in Christian ghettoes because they presume the return of Christ is imminent.[22]

What we do know is that we have been given a biblical mandate to love our neighbors as ourselves and to extend to others the blessings we have received.

GOD'S RELATIONSHIP WITH ISRAEL—
WHAT'S AMERICA GOT TO DO WITH IT?

Among Evangelicals, there is always going to be a positive posture and attitude toward Jews, because the majority of Evangelicals believe as a religious tenet that the Jews are God's chosen people and that God continues to have a covenantal relationship with them.

I was taught this from the time I was a child. I can remember my mother calling me in, during the Suez Crisis in 1956, and explaining to me as we were watching television and she was making biscuits, "Richard, the Jews are God's chosen people. God blesses those who bless the Jews, and God curses those who curse the Jews, and God gave that land to the Jewish people forever." She went on to explain that when you curse the Jews, what happens to you is what happened to Germany: you get obliterated, as Germany did in 1945.

I happened to tell this story to Dr. Jim Dobson, and he responded with a story from his own boyhood, when his father, a Nazarene pastor, called him in to listen on the radio to the UN vote in 1947, creating a Jewish state (established in 1948). "Jim," his father said to him, "that's the fulfillment of biblical prophecy."

Among some Evangelicals—I include myself here—there is always going to be support for Israel's right to exist within secure borders and support for America's obligation to aid the Jews because of God's special relationship with them.

However, many other Evangelicals reject the idea that Israel has a special relationship with God because they adhere to so-called replacement theology— that is, God's new covenant in Christ replaces Israel as the people of God with the church as the people of God. For these Evangelicals, Israel's status as a nation today has nothing to do with the Israel of Old Testament history. Nevertheless, they can still find reason to support Israel's right to exist within safe boundaries as the only current stable democracy in the Middle East.

Therefore, American Christians can find theologically sound and moral reasons for sharing common ground in supporting Israel's right to exist within safe borders as well as in supporting the establishment of an independent, democratic Palestinian state in the West Bank and Gaza that will live at peace with Israel.[23]

The question of whether God still has a special relationship with Israel can run parallel to the reality that God has uniquely blessed America, and therefore we have a responsibility to share that blessing with others. The reality of our obligation to support, defend, and expand freedom is entirely separate from the question of biblical prophecy.

LIVING OUT OUR LEGACY

If America's legacy is freedom, some ask, then why is American history built on the back of subjugated races such as African-Americans and Native Americans?

Belief in God had a lot to do with bringing an end to the evils of slavery—and, a century later, correcting much of its lingering effect through the biblical ideals that drove the Civil Rights Movement.

Unfortunately, misguided belief in God also had a lot to do with perpetuating the institution of slavery, and it also played a role in our unconscionable treatment of Native Americans. This in no way excuses our abhorrent treatment of Native Americans and our culpability in the severe cultural problems they have suffered since.

America has failed at key points to live up to our ideals of liberty and justice for all human beings. We have worked to rectify our failings; however, we have sometimes disagreed on how to do so. We need not make perfection the enemy of the good. We fought a terrible war on our own soil to overcome the horrors of slavery, and today the standard of living of African-Americans is higher than it is in any nation-state in Africa. And I don't see many minorities emigrating to a better life elsewhere. Instead, they continue to come to the United States, not just for better material lives, but also for a freedom that many of them do not have in their countries of origin.

Senator Joseph Lieberman describes an experience in which the special influence of the United States in extending freedom around the world was vividly manifest.

The most electric moment of my sixteen months in Washington came during Lech Walesa's speech to the Congress, when he described how the American ideal of freedom had inspired and sustained him and the rest of the Solidarity movement during their darkest days. We're finding the same response in the rest of Eastern

Europe and throughout the world. This is our strength, this powerful two-hundred-year-old democratic idea of our Founding Fathers, and it must be the foundation of our foreign policy. Any time we sacrifice principles for what appear to be short-term international political gains, we lose—if not in the short term, then eventually.[24]

As Dr. King called upon us to do, we are living out the legacy of our founding documents. We are continuing to expand the concept that "all men are created equal" to ever greater numbers of our own citizens—first to slaves and then to women—so that even today we have a far more inclusive definition of freedom and a far more inclusive practice of freedom than any other country in the world. But America has never been just a geographic place; it has always been an idea. That is why people can become American in a way that they cannot become German, French, or Japanese. People from all ethnic backgrounds come to America, and when they embrace and pledge their allegiance to American ideals, they become Americans.

It is my moral conviction as an individual citizen that America does have a special role to play in the world. As a Christian, I believe in providence, and so I affirm that God has providentially blessed the United States of America. I am also responsible to obey Jesus' teaching that to whom much is given, much is required. That doesn't give me the right to say, "We should do this because God said so." It is my responsibility in the public square to translate my religious argument into a moral argument that others can understand regardless of their religious differences. One doesn't have to be a Christian to believe that America has a special role to play in the world. Whether and how we will fulfill that role is a decision that will be made collectively, by the people, democratically. That's how we decide things in America.

America is not just a country with national interests. It is a cause, and that cause is freedom. If freedom is a God-given, unalienable right of every human being on the planet, then it is a God-given right not just for ourselves, but also for others. Therefore, it should be part of the foreign policy of the United States of America to promote freedom, to expand freedom, and whenever possible to protect and enlarge the realm of freedom in the world. And that freedom includes the choice either to acknowledge God or not to acknowledge God: *soul freedom.*

★ 10 ★

Soul Freedom—
a Divine Mandate?

I believe that God has planted in every human heart the desire to live in freedom. And even when that desire is crushed by tyranny for decades, it will rise again.

—GEORGE W. BUSH[1]

"Death by baptism"—that was the fate of Felix Manz, a leader of the sixteenth-century Swiss Anabaptists (literally "re-baptizers") and the first Protestant martyr to be killed by other Protestants. Manz was part of the so-called Radical Reformation, which dissented both from the Roman Catholic Church and from the Protestant Reformation in its insistence that the only true baptism was by immersion of a person old enough to make a confession of faith.

Manz and his small community in Zürich, Switzerland, baptized adults regardless of whether they had previously received infant baptism—a practice considered so heretical that in 1526 Zürich passed an edict declaring adult baptism by immersion by anyone not authorized by the official state church a crime punishable by death by drowning. Reformer Ulrich Zwingli and the Zürich council demanded that Manz recant, and when he refused, they bound his hands and knees to a pole behind his back and threw him into the icy waters of the Limmat River, at the north end of Lake Zürich.[2]

During the same period, German Anabaptist leader Balthasar Hübmaier, one of the greatest scholars and most eloquent preachers of his day, was advocating ultimate obedience to the Scriptures, and he could find no scriptural support for infant baptism. Hübmaier was also deeply troubled by the violent death sentences leveled upon religious dissenters, and he proposed more humane guidelines for distinguishing between theological disagreements versus outright disobedience to the Bible.

Nineteenth-century theologian and church historian Philip Schaff called Hübmaier "perhaps the first who taught the principle of universal religious liberty, on the ground that Christ came not to kill and to burn, but to save, and condemned the employment of force in his kingdom. He held that those only are heretics who willfully and wickedly oppose the holy Scriptures; and even these ought to be treated by no other than moral means of persuasion and instruction." For these views, as Schaff recounts, Hübmaier "was burned at the stake in Vienna, March 10, 1528, and died with pious joy; his wife, who encouraged him in his martyr spirit, was three days afterwards drowned in the Danube."[3]

And so began in modern history the Baptist concept of religious liberty, or *soul freedom*, an insistence that every individual has the right to decide what he or she will or won't believe, free of any external interference. As historian Walter Shurden defines it, "Soul freedom is the historic Baptist affirmation of the inalienable right and responsibility of every person to deal with God without the imposition of creed, the interference of clergy, or the intervention of civil government."[4]

In his discussion of Roger Williams's metaphor for the separation of church and state, Stephen Carter clarifies the reason for the wall between the two— "not that the wilderness needed protection from the garden—the wall was there to protect the garden from the wilderness. In particular, the garden needed protection from the wilderness so that the people who joined in community within it would be free to come to their understanding of God's will safe from the coercions of a society that might disagree."[5]

The radical concepts that Roger Williams was infusing into the American experiment came a century too late and a continent too far away to spare the lives of Felix Manz and Balthasar Hübmaier, who fell victim to a corrupted garden in league with the state. A pure garden could domesticate the wilderness, transforming society with the power of the gospel. However, if the wilderness was allowed to despoil the garden, one of the first freedoms to go would be religious liberty. "Williams was not worried that the people of the garden might have too much influence over the wilderness," Carter explains. "His worry was the other way around: 'The commonweal cannot with a spiritual rape force the consciences of all to one worship.'"[6]

Soul rape—Williams deliberately used such strong language to convey the absolute sanctity of individual conscience in regard to religion. A human being's relationship to God is so sacred that no other human being, no mere human institution, such as government, has the right to interfere with it. To do so is a fundamental violation of the human person.

Over a century later, Williams's views were incorporated into the Declaration of Independence: "We hold these truths to be self-evident, that all Men are created equal, that they are endowed by their Creator with certain unalienable Rights, that among these are Life, Liberty and the pursuit of Happiness. — That to secure these rights, Governments are instituted among Men, deriving their just Powers from the consent of the governed. . . ." Notice that these rights are established by divine ordinance—government does not create, originate, or grant them. It secures what has already been established by an authority higher still.

Catholic historian and philosopher Michael Novak illustrates this very point by observing the transcendent freedom of the soul under the state's most powerful and malicious—but ultimately futile—attempts to extinguish it.

In recent times we have learned that it is possible for humans to be free even in the prisons of the KGB. I have heard Soviet exile Natan Sharansky, for example, testify how he retained his liberty even in solitary confinement. Like so many prisoners before him, Sharansky discovered personally what Jefferson meant by calling human rights "unalienable." All the KGB required of Sharansky was that he confess his error, admit that he had been wrong. Yet Sharansky felt more powerfully the requirement of his own conscience, in the presence of another Judge. The KGB could restrict Sharansky's diet to bread and water, and could impose a series of other punitive measures, but it could not alienate him from his fundamental liberty. Sharansky maintained the freedom to say no. As he has testified, he found a nourishing, strengthening liberty at the very heart of creation, a liberty to say yes to the God who made him—and made him free—and no to his tormentors.

This liberty of conscience transcends any and all political orders. Human freedom rooted in God declares that all states and all political orders are under God, limited not omnipotent. States can crush or kill human beings, but they cannot alienate them from their responsibility to God and conscience.

But precisely because this freedom transcends all politics, it does not of itself constitute an order within which the liberties of human beings are secured. The purpose of instituting governments, as the American framers noted, was not to enumerate human rights but "to secure these rights."[7]

Every human being has a right to soul freedom, which is exactly what the United Nations' Universal Declaration of Human Freedoms affirms: "Everyone has the right to freedom of thought, conscience and religion; this right includes freedom to change his religion or belief, and freedom, either alone or in community with others and in public or private, to manifest his religion or belief in teaching, practice, worship and observance."[8]

Part of being human is a divinely protected, private sphere of the heart, mind, and soul where the freedom of conscience resides. This sacred space within each human being is inviolate. It is the innate foundation of human dignity, and it must be respected and nurtured, not crushed. Any attempt by governments to interfere with it, seek to repress it, or claim to have the right to control it is soul rape—the opposite of soul freedom.

"A STEADY AND MIGHTY INFLUENCE"

America's uniqueness as a nation founded upon the concept of soul freedom is at the heart of why this country is different from all others. Critics who cry "imperialism" at American attempts to extend the cause of soul freedom ignore the reality that America's historic legacy is solidly rooted in spreading this concept abroad. In the late nineteenth century, historian Philip Schaff—a Swiss citizen who emigrated to the United States—testified to American exceptionalism: "The example of the United States exerts a silent, but steady and mighty influence upon Europe in raising the idea of mere toleration to the higher plane of freedom, in emancipating religion from the control of civil government, and in proving the advantages of the primitive practice of ecclesiastical self-support and self-government."[9]

Our forebears believed this continent was preserved until it could be colonized and settled by people who came to obtain religious freedom for themselves and would extend it eventually to others. And it was in this country, as an extension of British civilization, that the idea of religious freedom found fertile soil, took root, and flourished as it became part of our founding documents in the Declaration of Independence and the Constitution.

As President Bush said in his second inaugural address, freedom is a cause we will champion everywhere it is under attack (see appendix D).

> We will persistently clarify the moral choice before every ruler and nation: The moral choice between oppression, which is always wrong, and freedom, which is eternally right. We will not pretend that jailed dissidents prefer their chains, or that women welcome humiliation and servitude or that any human being aspires to live at the mercy of bullies. We will encourage reform in other governments by making clear that success in our relations will require the decent treatment of their own people. That is part of the foreign policy of this nation. America's belief in human dignity will guide our policies, yet rights must be more than the grudging concessions of dictators. They are secured by free dissent and participation of the government. In the long run there is no justice without freedom and there can be no human rights without human liberty.[10]

This country has a legacy of standing ready to work with all nations of goodwill in defense of freedom. I believe we must not give other nations veto power over this responsibility. When others are unwilling to act and we believe that freedom and human rights are at stake, we must retain the right to act in what we believe are the best interests of freedom—not to maximize American power, but because we are committed to the cause of freedom.

In 1946, the year I was born, many mandarins of American foreign policy were claiming that the Germans didn't want freedom. They claimed that the Germans had already tried democracy with the Weimar Republic after World War I, and it didn't work, that Germany was a militaristic society and would never have a successful democratic government. They said similar things about Japan—it was a feudal and medieval society, it would never accept a democratic government.

However, when the United States proposed that the question be put directly to the German and Japanese people, without a gun to their heads, whether *they* wanted to have a government that was accountable to them and protected their freedoms and liberties, they answered with a resounding yes, and they have continued to say yes for over half a century.

Former CIA director R. James Woolsey told the U.S. Senate that America's stand for religious freedom was needed to help Muslim democracies institute what the world recognized as universal rights to human freedom.

> Governments in the Muslim world—as elsewhere—must be held to their commitments to the Universal Declaration of Human Rights, which establishes that "freedom of thought, conscience and religion" is a right that belongs to the individual person, not a government or community. In doing so, they can invoke the Koranic injunction that there must be no compulsion in religion. By standing firm for religious freedom, America can help create the political space Muslim democrats and reformers need to establish tolerant, free societies that adhere to religious values as well as universally accepted human rights.[11]

As part of its weekly focus on religion, faith, and spirituality, *USA Today* ran a column by an army chaplain in Baghdad.

> In Saddam Hussein's Iraq, freedom of religion was severely limited. The government exercised repressive measures against any religious groupings or organizations deemed as not providing full political and social support to the regime.
>
> Iraqis are now faced with deciding, personally and collectively, what role religion will play going forward. Will one religion dominate? Will Islamic law play a large role?
>
> Right now, that's a subject of much debate and an issue at the heart of Iraq's fighting. As the conflict continues, U.S. soldiers, being tested so severely here in the same country, provide a living lesson about the greater power of freely chosen faith over the tyranny of state-imposed religious laws. . . . The only real faith is a chosen faith. I and other chaplains are sensitive to that. We aim to make faith available but not mandatory.[12]

The chaplain, Captain James Key, eloquently testified to the power of religious freedom in individual lives and across cultures:

> I see the transformative power of real—not coerced—faith in the young men and women who come to chapel Sunday morning with a Bible in one hand and an

M-16 or 9mm in the other hand as they pray with their eyes closed tightly, singing songs of praise and worship from the bottom of their hearts and the depth of their souls.

They show a dimension of what our nation is about. Individual Iraqis are now making choices to shape their nation's future. I hope they will come to have similar religious freedoms as we do in the USA. We might not be a perfect nation, but I'm thankful we still have the constitutional right to practice the religion of our choice without fear of persecution—or coercion.

Because whether you are a troop in the desert, civilian in America or an Iraqi citizen, faith—and the ability to openly practice it, or reject it—matters.[13]

Critics of our presence in Iraq call it American hegemony—but the results of our intervention in Afghanistan suggest that American intervention is viewed quite differently by those on the receiving end than by those on the observation deck. In the first national survey conducted in Afghanistan and sponsored by a news organization, an ABC poll revealed that 87 percent of all Afghanis consider the U.S.-led overthrow of the Taliban good for their country, and 91 percent prefer the present government to their former life under the Taliban—despite the severe difficulties with which they struggle: inadequate infrastructures, lack of basic services such as electricity, a dearth of education opportunities, and widespread poverty. And the Afghanis are in no hurry for a U.S. withdrawal: "Just 8 percent say the United States should leave now, and another 6 percent say it should withdraw within the next year. The most common answer by far: Sixty-five percent say U.S. forces should leave Afghanistan 'only after security is restored.'"[14]

In an editorial on the tragic genocides occurring in Sudan, the *Wall Street Journal* observed what happens when the American commitment to freedom and human rights is *not* extended through military intervention in a corrupt regime.

At places like Davos and Harvard, the world's sages rarely stop fretting about the dangers of a too powerful America. Well, if you want to know what the world looks like without U.S. leadership, Exhibit A is Darfur in Sudan.

Today's leading authority on Darfur is the political philosopher Thomas Hobbes, who prophesied a world "nasty, brutish and short."[15]

The editorial went on to cite the abject failure of the rest of the global community to do anything about the atrocities, noting the self-interests of various members in their political or economic ties to Arab leadership in Khartoum. In a litany of virtual indictments, the *Wall Street Journal* went down the list of those who passively or actively blocked any attempts to hold the leadership in Sudan accountable: the United Nations, whose peace-making machinery was stalled by Russian, Chinese, and Arab Security Council members; the Arab League; the African Union; and Europe—especially France, which already has military bases in the region. In their collective refusal to act, they left UN Secretary-General Kofi Annan back on President Bush's doorstep: "Amid this global abdication, Mr. Annan finally decided . . . to call in the American cavalry," the *Wall Street Journal* commented.[16]

President Bush responded by proposing a NATO-supervised UN peacekeeping force, but the UN envoy to Sudan backed down under threats from the Sudanese government, and the global community once again failed to mount any attempt to stop the slaughter and aid the millions suffering in Darfur.

So that leaves . . . guess who? The cowboy President, the American unilateralists, the Yankee imperialists—or, to put it another way, the only nation with the will and wallet to provide order in an otherwise Hobbesian world. However, that will and wallet are being stretched today in Iraq and elsewhere, and Mr. Bush is rightly wary of committing more American blood and treasure to a conflict in Sudan that the rest of the world doesn't seem serious about ending in any event. One lesson of Darfur is that there really are limits to American power, and in its absence the world's savages have freer reign.[17]

The editors of the *Wall Street Journal* testified to the reality of the American legacy abroad: not a theology of empire, but a record of liberation; not a deluded presumption that America is different, but the evidence of American exceptionalism in plain—and painful—view.

This realistic assessment of American intervention abroad stands in stark contrast to the Religious Left's simplistic denunciation of foreign policy based on a concept of sacred obligation as nothing more than right-wing rhetoric of a righteous empire. For example, Richard Pierard, professor at Gordon College, applauds Jim Wallis for advancing the "genuine" gospel of Jesus Christ versus the "phony gospel perpetrated by right-wing strategists." He parrots Wallis's tired liberal critique—"How did the Jesus portrayed in the Gospels become pro-rich, pro-war, and pro-American?"—with a cheap shot at those who dare mix God and foreign policy in support of anything resembling conservative views of America's global role: "Perhaps Evangelicals will recover the holistic biblical vision of justice that was surrendered when they moved into the right wing of Caesar's palace."[18]

A *truly* holistic biblical vision of justice, however, will include the affirmation that human freedom is a universal gift from the Creator.

WHAT'S GOD GOT TO DO WITH SOUL FREEDOM?

If God is the giver of the fundamental human right to religious liberty, then no merely human power may rightly take it away. Baptists refer to this right as "soul competency."

> What does "soul competency" mean? Various terms have been used for this concept, such as soul freedom, freedom of conscience and soul competency. Basically it means the God-given freedom and ability of persons to know and respond to God's will. Baptists believe that God gives people competency—that is ability—to make choices. Human beings are not puppets or machines. *Baptists emphasize that this ability is not a mere human characteristic, but a gift from God.*[19]

If you take God out of it, this right becomes a merely human assertion. If it is humanly discerned and granted, then other human beings can infringe upon, impugn, imprison, or redefine it. The French Revolution was based on moral claims, but they were man-made and thus literally *unfounded*, not God-given. The so-called Goddess of Reason proved to be a far inferior guarantor of basic rights than the God of the Bible. This is one reason the French Revolution deteriorated into the Reign of Terror, and the American Revolution did not.

The twentieth century bore horrific witness to how a purely secular, religion-free worldview inevitably leads downhill to soul imprisonment. Note, for example, Josef Stalin's brutal annihilation of tens of millions of his own citizens, Mao

Tse-tung's even bloodier Cultural Revolution, and Cambodia's killing fields under Pol Pot and the Khmer Rouge.

This is not to deny that religion also has bloodstained hands, as the violence of the Inquisition, the Christian-Muslim wars of the Crusades, and the long history of deadly Protestant-Catholic conflicts demonstrate all too well. When corrupt religion takes on an unholy power, it manifests the same impulse to crush soul freedom: to seek to control and imprison the soul by denying the right of individuals to make up their own minds. Religious freedom and religious dictatorship are diametrically opposed.

Terrible things have been done in the name of religion, but not the kind of religion I profess, nor the kind of religion that most people of faith in America want for our society. Still, the overwhelming majority of the worst atrocities against human beings in the twentieth century were committed not in the name of religion, but in the name of consciously atheistic or secularist ideologies such as Nazism, Fascism, and Communism. In these systems, either God is subordinated as a prop for the ideology, or there is no God; the only absolute is the state.

Without an understanding of transcendent authority, it is not possible to sustain or support soul freedom. If anything goes, then moral relativism can— and often does—devolve into violent power struggles. Philip Schaff warned that a society without respect for the importance of religion in society is without respect for the responsibilities that come with human freedom.

> True liberty is a positive force, regulated by law; false liberty is a negative force, a release from restraint. True liberty is the moral power of self-government; the liberty of infidels and anarchists is carnal licentiousness. The American separation of church and state rests on respect for the church; the infidel separation, on indifference and hatred of the church, and of religion itself. . . . The infidel theory was tried and failed in the first Revolution of France. It began with toleration, and ended with the abolition of Christianity, and with the reign of terror, which in turn prepared the way for military despotism as the only means of saving society from anarchy and ruin.[20]

This necessity for the "moral power" of self-government, as Schaff phrased it, is the same call that George W. Bush made in his second inaugural address.

President Bush affirmed the importance of character, but he qualified it by declaring religious faith to be the foundation for it.

> In America's ideal of freedom, the public interest depends on private character— on integrity, and tolerance toward others, and the rule of conscience in our own lives. Self-government relies, in the end, on the governing of the self. That edifice of character is built in families, supported by communities with standards, and sustained in our national life by the truths of Sinai, the Sermon on the Mount, the words of the Koran, and the varied faiths of our people. Americans move forward in every generation by reaffirming all that is good and true that came before— ideals of justice and conduct that are the same yesterday, today, and forever.[21]

As a nation and as a people, we have been given tremendous resources. We have enjoyed tremendous privileges. With those undeserved resources and privileges come tremendous responsibilities to use them in a way that honors the God-given, universal rights of human beings. One of the ways in which we can do that is by seeking to expand the boundaries of freedom—including soul freedom. As a Christian, I believe this to be a divinely ordained mandate for human society. It is not necessary to be a Christian, however, to affirm soul freedom as a universally recognized human right. It is not necessary to be religious to recognize that American influence in extending the freedom given to us is not a doctrine of pride and privilege, but rather a doctrine of obligation, responsibility, sacrifice, and service.

American exceptionalism is not an attempt to force the American way of life on the world. It is an assertion that human freedom and liberty of conscience are universal truths applicable to all human beings and that America has, because of its past blessings, a unique obligation to champion these universal values in the world.

America's legacy of freedom *is* rooted in religiously informed convictions. The freedom we have been given is the same freedom to which all human beings—not just Americans—are entitled. The great "self-evident" truths of the Declaration are *universal* truths. *All* of us have been created equal. *All* of us have been endowed by our Creator with unalienable rights. It's enough to make even an atheist in a foxhole whisper, "God bless America."

★ 11 ★

What Does It Mean to Say, "God Bless America"?

We have been the recipients of the choicest bounties of Heaven. We have been preserved these many years in peace and prosperity. We have grown in numbers, wealth and power as no other nation has ever grown.

But we have forgotten God. We have forgotten the gracious Hand which preserved us in peace, and multiplied and enriched and strengthened us; and we have vainly imagined, in the deceitfulness of our hearts, that all these blessings were produced by some superior wisdom and virtue of our own.

—ABRAHAM LINCOLN[1]

On two tragic occasions within the last hundred years, America suffered attacks on the homeland. The first was at Pearl Harbor on December 7, 1941. The second was the coordinated assaults on September 11, 2001, on the Twin Towers of the World Trade Center in New York City and the Pentagon in Washington, D.C. (The successful thwarting, by the passengers of Flight 93, of the attack intended to destroy the Capitol building should be viewed as the first heroic counterattack in the War on Terror.) In the wake of both attacks, one particular song was heard and sung over and over all around the country, as if it were our national anthem: Irving Berlin's "God Bless America."

The phrase "God bless America" became a national benediction in the wake of 9/11, as millions of Americans displayed it via bumper stickers, window displays, lapel buttons, billboards, and even personal tattoos. It seemed to be the mantra the country needed to chant as a form of self-therapy in the early recovery period from such an unprecedented catastrophe. It was also an expression of devout fervor on the part of millions of Americans who believe in God and said it as a prayer for America's healing and future protection.

That seems to have been composer Berlin's intent for the song—a national prayer—when he revised the lyrics for Kate Smith, who first sang it on her radio show in observance of Armistice Day (now Veterans Day) in 1938. Berlin's first version of the song was prepared for an entertaining military revue, but his revision, written when the storm clouds of the Third Reich were darkening the sky over Europe, reflected a more serious and prayerful intent. Berlin, a Jewish immigrant to the United States, illustrates the fact that anyone can embrace being an American by accepting and affirming America's creed—those self-evident truths proclaimed in the Declaration of Independence.

In times of trauma and grief, it is common for people to turn their attention to God in a more intense and concentrated way—sometimes in fearful or angry questioning, but more often for comfort, protection, and a sense of eternal perspective on the tragedies of our frail and vulnerable lives. Clearly, a national tragedy brings people together in a spirit of community, in a need to mount a common defense and affirm their unity in the face of attack. The frequent occasions on which "God Bless America" was sung after 9/11—whether by U.S. Congressional representatives gathered on the steps of the Capitol for a press conference the night of September 11, spontaneously breaking into song; by baseball fans at Yankee Stadium singing along with tenor Ronan Tynan during the seventh-inning stretch; or by neighbors and friends at community gatherings—were as close as the country has ever come to praying in unison.

Church attendance spiked sharply in the immediate aftermath of 9/11, but soon dropped off to previous levels. The country found itself asking deep and searching questions, among them what Americans really do and don't believe, and how much it matters.

One of the country's self-reflective questions that kept popping up was, "What do we mean when we say, 'God bless America'?" Alternatives surfaced, such as "God bless everyone," as voices began to line up on opposing sides of the response. The "God, guts, 'n' guns" crowd swelled its chest in furious outrage, demanding that we inflict immediate and violent revenge. Conservative talk show hosts offered lurid descriptions of what we ought to do to those who attacked us. Meanwhile, the "I think; therefore I am a liberal" crowd denounced the perpetrators, but pointed a finger of blame at U.S. policy and national arrogance for inciting such hatred of America in Islamic countries.

In a nation with such a clamorous diversity of views on the role of religion in public life, has the phrase "God bless America" lost so much meaning that it is no longer useful as a collective expression?

UNPACKING A LOADED PHRASE

Some condemn "God bless America" as code language for views with which they disagree. "[Faith] prefers international community over nationalist religion. . . .

'God bless America' is found nowhere in the Bible,"[2] declares Jim Wallis, decrying what he perceives to be an illegitimate and dangerous distortion of Christianity in a form of patriotic, civil religion. He believes this kind of blurring of boundaries—perpetuated, he says, by the Religious Right—fuels the Bush administration's theological pretensions to empire.

In a review of Wallis's book *God's Politics*, scholar Paul Marshall points out that the Religious Left is marked in part by a theological suspicion of the state as a "Caesar," in opposition to Christ, "to be addressed prophetically or else shunned." However, the "new left," as Marshall calls it, "while suspicious of military and police power, has in leftist fashion frequently called for extensive government action." He then goes on to recall an incident that illuminates the contradictions inherent in the Left's condemnation of American distortions of biblical themes.

> I was once on a panel with a representative of this view who invoked the common trope of equating government in Romans 13 with the Beast in Revelation 13, and hence denounced "Caesar" as, basically, the Antichrist. Later, he called for a national health insurance plan, apparently oblivious of the fact that calling on the Antichrist to monopolize health care funding would be, to say the least, theologically and otherwise problematic.[3]

Others question the wisdom of saying, "God bless America," because it can be appropriated by the majority to claim superiority over others. In the wake of 9/11, the Pew Forum on Religion & Public Life sponsored a discussion among leaders from different religious backgrounds on the subject "God Bless America: Reflections on Civil Religion after September 11." Sikh leader Manjit Singh cautioned:

> When people say "God bless America," it brings up two thoughts. First, whose God? Whose God are we referring to? Is this referenced to a Christian God or to a universal God that is the creator of all the creation? Most Americans, I think it's fair to say, assume that it reflects and refers to a Judeo-Christian God.
>
> Second, it is also, again, fair and safe to assume that most Americans seem to think that God has some special investment in them when they hear God bless America. And this is easily interpreted as, God bless us, of all the people.[4]

Singh was right that "God bless America" can be misspoken as a way of saying, "God bless us above all others." And as Singh, representing an ethnic and a religious minority, would know too well, it can also be misused to say, "God bless us because we are (white, Christian) Americans."

Still others, such as Madeleine Albright, cautiously commend this phrase as a way of expressing hope for the best of what America has to offer as "a country of abundant resources, momentous accomplishments, and unique capabilities." We have "the right to ask—but never to insist or simply assume—that God bless America."[5]

Conservatives can make the mistake in saying, "God bless America," of mixing nationalism with religion by assuming that God is on their side, or in hindsight claiming God's favor upon their actions to invoke an absolute stamp of approval on their own partisan positions. As Lincoln pointed out in his second inaugural address, the two sides in the Civil War read the same Bible and prayed to the same God, yet each presumed that God was on their side and invoked His aid against the other—a logical contradiction. Perhaps, Lincoln reflected, God was on neither one's side, but simply willed to remove the evil of slavery and allowed both parties in the conflict to suffer the consequences of the nation's sin.

Furthermore, conservatives can err by claiming that America once was, and ought to return to being, a Christian nation. That is not just a historical error; it is also a theological error, because it risks conflating an earthly nation with the heavenly kingdom of God. If that is what is meant by "God bless America," then the phrase becomes an expression not of piety, but of idolatry.

The secular liberal bias in dismissing the legitimacy of saying, "God bless America," is often based in an aversion to moral absolutes. Since religion makes absolute claims about right and wrong, it poses a challenge to moral subjectivism or relativism. Liberals' most prominent value tends to be personal freedom. Their ultimate value is often individual autonomy. This is the fatal blind spot of the boomer generation: the presumption that they have the right to do whatever they please, whenever they want, with whomever they want, and nobody else has any right to judge them for it because it's nobody's business but theirs.

That's just not true. We are social beings living in social structures. If I am unfaithful to my wife, my wrongdoing has enormous consequences for my wife, my children, everyone with whom I have a circle of influence, and society. John

Donne said that "no man is an island entire unto himself—every man is a piece of the continent, a part of the main."[6] My behavior results in concentric circles of consequences. It's not all about me. I don't have the right to fulfill my perceived needs at others' expense, or at the cost of damaging the moral environment in which we shape our lives and rear our children.

To contain and marginalize moral absolutes, liberals tend to consign religion to a private sphere, attempting to limit its realm to overtly "religious" matters that have no place, they argue, in public life. This is a patronizing attempt to keep religious people in their place (i.e., pulpit, pew, and hearth, not policy arena) and sweep public life clean of all religious expressions in the name of separation of church and state. It is a form of segregation, driving religious faith to the fringes of the culture and, as Stephen Carter puts it, reducing it to the status of a hobby, such as model airplane building.[7] If it is therapeutic and it helps you to relax, that's fine, but it has nothing to say about anything important in public life.

As Stephen Carter points out, religion has to do with all of life; it has no "sphere," but the law today often behaves as though it does.

> We have turned poor Roger Williams inside out. The wall of separation is no longer for the protection of the people of the garden; it is for the protection of the people of the wilderness. And what is the evil against which the people of the wilderness need protection? Why, it is *the ideas, the words, the persuasions of the people of the garden*—the very things the wall itself was originally designed to nurture. . . . And speaking the right words—or avoiding the wrong ones—now turns out to be the only way the church is able to preserve such tatters of protection for religious liberty as the state now offers.
>
> So the wall of separation turns out to be not a garden wall but a prison wall, surrounding the church to keep the people of the garden inside.[8]

Furthermore, the liberal error is criticizing the Religious Right for presuming the moral superiority of their position. They object to the very notion of "sides," because they believe that God has no "side" on specific dimensions of human experience, and they are mortally offended when conservatives draw a clear line on specific moral issues, saying, in effect, "This is God's side, and we ought to get on it."

But liberals make the mistake of doing the very thing for which they criticize conservatives—either they pick and choose their own agenda of moral issues and invoke "personal rights" as the final board of appeal, or they grant automatic equality to all sides of an issue in the name of toleration to dodge discomfiting questions of moral absolutes. They criticize the Religious Right for assuming the moral superiority of their position, but the reason the Left finds that so offensive is that *they* assume the moral superiority of *their* position.

RECOVERING RELIGIOUS LANGUAGE

Are we at an impasse? Must we dismiss the phrase "God bless America" simply because it can be misused? Well, if that were the criterion, we would have nothing left to say.

America is a melting pot of religions as well as races and cultures. There is no way everyone can agree on a common definition of "God"—at best, we can affirm that people of religious faith will mean the God of their particular tradition and faith convictions when they say, "God bless America." Others who are undecided on what "God" does or doesn't mean to them are not forced to adhere to a particular religious creed simply by saying it. They might even recite or sing it if they so choose—simply as a social ritual that reflects the particularly religious character of Americans. The people most likely to feel excluded by it are those who don't believe in God at all. Their burden to bear is living in a country with a strong religious heritage and a vast majority who profess belief in God. If they are unhappy with this situation, they need to become Evangelists for atheism and make their case to the American people and seek to dissuade the majority of American citizens from their persistent belief in God. This is a free country. They ought to exercise their freedom of speech, rather than try to censor and silence a majority of Americans with whom they disagree.

But then, does "God bless America" become such a watered-down phrase that it is empty of meaning? No—any public expression of religious faith in this country, in which the majority of Americans feel comfortable participating, must of necessity be somewhat generic. It doesn't mean that using generic religious language is tantamount to creating a new, state-established religion called "civil religion." And neither does it mean that we are conjuring a divine being by committee, a generic substitute intended to replace the God of specific religious traditions.

So-called civil religion is an acknowledgment that America's population is preponderantly religious—and as such, religion has its place. It is a way of accommodating all people's rights to express their religious beliefs according to the dictates of their consciences. The religion of church, mosque, synagogue, and so forth is not a monolithic expression; it is a mind-bogglingly pluralistic expression of the American people. One way the government can accommodate that diversity is to express its basic, foundational-level agreement in the public square. That agreement is precisely what is expressed in the Declaration of Independence and echoed by presidents from Washington to Lincoln to FDR to George W. Bush.

Of course, civil religion does have its dangers, because a dumbed-down, bottom-shelf faith is hardly adequate for the purposes of religion, which involve defining ultimate values and addressing life's ultimate questions. Civil religion cannot replace personal faith, but it can be society's way of acknowledging the central role religion has played in American life and protecting a place for faith in the public square. It should in no way be considered a substitute for deep faith convictions—whether Baha'i, Buddhist, Catholic, Hindu, Jewish, Muslim, Protestant, Sikh, or any other tradition. It is merely society's way of accommodating religion in general without favoring a particular faith over other faiths.

Civil religion can also provide a shared space in which people of varying religious traditions can bring their faith convictions to public debate in a pluralistic society. For example, a person of profound Evangelical or Catholic faith believes that the taking of an unborn baby's life is with very rare exceptions an abomination to God as part of his or her understanding of God's transcendent moral order. When people of faith enter the public arena, they have an obligation not to stake a religious claim by saying, "The Bible says this, so this is the way it must be," but to translate that belief into a moral argument. As Rita Spillenger, executive director of the American Civil Liberties Union in Arkansas, observes:

> The truth is that most people have values—as a nation our job is to find the common ground. Almost everyone agrees that killing is wrong; not everyone agrees

that state executions are. So we compromise, and compromise involves making rational arguments and providing evidence for your point of view. In a diverse culture like ours you cannot say, "Girls should become housewives because God says so," and expect laws to be changed accordingly. Or rather, you can say so, but it is naive to think that that suffices as a political argument. Since we come together with different ideas about God, anyone who wants to be taken seriously, as the Religious Right says it does, must speak in a language we all share.[9]

To earn the right to be listened to in a pluralistic society, people of deeply religious convictions must make their case to their fellow citizens in the context of, not because of, the specific tenets of their particular tradition. The best way to do this, I think, is with the language of morality (including justice) versus immorality (including injustice).

The argument against abortion should be made in language and terms that are accessible to people of every faith and even those professing no faith. Instead of claiming that a woman's personal rights are defined by the God of the Bible, we can say that abortion constitutes a grave imposition on the rights of a nonconsenting person, the unborn baby, and the state should protect the child, like everyone else, against so serious an injustice. This was the same way in which Martin Luther King Jr., who was a Baptist minister, couched his arguments for racial equality in moral terms of right and wrong, justice and injustice. This is not a counsel of deception. On the contrary, it is an admonition to tell the whole truth about the God we worship—a God of love, virtue, and justice.

We don't have a right to assume that people should automatically accept our arguments because we say, "Thus saith the Lord." But we do have a right to bring our understanding of a transcendent moral order to our understanding of public policy. A secular minority does not have the right to censor and disqualify a religious majority from participation in the public policy issues of the day. Separation of church and state was never intended to build a wall of separation between the religiously informed moral values of its citizens and the public square. It was intended to build a wall of separation between the institution of the state and the institution of the church. In the First Amendment, all of the prohibitions refer to what the government cannot do, not to what the people of faith cannot do.

WHY WE NEED GOD IN AMERICA

When "God Bless America" is sung, it often provokes a strong emotional response. The lyrics are eloquent and the melody is stirring, but the reasons run deeper than the personal associations they conjure for each of us. Most Americans really do believe there is something special about this nation, that our country as a whole is greater than the sum of its parts. Part of being American is to believe that we are not just a country, but also a cause. The concept of "cause" connotes becoming part of something bigger than yourself, something that will outlive you, a bigger "whole" that elevates and ennobles you as you dedicate yourself to it.

George Mason University Law School professor Peter Berkowitz was a participant in the Pew Forum on Religion & Public Life discussion after 9/11, and he suggested that America's lowest-common-denominator shared belief may simply be our insistence that freedom and equality are self-evident truths.

> Then you take a step back and look at America's many achievements, the production of goods and services in unprecedented abundance, the absorption of large numbers of immigrants from every corner of the globe, the continuing process of incorporating the previously excluded in the nation's social and economic and political life, the spearheading of international humanitarian relief efforts around the world. Then you compare our foibles and foolishnesses and flaws to the shortcomings of our neighbors, our allies, our enemies, indeed to those of all the other states and forms of political organization that have come and gone since humanity learned to walk and talk and organize its collective life around claims and counterclaims about justice, and then you find it hard to resist the conclusion that one of the chief reasons that America is worth defending is because of our achievement in producing and sustaining a way of life that embodies this moral principle, or is it core faith in individual freedom and human equality.[10]

As John Adams said in 1798, however, we need a citizenry with a strong religious and moral character to sustain the American experiment successfully. Our government is "insufficient" for any other. Religion is not the only guardian of right and wrong, but historically it has proven to have the most staying power.

You can be a person with an internal moral compass that points to right and wrong, and you can try to live a moral life without being religious. History, however, would tell us you are not going to be nearly as successful at it. Jesus said that you can choose to build your house on sand and watch it wash away when the tide comes in, or you can choose to build it on rock and weather the storms.[11] If you don't base your moral values on a foundation external to yourself, something greater than human wisdom alone, then all you have is human insight. That has proven historically to be an unstable foundation in times of stress and crisis.

When conservatives talk about going back to the good old days, they overlook the reality that the good old days had some blind spots that needed addressing. They also sometimes overlook the fact that you can't force people to act morally—long term, at least—by government mandate, regulation, and force. True change takes place in hearts and minds, which will be reflected in the people's governments and in the people's courts. It is a fallacy to assume that the government and the courts can produce a moral system in people or do much more than help preserve a decent moral environment. Even if our government permitted it, which it doesn't, you can't simply declare this country to be one that affirms and practices Judeo-Christian values rooted in biblical authority. It can only *become* such a country through transformation of hearts and minds. It is not the government's job to do that any more than it is the government's role to prescribe or to prohibit religion.

The need for moral reformation impelled President Lincoln to proclaim a national day of prayer and fasting to help bind up the nation's postwar wounds.

And, insomuch as we know that, by His divine law, nations like individuals are subjected to punishments and chastisement in this world, may we not justly fear that the awful calamity of civil war, which now desolates the land, may be but a punishment inflicted upon us for our presumptuous sins to the needful end of our national reformation as a whole people?

We have been the recipients of the choicest bounties of Heaven. We have been preserved these many years in peace and prosperity. We have grown in numbers, wealth and power as no other nation has ever grown.

But we have forgotten God. We have forgotten the gracious Hand which preserved us in peace, and multiplied and enriched and strengthened us; and we have vainly imagined, in the deceitfulness of our hearts, that all these blessings were produced by some superior wisdom and virtue of our own.

Intoxicated with unbroken success, we have become too self-sufficient to feel the necessity of redeeming and preserving grace, too proud to pray to the God that made us!

It behooves us then to humble ourselves before the offended Power, to confess our national sins and to pray for clemency and forgiveness.[12]

We need God in America because we need a bedrock foundation for our national character that is external to ourselves. We need to be reminded of our accountability to a transcendent moral authority beyond human capacity to create or dismantle, because history shows that is the only sure way to preserve the self-evident, divinely established rights on which this nation is founded.

This does not mean it is right or desirable for us to have Christianity established as the official or unofficial faith of the nation. That would be detrimental to America. It would certainly be detrimental to Christianity to subsume or to blur the distinction between the Christian faith and our nation. That blurring of nation and religious ideology prepared the ground for Nazism in post–World War I Germany, as too many Christians began to assume that being German and being Christian were the same thing.

People have the right to bring their moral values to bear on public policy debates and to be heard regardless of the underlying convictions that inform those values—although in the course of presenting them, they may well appeal to their religious convictions, hoping to persuade others of them. Then society decides through public debate and the ballot box what public policies the people want to implement.

SPEAKING OUT

Senator Joseph Lieberman has pointed out that when you try to exclude religious values from the public square, you leave untapped a very rich mine of moral insight and truth that our society sorely needs.

This is another part of the First Amendment: everybody has a right to petition their government . . . in terms that are relevant to themselves. And some of that will be faith-based, some of it will be [a] totally secularly based sense of justice or morality. . . . In the end the democratic process will decide, Congress will decide, the courts will decide. But I think that the public square is greatly strengthened and enriched when people are prepared to speak, not just about secular notions of justice, but about the moral sense that our faith gives us. And again, I want to say that to me that is not un-American, that is very American. Our Constitution says we don't establish a religion, but it also says everybody has freedom of religion, and everybody has the right to speak their mind. And if your mind is faith-based, God bless you. Speak your mind.[13]

The government's job is to accommodate maximally the right of American citizens to express their religious convictions and beliefs when they choose to do so or not. Whether their expressions of faith offend advocates of some other faith or secular humanists is irrelevant. Whether secular humanists' declarations and manifestos offend me as a Christian is irrelevant. There is no constitutional guarantee against being offended. There *is* a constitutional guarantee of free exercise of religion.

An example from earlier in our history illustrates this point of freedom in the face of offense. In the mid-nineteenth century, the Kansas-Nebraska Act of 1854 was pending before Congress. Its passage would have expanded slavery into areas previously designated as free territory. A group of three thousand New England clergymen signed a petition against its passage, which they sent to the United States Senate.

The proslavery senators were apoplectic at the fact that (three thousand) *preachers* would dare to interfere in the political life of the nation. Illinois Senator Stephen Douglas, perhaps best known for his debates with Abraham Lincoln, said, "We find a large body of preachers, perhaps three thousand, following the lead of a circular which was issued by the Abolitionist confederates in this body, calculated to deceive and mislead the public, have here come forward, with atrocious falsehood and atrocious calumny against this Senate, desecrated the pulpit, and prostituted the sacred desk to the miserable and corrupting influence of party politics."[14]

That sounds amazingly similar to much of the national media's criticism of Evangelical preachers' participation in the policy debates of the presidential election in 2004.

"These political preachers ought to be rebuked," Douglas went on to say, "and required to confine themselves to their vocation."[15] Senator James Mason of Virginia added his voice to the baying of protestors, denouncing the action of the clergymen as an absolute abomination: "I understand this petition to come from a class who have put aside their character as citizens. It comes from a class who style themselves in the petition, ministers of the Gospel and not citizens. . . . Sir, ministers of the Gospel are unknown to this government, and God forbid the day should ever come when they shall be known to it."[16]

Sam Houston, at that time a senator from Texas, before he was elected governor, responded to the attacks on the petitioners, saying, "I do not think there is anything very derogatory to our institutions in the ministers of the Gospel expressing their opinions. They have a right to do it. No man can be a minister without first being a man. He has political rights; he also has the rights of a missionary of the Savior, and he is not disenfranchised by his vocation."

Senator Houston went on to say, "Certain political restrictions may be laid upon him; he may be disqualified from serving in the legislatures of the State, but that does not discharge him from political and civil obligations to his country. He has a right to contribute, as far he thinks necessary, to the sustentation of institutions. He has a right to interpose his voice as one of its citizens against the adoption of any measure which he believes will injure the nation."[17] Of course, one needs to understand that Houston was a staunch Unionist.

Proslavery senators calling for a clear separation between those representing the church and the affairs of the state argued that the petition should not even be received or considered, but torn up and thrown away. In the end, the preachers, not the senators, won the day because they refused to sit down and shut up even when told to do so by some members of the esteemed United States Senate.

Those antislavery preachers understood a simple fact about America that their Senate opponents did not: even in the face of those who would shut them down, most Americans consider it their civic right and obligation to allow the "salt" of the gospel to season public policy. They will continue to talk about God and how they conceive his concerns for justice even when they are told to keep silent about Him—such is our American core value of religious liberty.

THE FUTURE OF RELIGION IN AMERICA?

Before Dwight D. Eisenhower became president of the United States, while he was president of Columbia University (1948–53), he initiated a conference called the American Assembly, designed on a town-hall concept, to bring Americans of divergent viewpoints together to talk about different issues. After half a century, the assembly finally concluded that religion was important enough to address.

In 2000 I participated in the 96th American Assembly, which gathered fifty-seven men and women from government, business, labor, law, academia, the media, nonprofit organization (such as People for the American Way and Americans United for Separation of Church and State), and fourteen religions and faith-based organizations for three days "to define policies and actions concerning the role of religion in American public life." The assembly "sought to identify as wide a circle as possible of shared values among the many religions in the United States in order to help create an atmosphere of mutual respect in public life [and enable] individuals to discuss religious differences in a less divisive manner, whereby shared values could be used to help resolve non-religious issues."[18]

Our conclusions called for a renewed appreciation of the importance of religion in all spheres of life and stressed the need for robust public dialogue.

> Our deep commitment to these principles leads us to emphasize the importance of vigorous religious involvement in public policy and civic life. Americans should recognize they live in a country with strong and flexible institutions and a remarkable capacity for living with and sometimes resolving intensely conflicting views without recourse to violence. Religious voices are a vital component of our national conversation and should be heard in the public square.
>
> We reject the notion that religion is exclusively a private matter relegated to the homes and sacred meeting places of the faithful primarily for two reasons. First,

religious convictions of individuals cannot be severed from their daily lives. People of faith in business, law, medicine, education, and other sectors should not be required to divorce their faith from their professions. Second, many religious communities have a rich tradition of constructive social engagement, and our nation benefits from their work in such varied areas as social justice, civil rights, and ethics.

We encourage people of faith to foster the emergence of a new American generation, one that better comprehends the significance of the increasing religious pluralism in this nation and its implications for advancing civic dialogue. This will require people of faith to seek to communicate with one another and Americans of no religious convictions in ways that enhance mutual understanding and respect for the civil liberties of everyone.[19]

These recommendations are critically important to the future of America if demographics are destiny, because it would appear that the country is likely to become even more religious in the next several generations. Demographers such as Philip Longman have cited a correlation between religious conviction and high fertility, noting that younger Americans seem to be far more socially conservative than their parents' and grandparents' generations.[20] Longman observed that married couples with children voted 59 percent for George Bush and single women voted 62 percent for John Kerry. Consequently, the states that Bush carried had a 12 percent higher average birthrate than the states John Kerry won. Married couples with children have more influence than single women on the next generation of Americans simply because they are raising more of the children. If these trends hold, we will have an increasingly socially conservative population that believes in a transcendent moral order, although they may disagree about the points of origin and the details of that transcendent order.

If that population shift occurs, and we have a government that is still operating under a burgeoning secular spirit of rationalism and subjectivism, our governing structures will increasingly lose their moral authority and viability with an ever-growing majority of the American people—something that should concern all Americans who believe in representative self-government.

We have always been a moral and religious people—and evidently we are becoming more so, according to a January 2006 poll conducted by the Barna Research Group. The percentage of the United States that can be classified by their beliefs as "born again" (not self-identifying by that phrase) has risen in the last two decades from 31 percent to 45 percent.[21]

As one of the primary contributors to our founding documents and our second U.S. president, John Adams, cautioned, our government is wholly inadequate for a people who are *not* moral and religious. America was a new and exciting experiment combining Enlightenment theories of self-government with Judeo-Christian values. The degree of liberty Americans have enjoyed is dependent on a government that treads lightly. A government can tread lightly without inviting chaos and license only in a society where the majority of the people obey the law voluntarily, not simply from fear of punishment, but because they are acutely aware of their accountability to a transcendent moral order for the way in which they live their lives.

Not just our social fabric is at stake in what God's got to do with America, therefore; our liberty is as well. If we were to reach a point at which most Americans no longer believed in a transcendent moral order and did not feel an internal obligation to do the right thing even when no one was watching, the consequence would be chaos, reduced liberty, or both. Forced to choose, most people would opt for order over chaos, even at the loss of significant liberty.

When Christians say, "God bless America," they understand there is a connection between personal responsibility and faithfulness to God and the experience of divine blessing. This connection is explicit in God's promise in 2 Chronicles 7:14: "If my people, who are called by my name, will humble themselves and pray and seek my face and turn from their wicked ways, then will I hear from heaven and will forgive their sin and will heal their land." This promise originally applied to the believers in Israel but now applies to believers wherever they reside. It is not exclusive to Americans—it could apply to believers in England, Germany, Korea, Japan, Brazil, Guatemala, Mozambique, South Africa, or anywhere else. As an American Christian, I apply it to believers in the United States.

I believe that if America is exceptional, it is not because we made it that way. It is because we experienced God's undeserved blessings upon this nation. This is a doctrine of obligation, responsibility, sacrifice, and service—not of pride, privilege, and prejudice—and it is founded on a very basic spiritual and biblical principle: to whom much is given, much is required.

God's blessing is always grace—that is what makes it a blessing, not a reward.

When we say, "God bless America," we are asking God to treat our nation better than we deserve, even if we do repent and seek His face. If enough Americans respond in this way, we could reach a divine tipping point of heal-the-land blessing.[22]

We can affirm the "God bless" portion of the phrase, therefore, as a way of reclaiming what historically has been best about our country and as a way of making sure that we carry it forward to define our future in new and more promising ways. It is a way of honoring Lincoln's eloquent warning, lest we forget "the gracious Hand which preserved us in peace, and multiplied and enriched and strengthened us," and lest we "vainly imagine, in the deceitfulness of our hearts, that all these blessings were produced by some superior wisdom and virtue of our own."[23]

But what of the "America" we ask God to bless—is it a piece of geography, a parcel of real estate, a designated territory on a map? Or is it an idea, a belief, a creed, an understanding of humanity that we believe comes from God?

Our current immigration debate sometimes overlooks the fact that unless we are Native Americans, we are all immigrants or are descended from immigrants. Anyone can become an American. It doesn't have so much to do with racial or ethnic heritage or the amount of time we have spent in a particular place as it does with affirmation of a particular credo and set of beliefs.

So when we say, "God bless America," we are not just saying, God bless this nation of people who inhabit this geographical territory. We are saying, God bless and spread the idea of America, so that all people—Arab, Jew, Japanese, Chinese, Russian, African—can live in the equality and human dignity and freedom to which the laws of nature and nature's God entitle them. We are reciting, together, a prayer, a hope, a dream, a vision—that all men and women yearning to breathe freely may live in the liberty and equality that are their God-given birthrights—not just here, but everywhere.

Indeed—God bless America, and God bless everyone!

★ Appendix A ★

A Modest Proposal for Religious Accommodation in Public Schools

Some who oppose religious expression in public schools cite as a reason for their opposition their concern that religious pluralism would require public schools, or other government entities, to accommodate all religious expressions. They argue that if the door is opened to the Christian, Jewish, and Muslim faiths, public schools would be required to open themselves to any religion at all—even Satanism—which might involve practices that at worst would be illegal and at best would be morally and spiritually reprehensible to the vast majority of the school community.

First, I am not sure that most Americans in most communities would find such a potential eventuality any more unacceptable than they do the critics' current secular solution—an avoidance of any voluntary, student-initiated, student-led, student-content-dictated religious expression, which rather than honoring diversity simply creates an artificial, "religion-free" zone through religious apartheid.

Second, accommodation by school officials of student-initiated, student-led, student-content-dictated religious expression does not and never has included acceptance of illegal or dangerous behavior. For example, sexual copulation in public is illegal, even if it were argued that it was an act of worship to some ancient fertility goddess.

Third, such accommodation of student-initiated, student-led, student-content-dictated religious expression in public settings would necessarily reflect the religious makeup of individual communities. Religious and non-religious minorities would not have the right to equal time, only the right to equal access. Equality of opportunity does not require equality of accommodation time. This is preferable to the current situation in which those minorities who wish no accommodation of religious expression effectively silence, suppress, and censor such expression by the community majorities, who most often are adherents of some faith tradition.

For example, if students decided they wanted to have their school accommodate student-initiated, student-led, student-content-dictated (with the understanding that illegal actions are proscribed) religious expression before school athletic events, then the school officials would work out a schedule for student volunteers who wished to express their religious viewpoint to have an opportunity to do so in accordance with how prominent their particular faith was within that student community (making certain that *all* viewpoints that wished to be accommodated were included). So all students would have the opportunity to "opt in" to participating as well as "opt out" from being present during such student religious expression.

If the student body were 40 percent Catholic, 40 percent Protestant, 10 percent Jewish, and 10 percent other or no faith, then opportunities would be allotted accordingly. Would that mean students would be exposed at some part in the school year to a fellow student invoking the blessings of the earth goddess Gia? Yes, if adherents of that particular "deity" were present in the student body and wished to invoke. Would students possibly be exposed to a brief discourse on a fellow student's disbelief in God and his or her belief in the spirit of man? Yes, if students of atheistic belief volunteered to be accommodated.

It seems to me such an incidence would be a small price to pay for affirming and celebrating the religious diversity we say we prize as a society.

And by the way, the religious makeup of the school community would change from year to year and decade to decade. As adherents of various religious traditions successfully espoused their beliefs in the community, their percentage of the community's population would rise, as would their opportunities for accommodation.

For instance, in early federalist Rhode Island, the accommodation would have been overwhelmingly Protestant. Now, since Rhode Island is by percentage the most Catholic state in the nation, the Catholic students' opportunity for expression would greatly increase. Similarly, in some sections of Greater Detroit and Los Angeles, the majority would be Muslim or Buddhist, respectively.

Is such a model perfect? No. We should beware, however, of making the perfect the enemy of the good. This accommodation model is certainly preferable to turning our public schools into sterile, "no-religion" zones.

And it is certainly a better model than the earlier solution (through the early 1960s) to the question of religious expression in public schools—government-espoused acknowledgment of the majority faith—which was unacceptable, even with the student option to opt out, or not participate in such government-led acknowledgments. Government-sponsored acknowledgment of the majority faith violates the rights of all people of other faiths or no faith because it puts the government on the side of a particular faith tradition to the exclusion of all others.

★ Appendix B ★

The Barmen Declaration[1]

I. An Appeal to the Evangelical Congregation and Christians in Germany

The Confessional Synod of the German Evangelical Church met in Barmen, May 29–31, 1934. Here representatives from all the German Confessional Churches met with one accord in a confession of the one Lord of the one, holy, apostolic Church. In fidelity to their Confession of Faith, members of Lutheran, Reformed, and United Churches sought a common message for the need and temptation of the Church in our day. With gratitude to God they are convinced that they have been given a common word to utter. It was not their intention to found a new Church or to form a union. For nothing was farther from their minds than the abolition of the confessional status of our Churches. Their intention was, rather, to withstand in faith and unanimity the destruction of the Confession of Faith, and thus of the Evangelical Church in Germany. In opposition to attempts to establish the unity of the German Evangelical Church by means of false doctrine, by the use of force and insincere practices, the Confessional Synod insists that the unity of the Evangelical Churches in Germany can come only from the Word of God in faith through the Holy Spirit. Thus alone is the Church renewed.

Therefore the Confessional Synod calls upon the congregations to range themselves behind it in prayer, and steadfastly to gather around those pastors and teachers who are loyal to the Confessions.

Be not deceived by loose talk, as if we meant to oppose the unity of the German nation! Do not listen to the seducers who pervert our intentions, as if we wanted to break up the unity of the German Evangelical Church or to forsake the Confessions of the Fathers!

Try the spirits whether they are of God! Prove also the words of the Confessional Synod of the German Evangelical Church to see whether they agree with Holy Scripture and with the Confessions of the Fathers.

If you find that we are speaking contrary to Scripture, then do not listen to us! But if you find that we are taking our stand upon Scripture, then let no fear or temptation keep you from treading with us the path of faith and obedience to the Word of God, in order that God's people be of one mind upon earth and that we in faith experience what he himself has said: "I will never leave you, nor forsake you." Therefore, "Fear not, little flock, for it is your Father's good pleasure to give you the kingdom."

II. Theological Declaration Concerning the Present Situation of the German Evangelical Church

According to the opening words of its constitution of July 11, 1933, the German Evangelical Church is a federation of Confessional Churches that grew out of the Reformation and that enjoy equal rights. The theological basis for the unification of these Churches is laid down in Article 1 and Article 2(1) of the constitution of the German Evangelical Church that was recognized by the Reich Government on July 14, 1933:

Article 1. The inviolable foundation of the German Evangelical Church is the gospel of Jesus Christ as it is attested for us in Holy Scripture and brought to light again in the Confessions of the Reformation. The full powers that the Church needs for its mission are hereby determined and limited.

Article 2(1). The German Evangelical Church is divided into member Churches (Landeskirchen).

We, the representatives of Lutheran, Reformed, and United Churches, of free synods, Church assemblies, and parish organizations united in the Confessional Synod of the German Evangelical Church, declare that we stand together on the ground of the German Evangelical Church as a federation of German Confessional Churches. We are bound together by the confession of the one Lord of the one, holy, catholic, and apostolic Church.

We publicly declare before all Evangelical Churches in Germany that what they hold in common in this Confession is grievously imperiled, and with it the unity of the German Evangelical Church. It is threatened by the teaching methods and actions of the ruling Church party of the "German Christians" and of the Church administration carried on by them. These have become more and more apparent during the first year of the existence of the German Evangelical Church. This threat consists in the fact that the theological basis, in which the German Evangelical Church is united, has been continually and systematically thwarted and rendered ineffective by alien principles, on the part of the leaders and spokesmen of the "German Christians" as well as on the part of the Church administration. When these principles are held to be valid, then, according to all the Confessions in force among us, the Church ceases to be the Church and the German Evangelical Church, as a federation of Confessional Churches, becomes intrinsically impossible.

As members of Lutheran, Reformed, and United Churches, we may and must speak with one voice in this matter today. Precisely because we want to be and to remain faithful to our various Confessions, we may not keep silent, since we believe that we have been given a common message to utter in a time of common need and temptation. We commend to God what this may mean for the interrelations of the Confessional Churches.

In view of the errors of the "German Christians" of the present Reich Church government which are devastating the Church and also therefore breaking up the unity of the German Evangelical Church, we confess the following Evangelical truths:

1. "I am the way, and the truth, and the life; no one comes to the Father, but by me." (John 14:6.) "Truly, truly, I say to you, he who does not enter the sheep fold by the door but climbs in by another way, that man is a thief and a robber. . . . I am the door; if anyone enters by me, he will be saved." (John 10:1, 9.)

    Jesus Christ, as he is attested for us in Holy Scripture, is the one

Word of God which we have to hear and which we have to trust and obey in life and in death.

We reject the false doctrine, as though the Church could and would have to acknowledge as a source of its proclamation, apart from and besides this one Word of God, still other events and powers, figures and truths, as God's revelation.

2. "Christ Jesus, whom God made our wisdom, our righteousness and sanctification and redemption." (1 Cor. 1:30.)

As Jesus Christ is God's assurance of the forgiveness of all our sins, so in the same way and with the same seriousness he is also God's mighty claim upon our whole life. Through him befalls us a joyful deliverance from the godless fetters of this world for a free, grateful service to his creatures.

We reject the false doctrine, as though there were areas of our life in which we would not belong to Jesus Christ, but to other lords—areas in which we would not need justification and sanctification through him.

3. "Rather, speaking the truth in love, we are to grow up in every way into him who is the head, into Christ, from whom the whole body [is] joined and knit together." (Eph. 4:15, 16.)

The Christian Church is the congregation of the brethren in which Jesus Christ acts presently as the Lord in Word and sacrament through the Holy Spirit. As the Church of pardoned sinners, it has to testify in the midst of a sinful world, with its faith as with its obedience, with its message as with its order, that it is solely his property, and that it lives and wants to live solely from his comfort and from his direction in the expectation of his appearance.

We reject the false doctrine, as though the Church were permitted to abandon the form of its message and order to its own pleasure or to changes in prevailing ideological and political convictions.

4. "You know that the rulers of the Gentiles lord it over them, and their great men exercise authority over them. It shall not be so among you; but whoever would be great among you must be your servant." (Matt. 20:25, 26.)

The various offices in the Church do not establish a dominion of some over the others; on the contrary, they are for the exercise of the ministry entrusted to and enjoined upon the whole congregation.

We reject the false doctrine, as though the Church, apart from this ministry, could and were permitted to give to itself, or allow to be given to it, special leaders vested with ruling powers.

5. "Fear God. Honor the emperor." (1 Peter 2:17.)

Scripture tells us that, in the as yet unredeemed world in which the Church also exists, the State has by divine appointment the task of providing for justice and peace. [It fulfills this task] by means of the threat and exercise of force, according to the measure of human judgment and human ability. The Church acknowledges the benefit of this divine appointment in gratitude and reverence before him. It calls to mind the Kingdom of God, God's commandment and righteousness, and thereby the responsibility both of rulers and of the ruled. It trusts and obeys the power of the Word by which God upholds all things.

We reject the false doctrine, as though the State, over and beyond its special commission, should and could become the single and totalitarian order of human life, thus fulfilling the Church's vocation as well.

We reject the false doctrine, as though the Church, over and beyond its special commission, should and could appropriate the characteristics, the tasks, and the dignity of the State, thus itself becoming an organ of the State.

6. "Lo, I am with you always, to the close of the age." (Matt. 28:20.) "The word of God is not fettered." (2 Tim. 2:9.)

The Church's commission, upon which its freedom is founded, consists in delivering the message of the free grace of God to all people in Christ's stead, and therefore in the ministry of his own Word and work through sermon and sacrament.

We reject the false doctrine, as though the Church in human arrogance could place the Word and work of the Lord in the service of any arbitrarily chosen desires, purposes, and plans.

The Confessional Synod of the German Evangelical Church declares that it sees in the acknowledgment of these truths and in the rejection of these errors the indispensable theological basis of the German Evangelical Church as a federation of Confessional Churches. It invites all who are able to accept its declaration to be mindful of these theological principles in their decisions in Church politics. It entreats all whom it concerns to return to the unity of faith, love, and hope.

★ Appendix C ★

Bibles and Scripture Passages Used by Presidents in Taking the Oath of Office

The information below is part of an American Memory collection, "I Do Solemnly Swear . . .": Presidential Inaugurations, at the Library of Congress, courtesy of the Architect of the Capitol. It was compiled by the Office of the Curator from contemporary accounts and other sources in the files of the Architect of the Capitol.

PRESIDENT	DATE	EDITION
George Washington	1789	Genesis 49:13^2 (Masonic Bible); opened at random due to haste
George Washington	1793	Not known
John Adams	1797	Not known
Thomas Jefferson	1801, 1805	Not known

James Madison	1809, 1813	Not known
James Monroe	1817, 1821	Not known
John Q. Adams	1825	Not known
Andrew Jackson	1829, 1833	Not known
Martin Van Buren	1837	Proverbs 3:17[3]
William H. Harrison	1841	Not known
John Tyler	1841	Not known
James K. Polk	1845	Not known
Zachary Taylor	1849	Not known
Millard Fillmore	1850	Not known
Franklin Pierce	1853	Affirmed instead of swearing the oath; did not kiss Bible
James Buchanan	1857	Not known
Abraham Lincoln	1861	Opened at random
Abraham Lincoln	1865	Matthew 7:1; 18:7; Revelations 16:7[4]
Andrew Johnson	1865	Proverbs 21
Ulysses S. Grant	1869	Not known
Ulysses S. Grant	1873	Isaiah 11:1–3[5]
Rutherford B. Hayes	1877	Privately, no Bible; publicly, Psalm 118:11–135[5]
James A. Garfield	1881	Proverbs 21:1[5, 6]
Chester A. Arthur	1881	Privately, no Bible; Psalm 31:1–3[5, 6]

Appendix C

Grover Cleveland	1885	Psalm 112:4-10; Bible opened by Chief Justice and by chance it fell to this Psalm[7]
Benjamin Harrison	1889	Psalm 121:1-6[5]
Grover Cleveland	1893	Psalm 91:12-16[5]
William McKinley	1897	II Chron. 1:10; Bible given to him by Methodist church congregation[8]
William McKinley	1901	Proverbs 16[5]
Theodore Roosevelt	1901	No Bible
Theodore Roosevelt	1905	James 1:22-23[5]
William Howard Taft	1909	I Kings 3:9-11[5]
Woodrow Wilson	1913	Psalm 119[5]
Woodrow Wilson	1917	Privately, not known; publicly, Psalm 46[9]
Warren G. Harding	1921	Micah 6:8 (Washington Bible)[5]
Calvin Coolidge	1923	Not known
Calvin Coolidge	1925	John 1
Herbert C. Hoover	1929	Proverbs 29:18[5]
Franklin D. Roosevelt	1933, 1937 1941, 1945	I Corinthians 13[5]
Harry S. Truman	1945	Closed Bible held in left hand; right hand on upper cover[10]
Harry S. Truman	1949	Matthew 5:3-11 and Exodus 20:3-17[11]

APPENDIX C

Dwight D. Eisenhower	1953	Psalm 127:1 (Washington Bible) and II Chronicles 7:14 (West Point Bible)[12]
Dwight D. Eisenhower	1957	Privately, not known; publicly, Psalm 33:12 (West Point Bible)[13]
John F. Kennedy	1961	Closed Bible[14]
Lyndon B. Johnson	1963	Missal[15]
Lyndon B. Johnson	1965	Closed family Bible[16]
Richard M. Nixon	1969, 1973	Two family Bibles, both open to Isaiah 2:4[17]
Gerald R. Ford	1974	Proverbs 3:5–6[18]
James E. Carter	1977	Family Bible open to Micah 6:8[19]
Ronald W. Reagan	1981, 1985	Mother's Bible open to II Chronicles 7:14[20] (both privately and publicly in 1985)
George H. W. Bush	1989	Washington's Masonic Bible opened at random in the center; family Bible on top opened to Matthew 5
William J. Clinton	1993	King James Bible, given to him by grandmother, open to Galatians 6:8
William J. Clinton	1997	King James Bible, given to him by grandmother, open to Isaiah 58:12[21]
George W. Bush	2001	Closed family Bible[22]
George W. Bush	2005	Family Bible open to Isaiah 40:31[23]

★ Appendix D ★

Presidential Addresses

Abraham Lincoln
Gettysburg Address
Second Inaugural Address

Franklin D. Roosevelt
"The Four Freedoms"
D-day Prayer

John F. Kennedy
Address to the Greater Houston Ministerial Association
Inaugural Address
Remarks Prepared for Delivery at the Trade Mart in Dallas

George W. Bush
First Inaugural Address
Second Inaugural Address

APPENDIX D

ABRAHAM LINCOLN'S GETTYSBURG ADDRESS[24]
November 19, 1863

FOURSCORE and seven years ago our fathers brought forth on this continent a new nation, conceived in liberty, and dedicated to the proposition that all men are created equal.

Now we are engaged in a great civil war, testing whether that nation, or any nation so conceived and so dedicated, can long endure. We are met on a great battlefield of that war. We have come to dedicate a portion of that field as a final resting-place for those who here gave their lives that that nation might live. It is altogether fitting and proper that we should do this. But, in a larger sense, we cannot dedicate, we cannot consecrate, we cannot hallow, this ground. The brave men, living and dead, who struggled here have consecrated it, far above our poor power to add or detract. The world will little note, nor long remember what we say here, but it can never forget what they did here. It is for us the living, rather, to be dedicated here to the unfinished work which they who fought here have thus far so nobly advanced. It is rather for us to be here dedicated to the great task remaining before us—that from these honored dead we take increased devotion to that cause for which they gave the last full measure of devotion—that we here highly resolve that these dead shall not have died in vain—that this nation, under God, shall have a new birth of freedom and that government of the people, by the people, for the people, shall not perish from the earth.

ABRAHAM LINCOLN'S SECOND INAUGURAL ADDRESS[25]
March 4, 1865

Fellow Countrymen:

At this second appearing to take the oath of the presidential office, there is less occasion for an extended address than there was at the first. Then a statement somewhat in detail of a course to be pursued seemed fitting and proper. Now, at the expiration of four years, during which public declarations have been constantly called forth on every point and phase of the great contest which still absorbs the attention, and engrosses the energies of the nation, little that is new could be presented. The progress of our arms, upon which all else chiefly depends, is as well known to the public as to myself, and it is, I trust, reasonably satisfactory and encouraging to all. With high hope for the future, no prediction in regard to it is ventured.

On the occasion corresponding to this four years ago all thoughts were anxiously directed to an impending civil war. All dreaded it, all sought to avert it. While the inaugural address was being delivered from this place, devoted altogether to *saving* the Union without war, urgent agents were in the city seeking to *destroy* it without war—seeking to dissolve the Union, and divide effects by negotiation. Both parties deprecated war; but one of them would *make* war rather than let the nation survive, and the other would *accept* war rather than let it perish, and the war came.

One-eighth of the whole population were colored slaves, not distributed generally over the Union, but localized in the southern part of it. These slaves constituted a peculiar and powerful interest. All knew that this interest was somehow the cause of the war. To strengthen, perpetuate, and extend this interest was the object for which the insurgents would rend the Union even by war, while the Government claimed no right to do more than to restrict the territorial enlargement of it. Neither party expected for the war the magnitude or the duration which it has already attained. Neither anticipated that the *cause* of the conflict might cease with or even before the conflict itself should cease. Each looked for an easier triumph, and a result less fundamental and astounding. Both read the same Bible and pray to the same God, and each invokes His aid against the other. It may seem strange that any men should dare to ask a just God's assistance in wringing their bread from the sweat of other men's faces, but let us judge not, that we be not judged. The prayers of both could not be answered. That of neither has been answered fully. The Almighty has His own purposes. "Woe unto the world because of offenses; for it must needs be that offenses come, but woe to that man by whom the offense cometh." If we shall suppose that American slavery is one of those offenses which, in the providence of God, must needs come, but which, having continued through His appointed time, He now wills to remove, and that He gives to both North and South this terrible war as the woe due to those by whom the offense came, shall we discern therein any departure from those divine attributes which the believers in a living God always ascribe to

Him? Fondly do we hope, fervently do we pray, that this mighty scourge of war may speedily pass away. Yet, if God wills that it continue until all the wealth piled by the bondsman's two hundred and fifty years of unrequited toil shall be sunk, and until every drop of blood drawn with the lash shall be paid by another drawn with the sword, as was said three thousand years ago, so still it must be said "the judgments of the Lord are true and righteous altogether."

With malice toward none, with charity for all, with firmness in the right as God gives us to see the right, let us strive on to finish the work we are in, to bind up the nation's wounds, to care for him who shall have borne the battle and for his widow and his orphan, to do all which may achieve and cherish a just and a lasting peace among ourselves, and with all nations.

EXCERPTS FROM FRANKLIN D. ROOSEVELT'S "FOUR FREEDOMS" SPEECH[26]
Annual Message to Congress, January 6, 1941

Mr. President, Mr. Speaker, Members of the Seventy-seventh Congress:

I address you, the Members of the Seventy-seventh Congress, at a moment unprecedented in the history of the Union. I use the word "unprecedented," because at no previous time has American security been as seriously threatened from without as it is today. . . .

. . . The American people have unalterably set their faces against that tyranny.

Every realist knows that the democratic way of life is at this moment being directly assailed in every part of the world—assailed either by arms, or by secret spreading of poisonous propaganda by those who seek to destroy unity and promote discord in nations that are still at peace. . . .

Armed defense of democratic existence is now being gallantly waged in four continents. If that defense fails, all the population and all the resources of Europe, Asia, Africa and Australasia will be dominated by the conquerors. Let us remember that the total of those populations and their resources in those four continents greatly exceeds the sum total of the population and the resources of the whole of the Western Hemisphere—many times over.

In times like these it is immature—and incidentally, untrue—for anybody to brag that an unprepaRed America, single-handed, and with one hand tied behind its back, can hold off the whole world.

No realistic American can expect from a dictator's peace international generosity, or return of true independence, or world disarmament, or freedom of expression, or freedom of religion—or even good business.

Such a peace would bring no security for us or for our neighbors. "Those, who would give up essential liberty to purchase a little temporary safety, deserve neither liberty nor safety."

As a nation, we may take pride in the fact that we are softhearted; but we cannot afford to be soft-headed. . . .

The need of the moment is that our actions and our policy should be devoted primarily—almost exclusively—to meeting this foreign peril. For all our domestic problems are now a part of the great emergency.

Just as our national policy in internal affairs has been based upon a decent respect for the rights and the dignity of all our fellow men within our gates, so our national policy in foreign affairs has been based on a decent respect for the rights and dignity of all nations, large and small. And the justice of morality must and will win in the end.

Our national policy is this:

First, by an impressive expression of the public will and without regard to partisanship, we are committed to all-inclusive national defense.

Second, by an impressive expression of the public will and without regard to partisanship, we are committed to full support of all those resolute peoples, everywhere, who are resisting aggression and are thereby keeping war away from our Hemisphere. By this support, we express our determination that the democratic cause shall prevail; and we strengthen the defense and the security of our own nation.

Third, by an impressive expression of the public will and without regard to partisanship, we are committed to the proposition that principles of morality and considerations for our own security will never permit us to acquiesce in a peace dictated by aggressors and sponsored by appeasers. We know that enduring peace cannot be bought at the cost of other people's freedom. . . .

In the future days, which we seek to make secure, we look forward to a world founded upon four essential human freedoms.

The first is freedom of speech and expression—everywhere in the world.

The second is freedom of every person to worship God in his own way—everywhere in the world.

The third is freedom from want—which, translated into world terms, means economic understandings which will secure to every nation a healthy peacetime life for its inhabitants—everywhere in the world.

The fourth is freedom from fear—which, translated into world terms, means a world-wide reduction of armaments to such a point and in such a thorough fashion that no nation will be in a position to commit an act of physical aggression against any neighbor—anywhere in the world.

That is no vision of a distant millennium. It is a definite basis for a kind of world attainable in our own time and generation. That kind of world is the very antithesis of the so-called new order of tyranny which the dictators seek to create with the crash of a bomb.

To that new order we oppose the greater conception—the moral order. A good society is able to face schemes of world domination and foreign revolutions alike without fear.

Since the beginning of our American history, we have been engaged in change—in a perpetual peaceful revolution—a revolution which goes on steadily, quietly adjusting itself to changing conditions—without the concentration camp or the quick-lime in the ditch. The world order which we seek is the cooperation of free countries, working together in a friendly, civilized society.

This nation has placed its destiny in the hands and heads and hearts of its millions of free men and women; and its faith in freedom under the guidance of God. Freedom means the supremacy of human rights everywhere. Our support goes to those who struggle to gain those rights or keep them. Our strength is our unity of purpose. To that high concept there can be no end save victory.

FRANKLIN DELANO ROOSEVELT'S D-DAY PRAYER[27]
June 6, 1944

My fellow Americans: Last night, when I spoke with you about the fall of Rome, I knew at that moment that troops of the United States and our allies were crossing the Channel in another and greater operation. It has come to pass with success thus far.

And so, in this poignant hour, I ask you to join with me in prayer:

Almighty God: Our sons, pride of our Nation, this day have set upon a mighty endeavor, a struggle to preserve our Republic, our religion, and our civilization, and to set free a suffering humanity.

Lead them straight and true; give strength to their arms, stoutness to their hearts, steadfastness in their faith.

They will need Thy blessings. Their road will be long and hard. For the enemy is strong. He may hurl back our forces. Success may not come with rushing speed, but we shall return again and again; and we know that by Thy grace, and by the righteousness of our cause, our sons will triumph.

They will be sore tried, by night and by day, without rest—until the victory is won. The darkness will be rent by noise and flame. Men's souls will be shaken with the violences of war.

For these men are lately drawn from the ways of peace. They fight not for the lust of conquest. They fight to end conquest. They fight to liberate. They fight to let justice arise, and tolerance and good will among all Thy people. They yearn but for the end of battle, for their return to the haven of home.

Some will never return. Embrace these, Father, and receive them, Thy heroic servants, into Thy kingdom.

And for us at home—fathers, mothers, children, wives, sisters, and brothers of brave men overseas—whose thoughts and prayers are ever with them—help us, Almighty God, to rededicate ourselves in renewed faith in Thee in this hour of great sacrifice.

Many people have urged that I call the Nation into a single day of special prayer. But because the road is long and the desire is great, I ask that our people devote themselves in a continuance of prayer. As we rise to each new day, and again when each day is spent, let words of prayer be on our lips, invoking Thy help to our efforts.

Give us strength, too—strength in our daily tasks, to redouble the contributions we make in the physical and the material support of our armed forces.

And let our hearts be stout, to wait out the long travail, to bear sorrows that may come, to impart our courage unto our sons wheresoever they may be.

And, O Lord, give us Faith. Give us Faith in Thee; Faith in our sons; Faith in each other; Faith in our united crusade. Let not the keenness of our spirit ever be dulled. Let not the impacts of temporary events, of temporal matters of but fleeting moment, let not these deter us in our unconquerable purpose.

With Thy blessing, we shall prevail over the unholy forces of our enemy. Help us to conquer the apostles of greed and racial arrogancies. Lead us to the saving of our country, and with our sister Nations into a world unity that will spell a sure peace, a peace invulnerable to the schemings of unworthy men. And a peace that will let all men live in freedom, reaping the just rewards of their honest toil.

Thy will be done, Almighty God. Amen.

JOHN F. KENNEDY'S ADDRESS TO THE GREATER HOUSTON MINISTERIAL ASSOCIATION[28]
September 12, 1960

Reverend Meza, Reverend Reck, I'm grateful for your generous invitation to speak my views.

While the so-called religious issue is necessarily and properly the chief topic here tonight, I want to emphasize from the outset that we have far more critical issues to face in the 1960 election; the spread of Communist influence, until it now festers 90 miles off the coast of Florida—the humiliating treatment of our President and Vice President by those who no longer respect our power—the hungry children I saw in West Virginia, the old people who cannot pay their doctor bills, the families forced to give up their farms—an America with too many slums, with too few schools, and too late to the moon and outer space.

These are the real issues which should decide this campaign. And they are not religious issues—for war and hunger and ignorance and despair know no religious barriers.

But because I am a Catholic, and no Catholic has ever been elected President, the real issues in this campaign have been obscured—perhaps deliberately, in some quarters less responsible than this. So it is apparently necessary for me to state once again—not what kind of church I believe in, for that should be important only to me—but what kind of America I believe in.

Appendix D

I believe in an America where the separation of church and state is absolute—where no Catholic prelate would tell the President (should he be Catholic) how to act, and no Protestant minister would tell his parishioners for whom to vote—where no church or church school is granted any public funds or political preference—and where no man is denied public office merely because his religion differs from the President who might appoint him or the people who might elect him.

I believe in an America that is officially neither Catholic, Protestant nor Jewish—where no public official either requests or accepts instructions on public policy from the Pope, the National Council of Churches or any other ecclesiastical source—where no religious body seeks to impose its will directly or indirectly upon the general populace or the public acts of its officials—and where religious liberty is so indivisible that an act against one church is treated as an act against all.

For while this year it may be a Catholic against whom the finger of suspicion is pointed, in other years it has been, and may someday be again, a Jew—or a Quaker—or a Unitarian—or a Baptist. It was Virginia's harassment of Baptist preachers, for example, that helped lead to Jefferson's statute of religious freedom. Today I may be the victim—but tomorrow it may be you—until the whole fabric of our harmonious society is ripped at a time of great national peril.

Finally, I believe in an America where religious intolerance will someday end—where all men and all churches are treated as equal—where every man has the same right to attend or not attend the church of his choice—where there is no Catholic vote, no anti-Catholic vote, no bloc voting of any kind—and where Catholics, Protestants and Jews, at both the lay and pastoral level, will refrain from those attitudes of disdain and division which have so often marred their works in the past, and promote instead the American ideal of brotherhood.

That is the kind of America in which I believe. And it represents the kind of Presidency in which I believe—a great office that must neither be humbled by making it the instrument of any one religious group nor tarnished by arbitrarily withholding its occupancy from the members of any one religious group. I believe in a President whose religious views are his own private affair, neither imposed by him upon the nation or imposed by the nation upon him as a condition to holding that office.

I would not look with favor upon a President working to subvert the first amendment's guarantees of religious liberty. Nor would our system of checks and balances permit him to do so—and neither do I look with favor upon those who would work to subvert Article VI of the Constitution by requiring a religious test—even by indirection—for it. If they disagree with that safeguard they should be out openly working to repeal it.

I want a Chief Executive whose public acts are responsible to all groups and obligated to none—who can attend any ceremony, service or dinner his office may appropriately require of him—and whose fulfillment of his Presidential oath is not limited or conditioned by any religious oath, ritual or obligation.

This is the kind of America I believe in—and this is the kind I fought for in the South Pacific, and the kind my brother died for in Europe. No one suggested then that we may have a "divided loyalty," that we did "not believe in liberty," or that we belonged to a disloyal group that threatened the "freedoms for which our forefathers died."

And in fact this is the kind of America for which our forefathers died—when they fled here to escape religious test oaths that denied office to members of less favored churches—when they fought for the Constitution, the Bill of Rights, and the Virginia Statute of Religious Freedom—and when they fought at the shrine I visited today, the Alamo. For side by side with Bowie and Crockett died McCafferty and Bailey and Carey—but no one knows whether they were Catholic or not. For there was no religious test at the Alamo.

I ask you tonight to follow in that tradition—to judge me on the basis of my record of 14 years in Congress—on my declared stands against an Ambassador to the Vatican, against unconstitutional aid to parochial schools, and against any boycott of the public schools (which I have attended myself)—instead of judging me on the basis of these pamphlets and publications we all have seen that carefully select quotations out of context from the statements of Catholic church leaders, usually in other countries, frequently in other centuries, and always omitting, of course, the statement of the American Bishops in 1948 which strongly endorsed church-state separation, and which more nearly reflects the views of almost every American Catholic.

I do not consider these other quotations binding upon my public acts—why should you? But let me say, with respect to other countries, that I am wholly opposed to the state being used by any religious group, Catholic or Protestant, to compel, prohibit, or persecute the free exercise of any other religion. And I hope that you and I condemn with equal fervor those nations which deny their Presidency to Protestants and those which deny it to Catholics. And rather than cite the misdeeds of those who differ, I would cite the record of the Catholic Church in such nations as Ireland and France—and the independence of such statesmen as Adenauer and De Gaulle.

But let me stress again that these are my views—for contrary to common newspaper usage, I am not the Catholic candidate for President. I am the Democratic Party's candidate for President who happens also to be a Catholic. I do not speak for my church on public matters—and the church does not speak for me.

Whatever issue may come before me as President—on birth control, divorce, censorship, gambling or any other subject—I will make my decision in accordance with these views, in accordance with what my conscience tells me to be the national interest, and without regard to outside religious pressures or dictates. And no power or threat of punishment could cause me to decide otherwise.

But if the time should ever come—and I do not concede any conflict to be even remotely possible—when my office would require me to either violate my conscience or violate the national interest, then I would resign the office; and I hope any conscientious public servant would do the same.

But I do not intend to apologize for these views to my critics of either Catholic or Protestant faith—nor do I intend to disavow either my views or my church in order to win this election.

If I should lose on the real issues, I shall return to my seat in the Senate, satisfied that I had tried my best and was fairly judged. But if this election is decided on the basis that 40 million Americans lost their chance of being President on the day they were baptized, then it is the whole nation that will be the loser, in the eyes of Catholics and non-Catholics around the world, in the eyes of history, and in the eyes of our own people.

But if, on the other hand, I should win the election, then I shall devote every effort of mind and spirit to fulfilling the oath of the Presidency—practically identical, I might add, to the oath I have taken for 14 years in the Congress. For without reservation, I can "solemnly swear that I will faithfully execute the office of President of the United States, and will to the best of my ability preserve, protect, and defend the Constitution . . . so help me God."

JOHN F. KENNEDY'S INAUGURAL ADDRESS[29]
January 20, 1961

Vice President Johnson, Mr. Speaker, Mr. Chief Justice, President Eisenhower, Vice President Nixon, President Truman, Reverend Clergy, fellow citizens:

We observe today not a victory of party, but a celebration of freedom—symbolizing an end as well as a beginning—signifying renewal as well as change. For I have sworn before you and Almighty God the same solemn oath our forebears prescribed nearly a century and three-quarters ago.

The world is very different now. For man holds in his mortal hands the power to abolish all forms of human poverty and all forms of human life. And yet the same revolutionary beliefs for which our forebears fought are still at issue around the globe—the belief that the rights of man come not from the generosity of the state, but from the hand of God.

We dare not forget today that we are the heirs of that first revolution. Let the word go forth from this time and place, to friend and foe alike, that the torch has been passed to a new generation of Americans—born in this century, tempered by war, disciplined by a hard and bitter peace, proud of our ancient heritage, and unwilling to witness or permit the slow undoing of those human rights to which this nation has always been committed, and to which we are committed today at home and around the world.

Let every nation know, whether it wishes us well or ill, that we shall pay any price, bear any burden, meet any hardship, support any friend, oppose any foe to assure the survival and the success of liberty.

This much we pledge—and more.

To those old allies whose cultural and spiritual origins we share, we pledge the loyalty of faithful friends. United there is little we cannot do in a host of cooperative ventures. Divided there is little we can do—for we dare not meet a powerful challenge at odds and split asunder.

To those new states whom we welcome to the ranks of the free, we pledge our word that one form of colonial control shall not have passed away merely to be replaced by a far more iron tyranny. We shall not always expect to find them supporting our view. But we shall always hope to find them strongly supporting their own freedom—and to remember that, in the past, those who foolishly sought power by riding the back of the tiger ended up inside.

To those people in the huts and villages of half the globe struggling to break the bonds of mass misery, we pledge our best efforts to help them help themselves, for whatever period is required—not because the Communists may be doing it, not because we seek their votes, but because it is right. If a free society cannot help the many who are poor, it cannot save the few who are rich.

To our sister republics south of our border, we offer a special pledge: to convert our good words into good deeds, in a new alliance for progress to assist free men and free governments in casting off the chains of poverty. But this peaceful revolution of hope cannot become the prey of hostile powers. Let all our neighbors know that we shall join with them to oppose aggression or subversion anywhere in the Americas. And let every other power know that this hemisphere intends to remain the master of its own house.

To that world assembly of sovereign states, the United Nations, our last best hope in an age where the instruments of war have far outpaced the instruments of peace, we renew our pledge of support—to prevent it from becoming merely a forum for invective, to strengthen its shield of the new and the weak, and to enlarge the area in which its writ may run.

Finally, to those nations who would make themselves our adversary, we offer not a pledge but a request: that both sides begin anew the quest for peace, before the dark powers of destruction unleashed by science engulf all humanity in planned or accidental self-destruction.

We dare not tempt them with weakness. For only when our arms are sufficient beyond doubt can we be certain beyond doubt that they will never be employed.

But neither can two great and powerful groups of nations take comfort from our present course—both sides overburdened by the cost of modern weapons, both rightly alarmed by the steady spread of the deadly atom, yet both racing to alter that uncertain balance of terror that stays the hand of mankind's final war.

So let us begin anew—remembering on both sides that civility is not a sign of weakness, and sincerity is always subject to proof. Let us never negotiate out of fear. But let us never fear to negotiate.

Let both sides explore what problems unite us instead of belaboring those problems which divide us.

Let both sides, for the first time, formulate serious and precise proposals for the inspection and control of arms—and bring the absolute power to destroy other nations under the absolute control of all nations.

Let both sides seek to invoke the wonders of science instead of its terrors. Together let us explore the stars, conquer the deserts, eradicate disease, tap the ocean depths, and encourage the arts and commerce.

Let both sides unite to heed in all corners of the earth the command of Isaiah —to "undo the heavy burdens, and to let the oppressed go free" [Isaiah 58:6 KJV].

And if a beachhead of cooperation may push back the jungle of suspicion, let both sides join in creating a new endeavor, not a new balance of power, but a new world of law, where the strong are just and the weak secure and the peace preserved.

All this will not be finished in the first one hundred days. Nor will it be finished in the first one thousand days, nor in the life of this Administration, nor even perhaps in our lifetime on this planet. But let us begin.

In your hands, my fellow citizens, more than mine, will rest the final success or failure of our course. Since this country was founded, each generation of Americans has been summoned to give testimony to its national loyalty. The graves of young Americans who answered the call to service surround the globe.

Now the trumpet summons us again—not as a call to bear arms, though arms we need—not as a call to battle, though embattled we are—but a call to bear the burden of a long twilight struggle, year in and year out, "rejoicing in hope; patient in tribulation" [Romans 12:12 KJV]—a struggle against the common enemies of man: tyranny, poverty, disease and war itself.

Can we forge against these enemies a grand and global alliance, North and South, East and West, that can assure a more fruitful life for all mankind? Will you join in that historic effort?

In the long history of the world, only a few generations have been granted the role of defending freedom in its hour of maximum danger. I do not shrink from this responsibility—I welcome it. I do not believe that any of us would exchange places with any other people or any other generation. The energy, the faith, the devotion which we bring to this endeavor will light our country and all who serve it—and the glow from that fire can truly light the world.

And so, my fellow Americans: ask not what your country can do for you— ask what you can do for your country.

My fellow citizens of the world: ask not what America will do for you, but what together we can do for the freedom of man.

Finally, whether you are citizens of America or citizens of the world, ask of us here the same high standards of strength and sacrifice which we ask of you. With a good conscience our only sure reward, with history the final judge of our deeds, let us go forth to lead the land we love, asking His blessing and His help, but knowing that here on earth God's work must truly be our own.

REMARKS PREPARED FOR DELIVERY AT THE TRADE MART IN DALLAS BY JOHN F. KENNEDY[30]
November 22, 1963

I am honored to have this invitation to address the annual meeting of the Dallas Citizens Council, joined by the members of the Dallas Assembly—and pleased to have this opportunity to salute the Graduate Research Center of the Southwest.

It is fitting that these two symbols of Dallas progress are united in the sponsorship of this meeting. For they represent the best qualities, I am told, of leadership and learning in this city—and leadership and learning are indispensable to each other. The advancement of learning depends on community leadership for financial and political support, and the products of that learning, in turn, are essential to the leadership's hopes for continued progress and prosperity. It is not a coincidence that those communities possessing the best in research and graduate facilities—from MIT to Cal Tech—tend to attract the new and growing industries. I congratulate those of you here in Dallas who have recognized these basic facts through the creation of the unique and forward-looking Graduate Research Center.

This link between leadership and learning is not only essential at the community level. It is even more indispensable in world affairs. Ignorance and misinformation can handicap the progress of a city or a company, but they can, if allowed to prevail in foreign policy, handicap this country's security. In a world of complex and continuing problems, in a world full of frustrations and irritations, America's leadership must be guided by the lights of learning and reason, or else those who confuse rhetoric with reality and the plausible with the possible will gain the popular ascendancy with their seemingly swift and simple solutions to every world problem.

There will always be dissident voices heard in the land, expressing opposition without alternatives, finding fault but never favor, perceiving gloom on every side, and seeking influence without responsibility. Those voices are inevitable.

But today other voices are heard in the land—voices preaching doctrines wholly unrelated to reality, wholly unsuited to the sixties, doctrines which apparently assume that words will suffice without weapons, that vituperation is as good as victory, and that peace is a sign of weakness. At a time when the national debt is steadily being reduced in terms of its burden on our economy, they see that debt as the greatest single threat to our security. At a time when we are steadily reducing the number of Federal employees serving every thousand citizens, they fear those supposed hordes of civil servants far more than the actual hordes of opposing armies.

We cannot expect that everyone, to use the phrase of a decade ago, will "talk sense to the American people." But we can hope that fewer people will listen to nonsense. And the notion that this Nation is headed for defeat through deficit, or that strength is but a matter of slogans, is nothing but just plain nonsense.

I want to discuss with you today the status of our strength and our security because this question clearly calls for the most responsible qualities of leadership and the most enlightened products of scholarship. For this Nation's strength and security are not easily or cheaply obtained, nor are they quickly and simply explained. There are many kinds of strength and no one kind will suffice. Overwhelming nuclear strength cannot stop a guerrilla war. Formal pacts of alliance cannot stop internal subversion. Displays of material wealth cannot stop the disillusionment of diplomats subjected to discrimination.

Above all, words alone are not enough. The United States is a peaceful nation. And where our strength and determination are clear, our words need merely to convey conviction, not belligerence. If we are strong, our strength will speak for itself. If we are weak, words will be of no help.

I realize that this Nation often tends to identify turning-points in world affairs with the major addresses which preceded them. But it was not the Monroe Doctrine that kept all Europe away from this hemisphere—it was the strength of the British fleet and the width of the Atlantic Ocean. It was not General Marshall's speech at Harvard which kept communism out of Western Europe—it was the strength and stability made possible by our military and economic assistance.

In this administration also it has been necessary at times to issue specific warnings—warnings that we could not stand by and watch the Communists conquer Laos by force, or intervene in the Congo, or swallow West Berlin, or maintain offensive missiles on Cuba. But while our goals were at least temporarily obtained in these and other instances, our successful defense of freedom was due not to the words we used, but to the strength we stood ready to use on behalf of the principles we stand ready to defend.

This strength is composed of many different elements, ranging from the most massive deterrents to the most subtle influences. And all types of strength are needed—no one kind could do the job alone. Let us take a moment, therefore, to review this Nation's progress in each major area of strength.

I. First, as Secretary McNamara made clear in his address last Monday, the strategic nuclear power of the United States has been so greatly modernized and expanded in the last 1,000 days, by the rapid production and deployment of the most modern missile systems, that any and all potential aggressors are clearly confronted now with the impossibility of strategic victory—and the certainty of total destruction—if by reckless attack they should ever force upon us the necessity of a strategic reply.

In less than 3 years, we have increased by 50 percent the number of Polaris submarines scheduled to be in force by the next fiscal year, increased by more than 70 percent our total Polaris purchase program, increased by more than 75 percent our Minuteman purchase program, increased by 50 percent the portion of our strategic bombers on 15-minute alert, and increased by 100 percent the total number of nuclear weapons available in our strategic alert forces. Our security is further enhanced by the steps we have taken regarding these weapons to improve the speed and certainty of their response, their readiness at all times to respond, their ability to survive an attack, and their ability to be carefully controlled and directed through secure command operations.

II. But the lessons of the last decade have taught us that freedom cannot be defended by strategic nuclear power alone. We have, therefore, in the last 3 years accelerated the development and deployment of tactical nuclear weapons, and increased by 60 percent the tactical nuclear forces deployed in Western Europe.

Nor can Europe or any other continent rely on nuclear forces alone, whether they are strategic or tactical. We have radically improved the readiness of our conventional forces—increased by 45 percent the number of combat ready Army divisions, increased by 100 percent the procurement of modern Army weapons and equipment, increased by 100 percent our ship construction, conversion, and modernization program, increased by 100 percent our procurement of tactical aircraft, increased by 30 percent the number of tactical air squadrons, and increased the strength of the Marines. As last month's "Operation Big Lift"— which originated here in Texas—showed so clearly, this Nation is prepared as never before to move substantial numbers of men in surprisingly little time to advanced positions anywhere in the world. We have increased by 175 percent the procurement of airlift aircraft, and we have already achieved a 75 percent increase in our existing strategic airlift capability. Finally, moving beyond the traditional roles of our military forces, we have achieved an increase of nearly 600 percent in our special forces—those forces that are prepared to work with our allies and friends against the guerrillas, saboteurs, insurgents, and assassins who threaten freedom in a less direct but equally dangerous manner.

III. But American military might should not and need not stand alone against the ambitions of international communism. Our security and strength, in the last analysis, directly depend on the security and strength of others, and that is why our military and economic assistance plays such a key role in enabling those who live on the periphery of the Communist world to maintain their independence of choice. Our assistance to these nations can be painful, risky, and costly, as is true in Southeast Asia today. But we dare not weary of the task. For our assistance makes possible the stationing of 3 to 5 million allied troops along the Communist frontier at one-tenth the cost of maintaining a comparable number of American soldiers. A successful Communist breakthrough in these areas, necessitating direct United States intervention, would cost us several times as much as our entire foreign aid program, and might cost us heavily in American lives as well.

About 70 percent of our military assistance goes to nine key countries located on or near the borders of the Communist bloc—nine countries confronted directly or indirectly with the threat of Communist aggression—Viet-Nam, Free China, Korea, India, Pakistan, Thailand, Greece, Turkey, and Iran. No one of these countries possesses on its own the resources to maintain the forces which our own Chiefs of Staff think needed in the common interest. Reducing our efforts to train, equip, and assist their armies can only encourage Communist penetration and require in time the increased overseas deployment of American combat forces. And reducing the economic help needed to bolster these nations that undertake to help defend freedom can have the same disastrous result. In short, the $50 billion we spend each year on our own defense could well be ineffective without the $4 billion required for military and economic assistance.

Our foreign aid program is not growing in size; it is, on the contrary, smaller now than in previous years. It has had its weaknesses, but we have undertaken to correct them. And the proper way of treating weaknesses is to replace them with strength, not to increase those weaknesses by emasculating essential programs. Dollar for dollar, in or out of government, there is no better form of investment in our national security than our much-abused foreign aid program. We cannot afford to lose it. We can afford to maintain it. We can surely afford, for example, to do as much for our 19 needy neighbors of Latin America as the Communist bloc is sending to the island of Cuba alone.

IV. I have spoken of strength largely in terms of the deterrence and resistance of aggression and attack. But, in today's world, freedom can be lost without a shot being fired, by ballots as well as bullets. The success of our leadership is dependent upon respect for our mission in the world as well as our missiles— on a clearer recognition of the virtues of freedom as well as the evils of tyranny.

That is why our Information Agency has doubled the shortwave broadcasting power of the Voice of America and increased the number of broadcasting hours by 30 percent, increased Spanish language broadcasting to Cuba and Latin America from 1 to 9 hours a day, increased seven-fold to more than 3 to 5 million copies the number of American books being translated and published for Latin American readers, and taken a host of other steps to carry our message of truth and freedom to all the far corners of the earth.

And that is also why we have regained the initiative in the exploration of outer space, making an annual effort greater than the combined total of all space activities undertaken during the fifties, launching more than 130 vehicles into earth orbit, putting into actual operation valuable weather and communications satellites, and making it clear to all that the United States of America has no intention of finishing second in space.

This effort is expensive—but it pays its own way, for freedom and for America. For there is no longer any fear in the free world that a Communist lead in space will become a permanent assertion of supremacy and the basis of military superiority. There is no longer any doubt about the strength and skill of American science, American industry, American education, and the American free enterprise system. In short, our national space effort represents a great gain in, and a great resource of, our national strength—and both Texas and Texans are contributing greatly to this strength.

Finally, it should be clear by now that a nation can be no stronger abroad than she is at home. Only an America which practices what it preaches about equal rights and social justice will be respected by those whose choice affects our future. Only an America which has fully educated its citizens is fully capable of tackling the complex problems and perceiving the hidden dangers of the world in which we live. And only an America which is growing and prospering economically can sustain the worldwide defenses of freedom, while demonstrating to all concerned the opportunities of our system and society.

It is clear, therefore, that we are strengthening our security as well as our economy by our recent record increases in national income and output—by surging ahead of most of Western Europe in the rate of business expansion and the margin of corporate profits, by maintaining a more stable level of prices than almost any of our overseas competitors, and by cutting personal and corporate income taxes by some $11 billion, as I have proposed, to assure this Nation of the longest and strongest expansion in our peacetime economic history.

This Nation's total output—which 3 years ago was at the $500 billion mark—will soon pass $600 billion, for a record rise of over $100 billion in 3 years. For the first time in history we have 70 million men and women at work. For the first time in history average factory earnings have exceeded $100 a week. For the first time in history corporation profits after taxes—which have risen 43 percent in less than 3 years—have an annual level of $27.4 billion.

My friends and fellow citizens: I cite these facts and figures to make it clear that America today is stronger than ever before. Our adversaries have not abandoned their ambitions, our dangers have not diminished, our vigilance cannot be relaxed. But now we have the military, the scientific, and the economic strength to do whatever must be done for the preservation and promotion of freedom.

That strength will never be used in pursuit of aggressive ambitions—it will always be used in pursuit of peace. It will never be used to promote provocations—it will always be used to promote the peaceful settlement of disputes.

We in this country, in this generation, are—by destiny rather than choice—the watchmen on the walls of world freedom. We ask, therefore, that we may be worthy of our power and responsibility, that we may exercise our strength with wisdom and restraint, and that we may achieve in our time and for all time the ancient vision of "peace on earth, good will toward men."[31] That must always be our goal, and the righteousness of our cause must always underlie our strength. For as was written long ago: "except the Lord keep the city, the watchman waketh but in vain."

GEORGE W. BUSH'S FIRST INAUGURAL ADDRESS[32]
January 20, 2001

President Clinton, distinguished guests and my fellow citizens, the peaceful transfer of authority is rare in history, yet common in our country. With a simple oath, we affirm old traditions and make new beginnings.

As I begin, I thank President Clinton for his service to our nation.

And I thank Vice President Gore for a contest conducted with spirit and ended with grace.

I am honored and humbled to stand here, where so many of America's leaders have come before me, and so many will follow.

We have a place, all of us, in a long story—a story we continue, but whose end we will not see. It is the story of a new world that became a friend and liberator of the old, a story of a slave-holding society that became a servant of freedom, the story of a power that went into the world to protect but not possess, to defend but not to conquer.

It is the American story—a story of flawed and fallible people, united across the generations by grand and enduring ideals.

The grandest of these ideals is an unfolding American promise that everyone belongs, that everyone deserves a chance, that no insignificant person was ever born.

Americans are called to enact this promise in our lives and in our laws. And though our nation has sometimes halted, and sometimes delayed, we must follow no other course.

Through much of the last century, America's faith in freedom and democracy was a rock in a raging sea. Now it is a seed upon the wind, taking root in many nations.

Our democratic faith is more than the creed of our country, it is the inborn hope of our humanity, an ideal we carry but do not own, a trust we bear and pass along. And even after nearly 225 years, we have a long way yet to travel.

While many of our citizens prosper, others doubt the promise, even the justice, of our own country. The ambitions of some Americans are limited by failing schools and hidden prejudice and the circumstances of their birth. And sometimes our differences run so deep, it seems we share a continent, but not a country.

We do not accept this, and we will not allow it. Our unity, our union, is the serious work of leaders and citizens in every generation. And this is my solemn pledge: I will work to build a single nation of justice and opportunity.

I know this is in our reach, because we are guided by a power larger than ourselves who creates us equal in His image.

And we are confident in principles that unite and lead us onward.

America has never been united by blood or birth or soil. We are bound by ideals that move us beyond our backgrounds, lift us above our interests and teach us what it means to be citizens. Every child must be taught these principles. Every citizen must uphold them. And every immigrant, by embracing these ideals, makes our country more, not less, American.

Today, we affirm a new commitment to live out our nation's promise through civility, courage, compassion and character.

America, at its best, matches a commitment to principle with a concern for civility. A civil society demands from each of us good will and respect, fair dealing and forgiveness.

Some seem to believe that our politics can afford to be petty because, in a time of peace, the stakes of our debates appear small.

But the stakes for America are never small. If our country does not lead the cause of freedom, it will not be led. If we do not turn the hearts of children toward knowledge and character, we will lose their gifts and undermine their idealism. If we permit our economy to drift and decline, the vulnerable will suffer most.

We must live up to the calling we share. Civility is not a tactic or a sentiment. It is the determined choice of trust over cynicism, of community over chaos. And this commitment, if we keep it, is a way to shared accomplishment.

America, at its best, is also courageous.

Our national courage has been clear in times of depression and war, when defending common dangers defined our common good. Now we must choose if the example of our fathers and mothers will inspire us or condemn us. We must show courage in a time of blessing by confronting problems instead of passing them on to future generations.

Together, we will reclaim America's schools, before ignorance and apathy claim more young lives.

We will reform Social Security and Medicare, sparing our children from struggles we have the power to prevent. And we will reduce taxes, to recover the momentum of our economy and reward the effort and enterprise of working Americans.

We will build our defenses beyond challenge, lest weakness invite challenge.

We will confront weapons of mass destruction, so that a new century is spared new horrors.

The enemies of liberty and our country should make no mistake: America remains engaged in the world by history and by choice, shaping a balance of power that favors freedom. We will defend our allies and our interests. We will show purpose without arrogance. We will meet aggression and bad faith with resolve and strength. And to all nations, we will speak for the values that gave our nation birth.

America, at its best, is compassionate. In the quiet of American conscience, we know that deep, persistent poverty is unworthy of our nation's promise.

And whatever our views of its cause, we can agree that children at risk are not at fault. Abandonment and abuse are not acts of God, they are failures of love.

And the proliferation of prisons, however necessary, is no substitute for hope and order in our souls.

Where there is suffering, there is duty. Americans in need are not strangers, they are citizens, not problems, but priorities. And all of us are diminished when any are hopeless.

Government has great responsibilities for public safety and public health, for civil rights and common schools. Yet compassion is the work of a nation, not just a government.

And some needs and hurts are so deep they will only respond to a mentor's touch or a pastor's prayer. Church and charity, synagogue and mosque lend our communities their humanity, and they will have an honored place in our plans and in our laws.

Many in our country do not know the pain of poverty, but we can listen to those who do.

And I can pledge our nation to a goal: When we see that wounded traveler on the road to Jericho, we will not pass to the other side.

America, at its best, is a place where personal responsibility is valued and expected.

Encouraging responsibility is not a search for scapegoats, it is a call to conscience. And though it requires sacrifice, it brings a deeper fulfillment. We find the fullness of life not only in options, but in commitments. And we find that children and community are the commitments that set us free.

Our public interest depends on private character, on civic duty and family bonds and basic fairness, on uncounted, unhonored acts of decency which give direction to our freedom.

Sometimes in life we are called to do great things. But as a saint of our times has said, every day we are called to do small things with great love. The most important tasks of a democracy are done by everyone.

I will live and lead by these principles: to advance my convictions with civility, to pursue the public interest with courage, to speak for greater justice and compassion, to call for responsibility and try to live it as well.

In all these ways, I will bring the values of our history to the care of our times.

What you do is as important as anything government does. I ask you to seek a common good beyond your comfort; to defend needed reforms against easy attacks; to serve your nation, beginning with your neighbor. I ask you to be citizens: citizens, not spectators; citizens, not subjects; responsible citizens, building communities of service and a nation of character.

Americans are generous and strong and decent, not because we believe in ourselves, but because we hold beliefs beyond ourselves. When this spirit of citizenship is missing, no government program can replace it. When this spirit is present, no wrong can stand against it.

After the Declaration of Independence was signed, Virginia statesman John Page wrote to Thomas Jefferson: "We know the race is not to the swift nor the battle to the strong. Do you not think an angel rides in the whirlwind and directs this storm?"

Much time has passed since Jefferson arrived for his inauguration. The years and changes accumulate. But the themes of this day he would know: our nation's grand story of courage and its simple dream of dignity.

We are not this story's author, who fills time and eternity with his purpose. Yet his purpose is achieved in our duty, and our duty is fulfilled in service to one another.

Never tiring, never yielding, never finishing, we renew that purpose today, to make our country more just and generous, to affirm the dignity of our lives and every life.

This work continues. This story goes on. And an angel still rides in the whirlwind and directs this storm.

God bless you all, and God bless America.

GEORGE W. BUSH'S SECOND INAUGURAL ADDRESS[33]
January 20, 2005

Vice President Cheney, Mr. Chief Justice, President Carter, President Bush, President Clinton, reverend clergy, distinguished guests, fellow citizens:

On this day, prescribed by law and marked by ceremony, we celebrate the durable wisdom of our Constitution, and recall the deep commitments that unite our country. I am grateful for the honor of this hour, mindful of the consequential times in which we live, and determined to fulfill the oath that I have sworn and you have witnessed.

At this second gathering, our duties are defined not by the words I use, but by the history we have seen together. For a half century, America defended our own freedom by standing watch on distant borders. After the shipwreck of communism came years of relative quiet, years of repose, years of sabbatical—and then there came a day of fire.

We have seen our vulnerability—and we have seen its deepest source. For as long as whole regions of the world simmer in resentment and tyranny—prone to ideologies that feed hatred and excuse murder—violence will gather, and multiply in destructive power, and cross the most defended borders, and raise a mortal threat. There is only one force of history that can break the reign of hatred and resentment, and expose the pretensions of tyrants, and reward the hopes of the decent and tolerant, and that is the force of human freedom.

We are led, by events and common sense, to one conclusion: The survival of liberty in our land increasingly depends on the success of liberty in other lands. The best hope for peace in our world is the expansion of freedom in all the world.

America's vital interests and our deepest beliefs are now one. From the day of our Founding, we have proclaimed that every man and woman on this earth has rights, and dignity, and matchless value, because they bear the image of the Maker of Heaven and earth. Across the generations we have proclaimed the imperative of self-government, because no one is fit to be a master, and no one deserves to be a slave. Advancing these ideals is the mission that created our Nation. It is the honorable achievement of our fathers. Now it is the urgent requirement of our nation's security, and the calling of our time.

Appendix D

So it is the policy of the United States to seek and support the growth of democratic movements and institutions in every nation and culture, with the ultimate goal of ending tyranny in our world.

This is not primarily the task of arms, though we will defend ourselves and our friends by force of arms when necessary. Freedom, by its nature, must be chosen, and defended by citizens, and sustained by the rule of law and the protection of minorities. And when the soul of a nation finally speaks, the institutions that arise may reflect customs and traditions very different from our own. America will not impose our own style of government on the unwilling. Our goal instead is to help others find their own voice, attain their own freedom, and make their own way.

The great objective of ending tyranny is the concentrated work of generations. The difficulty of the task is no excuse for avoiding it. America's influence is not unlimited, but fortunately for the oppressed, America's influence is considerable, and we will use it confidently in freedom's cause.

My most solemn duty is to protect this nation and its people against further attacks and emerging threats. Some have unwisely chosen to test America's resolve, and have found it firm.

We will persistently clarify the choice before every ruler and every nation: The moral choice between oppression, which is always wrong, and freedom, which is eternally right. America will not pretend that jailed dissidents prefer their chains, or that women welcome humiliation and servitude, or that any human being aspires to live at the mercy of bullies.

We will encourage reform in other governments by making clear that success in our relations will require the decent treatment of their own people. America's belief in human dignity will guide our policies, yet rights must be more than the grudging concessions of dictators; they are secured by free dissent and the participation of the governed. In the long run, there is no justice without freedom, and there can be no human rights without human liberty.

Some, I know, have questioned the global appeal of liberty—though this time in history, four decades defined by the swiftest advance of freedom ever seen, is an odd time for doubt. Americans, of all people, should never be surprised by the power of our ideals. Eventually, the call of freedom comes to every mind and every soul. We do not accept the existence of permanent tyranny because we do not accept the possibility of permanent slavery. Liberty will come to those who love it.

Today, America speaks anew to the peoples of the world:

All who live in tyranny and hopelessness can know: The United States will not ignore your oppression, or excuse your oppressors. When you stand for your liberty, we will stand with you.

Democratic reformers facing repression, prison, or exile can know: America sees you for who you are: the future leaders of your free country.

The rulers of outlaw regimes can know that we still believe as Abraham Lincoln did: "Those who deny freedom to others deserve it not for themselves; and, under the rule of a just God, cannot long retain it."

The leaders of governments with long habits of control need to know: To serve your people you must learn to trust them. Start on this journey of progress and justice, and America will walk at your side.

And all the allies of the United States can know: We honor your friendship, we rely on your counsel, and we depend on your help. Division among free nations is a primary goal of freedom's enemies. The concerted effort of free nations to promote democracy is a prelude to our enemies' defeat.

Today, I also speak anew to my fellow citizens:

From all of you, I have asked patience in the hard task of securing America, which you have granted in good measure. Our country has accepted obligations that are difficult to fulfill, and would be dishonorable to abandon. Yet because we have acted in the great liberating tradition of this nation, tens of millions have achieved their freedom. And as hope kindles hope, millions more will find it. By our efforts, we have lit a fire as well—a fire in the minds of men. It warms those who feel its power, it burns those who fight its progress, and one day this untamed fire of freedom will reach the darkest corners of our world.

A few Americans have accepted the hardest duties in this cause - in the quiet work of intelligence and diplomacy . . . the idealistic work of helping raise up free governments . . . the dangerous and necessary work of fighting our enemies. Some have shown their devotion to our country in deaths that honored their whole lives—and we will always honor their names and their sacrifice.

All Americans have witnessed this idealism, and some for the first time. I ask our youngest citizens to believe the evidence of your eyes. You have seen duty and allegiance in the determined faces of our soldiers. You have seen that life is fragile, and evil is real, and courage triumphs. Make the choice to serve in a cause larger than your wants, larger than yourself—and in your days you will add not just to the wealth of our country, but to its character.

America has need of idealism and courage, because we have essential work at home—the unfinished work of American freedom. In a world moving toward liberty, we are determined to show the meaning and promise of liberty.

In America's ideal of freedom, citizens find the dignity and security of economic independence, instead of laboring on the edge of subsistence. This is the broader definition of liberty that motivated the Homestead Act, the Social Security Act, and the G.I. Bill of Rights. And now we will extend this vision by reforming great institutions to serve the needs of our time. To give every American a stake in the promise and future of our country, we will bring the highest standards to our schools, and build an ownership society. We will widen the ownership of homes and businesses, retirement savings and health insurance—preparing our people for the challenges of life in a free society. By making every citizen an agent of his or her own destiny, we will give our fellow Americans greater freedom from want and fear, and make our society more prosperous and just and equal.

In America's ideal of freedom, the public interest depends on private character —on integrity, and tolerance toward others, and the rule of conscience in our own lives. Self-government relies, in the end, on the governing of the self. That edifice of character is built in families, supported by communities with standards, and sustained in our national life by the truths of Sinai, the Sermon on the Mount, the words of the Koran, and the varied faiths of our people. Americans move forward in every generation by reaffirming all that is good and true that came before —ideals of justice and conduct that are the same yesterday, today, and forever.

In America's ideal of freedom, the exercise of rights is ennobled by service, and mercy, and a heart for the weak. Liberty for all does not mean independence from one another. Our nation relies on men and women who look after a neighbor and surround the lost with love. Americans, at our best, value the life we see in one another, and must always remember that even the unwanted have worth. And our country must abandon all the habits of racism, because we cannot carry the message of freedom and the baggage of bigotry at the same time.

From the perspective of a single day, including this day of dedication, the issues and questions before our country are many. From the viewpoint of centuries, the questions that come to us are narrowed and few. Did our generation advance the cause of freedom? And did our character bring credit to that cause?

These questions that judge us also unite us, because Americans of every party and background, Americans by choice and by birth, are bound to one another in the cause of freedom. We have known divisions, which must be healed to move forward in great purposes—and I will strive in good faith to heal them. Yet those divisions do not define America. We felt the unity and fellowship of our nation when freedom came under attack, and our response came like a single hand over a single heart. And we can feel that same unity and pride whenever America acts for good, and the victims of disaster are given hope, and the unjust encounter justice, and the captives are set free.

We go forward with complete confidence in the eventual triumph of freedom. Not because history runs on the wheels of inevitability; it is human choices that move events. Not because we consider ourselves a chosen nation; God moves and chooses as He wills. We have confidence because freedom is the permanent hope of mankind, the hunger in dark places, the longing of the soul. When our Founders declared a new order of the ages; when soldiers died in wave upon wave for a union based on liberty; when citizens marched in peaceful outrage under the banner "Freedom Now"—they were acting on an ancient hope that is meant to be fulfilled. History has an ebb and flow of justice, but history also has a visible direction, set by liberty and the Author of Liberty.

When the Declaration of Independence was first read in public and the Liberty Bell was sounded in celebration, a witness said, "It rang as if it meant something." In our time it means something still. America, in this young century, proclaims liberty throughout all the world, and to all the inhabitants thereof. Renewed in our strength—tested, but not weary—we are ready for the greatest achievements in the history of freedom.

May God bless you, and may He watch over the United States of America.

★ Appendix E ★

The Universal Declaration of Human Rights[34]

Adopted and proclaimed by General Assembly resolution 217 A (III) of 10 December 1948.

On December 10, 1948 the General Assembly of the United Nations adopted and proclaimed the Universal Declaration of Human Rights the full text of which appears in the following pages. Following this historic act the Assembly called upon all Member countries to publicize the text of the Declaration and "to cause it to be disseminated, displayed, read and expounded principally in schools and other educational institutions, without distinction based on the political status of countries or territories."

Preamble

Whereas recognition of the inherent dignity and of the equal and inalienable rights of all members of the human family is the foundation of freedom, justice and peace in the world,

Whereas disregard and contempt for human rights have resulted in barbarous acts which have outraged the conscience of mankind, and the advent of a world in which human beings shall enjoy freedom of speech and belief and freedom from fear and want has been proclaimed as the highest aspiration of the common people,

Whereas it is essential, if man is not to be compelled to have recourse, as a last resort, to rebellion against tyranny and oppression, that human rights should be protected by the rule of law,

Whereas it is essential to promote the development of friendly relations between nations,

Whereas the peoples of the United Nations have in the Charter reaffirmed their faith in fundamental human rights, in the dignity and worth of the human person and in the equal rights of men and women and have determined to promote social progress and better standards of life in larger freedom,

Whereas Member States have pledged themselves to achieve, in co-operation with the United Nations, the promotion of universal respect for and observance of human rights and fundamental freedoms,

Whereas a common understanding of these rights and freedoms is of the greatest importance for the full realization of this pledge,

Now, Therefore THE GENERAL ASSEMBLY proclaims THIS UNIVERSAL DECLARATION OF HUMAN RIGHTS as a common standard of achievement for all peoples and all nations, to the end that every individual and every organ of society, keeping this Declaration constantly in mind, shall strive by teaching and education to promote respect for these rights and freedoms and by progressive measures, national and international, to secure their universal and effective recognition and observance, both among the peoples of Member States themselves and among the peoples of territories under their jurisdiction.

Article 1.

All human beings are born free and equal in dignity and rights. They are endowed with reason and conscience and should act towards one another in a spirit of brotherhood.

Article 2.

Everyone is entitled to all the rights and freedoms set forth in this Declaration, without distinction of any kind, such as race, colour, sex, language, religion, political or other opinion, national or social origin, property, birth or other status. Furthermore, no distinction shall be made on the basis of the political, jurisdictional or international status of the country or territory to which a person belongs, whether it be independent, trust, non-self-governing or under any other limitation of sovereignty.

Article 3.
Everyone has the right to life, liberty and security of person.

Article 4.
No one shall be held in slavery or servitude; slavery and the slave trade shall be prohibited in all their forms.

Article 5.
No one shall be subjected to torture or to cruel, inhuman or degrading treatment or punishment.

Article 6.
Everyone has the right to recognition everywhere as a person before the law.

Article 7.
All are equal before the law and are entitled without any discrimination to equal protection of the law. All are entitled to equal protection against any discrimination in violation of this Declaration and against any incitement to such discrimination.

Article 8.
Everyone has the right to an effective remedy by the competent national tribunals for acts violating the fundamental rights granted him by the constitution or by law.

Article 9.
No one shall be subjected to arbitrary arrest, detention or exile.

Article 10.
Everyone is entitled in full equality to a fair and public hearing by an independent and impartial tribunal, in the determination of his rights and obligations and of any criminal charge against him.

Article 11.

(1) Everyone charged with a penal offence has the right to be presumed innocent until proved guilty according to law in a public trial at which he has had all the guarantees necessary for his defence.

(2) No one shall be held guilty of any penal offence on account of any act or omission which did not constitute a penal offence, under national or international law, at the time when it was committed. Nor shall a heavier penalty be imposed than the one that was applicable at the time the penal offence was committed.

Article 12.

No one shall be subjected to arbitrary interference with his privacy, family, home or correspondence, nor to attacks upon his honour and reputation. Everyone has the right to the protection of the law against such interference or attacks.

Article 13.

(1) Everyone has the right to freedom of movement and residence within the borders of each state.

(2) Everyone has the right to leave any country, including his own, and to return to his country.

Article 14.

(1) Everyone has the right to seek and to enjoy in other countries asylum from persecution.

(2) This right may not be invoked in the case of prosecutions genuinely arising from non-political crimes or from acts contrary to the purposes and principles of the United Nations.

Article 15.

(1) Everyone has the right to a nationality.

(2) No one shall be arbitrarily deprived of his nationality nor denied the right to change his nationality.

Article 16.

(1) Men and women of full age, without any limitation due to race, nationality or religion, have the right to marry and to found a family. They are entitled to equal rights as to marriage, during marriage and at its dissolution.

(2) Marriage shall be entered into only with the free and full consent of the intending spouses.

(3) The family is the natural and fundamental group unit of society and is entitled to protection by society and the State.

Article 17.

(1) Everyone has the right to own property alone as well as in association with others.

(2) No one shall be arbitrarily deprived of his property.

Article 18.

Everyone has the right to freedom of thought, conscience and religion; this right includes freedom to change his religion or belief, and freedom, either alone or in community with others and in public or private, to manifest his religion or belief in teaching, practice, worship and observance.

Article 19.

Everyone has the right to freedom of opinion and expression; this right includes freedom to hold opinions without interference and to seek, receive and impart information and ideas through any media and regardless of frontiers.

Article 20.

(1) Everyone has the right to freedom of peaceful assembly and association.

(2) No one may be compelled to belong to an association.

Article 21.

(1) Everyone has the right to take part in the government of his country, directly or through freely chosen representatives.

(2) Everyone has the right of equal access to public service in his country.

(3) The will of the people shall be the basis of the authority of government; this will shall be expressed in periodic and genuine elections which shall be by universal and equal suffrage and shall be held by secret vote or by equivalent free voting procedures.

Article 22.

Everyone, as a member of society, has the right to social security and is entitled to realization, through national effort and international co-operation and in accordance with the organization and resources of each State, of the economic, social and cultural rights indispensable for his dignity and the free development of his personality.

Article 23.

(1) Everyone has the right to work, to free choice of employment, to just and favourable conditions of work and to protection against unemployment.
(2) Everyone, without any discrimination, has the right to equal pay for equal work.
(3) Everyone who works has the right to just and favourable remuneration ensuring for himself and his family an existence worthy of human dignity, and supplemented, if necessary, by other means of social protection.
(4) Everyone has the right to form and to join trade unions for the protection of his interests.

Article 24.

Everyone has the right to rest and leisure, including reasonable limitation of working hours and periodic holidays with pay.

Article 25.

(1) Everyone has the right to a standard of living adequate for the health and well-being of himself and of his family, including food, clothing, housing and medical care and necessary social services, and the right to security in the event of unemployment, sickness, disability, widowhood, old age or other lack of livelihood in circumstances beyond his control.
(2) Motherhood and childhood are entitled to special care and assistance. All

children, whether born in or out of wedlock, shall enjoy the same social protection.

Article 26.

(1) Everyone has the right to education. Education shall be free, at least in the elementary and fundamental stages. Elementary education shall be compulsory. Technical and professional education shall be made generally available and higher education shall be equally accessible to all on the basis of merit.

(2) Education shall be directed to the full development of the human personality and to the strengthening of respect for human rights and fundamental freedoms. It shall promote understanding, tolerance and friendship among all nations, racial or religious groups, and shall further the activities of the United Nations for the maintenance of peace.

(3) Parents have a prior right to choose the kind of education that shall be given to their children.

Article 27.

(1) Everyone has the right freely to participate in the cultural life of the community, to enjoy the arts and to share in scientific advancement and its benefits.

(2) Everyone has the right to the protection of the moral and material interests resulting from any scientific, literary or artistic production of which he is the author.

Article 28.

Everyone is entitled to a social and international order in which the rights and freedoms set forth in this Declaration can be fully realized.

Article 29.

(1) Everyone has duties to the community in which alone the free and full development of his personality is possible.

(2) In the exercise of his rights and freedoms, everyone shall be subject only to such limitations as are determined by law solely for the purpose of securing due recognition and respect for the rights and freedoms of others and of

meeting the just requirements of morality, public order and the general welfare in a democratic society.

(3) These rights and freedoms may in no case be exercised contrary to the purposes and principles of the United Nations.

Article 30.

Nothing in this Declaration may be interpreted as implying for any State, group or person any right to engage in any activity or to perform any act aimed at the destruction of any of the rights and freedoms set forth herein.

★ Appendix F ★

Avoidance, Accommodation, and Acknowledgment: Comparison and Contrast

Religious Liberty—God alone is Lord of the conscience, and He has left it free from the doctrines and commandments of men which are contrary to His Word or not contained in it. Church and state should be separate. The state owes to every church protection and full freedom in the pursuit of its spiritual ends. In providing for such freedom, no ecclesiastical group or denomination should be favored by the state more than others. Civil government being ordained of God, it is the duty of Christians to render loyal obedience thereto in all things not contrary to the revealed will of God. The church should not resort to the civil power to carry on its work. The gospel of Christ contemplates spiritual means alone for the pursuit of its ends. The state has no right to impose penalties for religious opinions of any kind. The state has no right to impose taxes for the support of any form of religion. A free church in a free state is the Christian ideal, and this implies the right of free and unhindered access to God on the part of all men, and the right to form and propagate opinions in the sphere of religion without interference by the civil power.

Relevant Scripture passages: Genesis 1:27; 2:7; Matthew 6:6–7, 24; 16:26; 22:21; John 8:36; Acts 4:19–20; Romans 6:1–2; 13:1–7; Galatians 5:1, 13; Philippians 3:20; 1 Timothy 2:1–2; James 4:12; 1 Peter 2:12–17; 3:11–17; 4:12–19.[35]

Position	Separationist "Avoidance" Position	Accommodationists' "Accommodation" Position	Neo-establishment "Acknowledgment" Position
Definition	Seeks "avoidance" of religious expression in government locales (courts, schools, etc.)	Seeks government "accommodation" of individuals' rights to express religious beliefs in government locales	Seeks government "acknowledgment" for, and on behalf of, "the people" at government expense
Applied to religious expression	Would ban the wearing of Muslim headscarves, yarmulkes, or any other religious symbols by students or staff in public schools or employees in the workplace; would bar religious displays in such locales	Would accommodate but not require the wearing of any religious symbols in schools or in the workplace, according to the dictates of each person's conscience; would also accommodate religious displays initiated by students in schools and by employees in the workplace	Would give preference to symbols of the majority religion and would allow government-sponsored religious displays of the majority faith in schools and employer-sponsored displays of the majority faith in the workplace
Applied to public prayer at public school events	Opposes government-accommodated or -acknowledged prayer in public schools, even by students	Would seek government accommodation of each student-initiated, student-led, and student-content-dictated prayer according to the dictates of individual conscience in public schools, protecting both religious majority and religious minority students' right to pray as they so choose	Seeks government acknowledgment of student-initiated, student-led prayer in public schools, which could allow religious majority students to determine prayer and exclude religious minority students from participation
Applied to public displays of religious monuments or symbols	Opposes manger scenes or religious displays (e.g., the Ten Commandments) in government locales, such as courthouse lawns	Allows manger scenes or religious displays (e.g., the Ten Commandments) in government locales, such as courthouse lawns, as long as they are privately funded and no community religious group is excluded from displaying its symbols as well	Allows tax-funded religious displays in government locales determined by the majority either nationally or locally, county by county

★ Notes ★

Chapter 1: What's God Got to Do with America?

1. Sam Harris, *The End of Faith: Religion, Terror, and the Future of Reason* (New York: W. W. Norton, 2005), 48.
2. Chuck Baldwin, "No God, No Guns, No Guts," December 17, 2002, http://www. chuckbaldwinlive.com/bush17Dec02.html.
3. Clint Willis, ed., *The I Hate Ann Coulter, Bill O'Reilly, Rush Limbaugh, Michael Savage, Sean Hannity . . . Reader: The Hideous Truth about America's Ugliest Conservatives* (New York: Thunder's Mouth/Avalon Press, 2004), back cover copy.
4. Steve Farkas, Jean Johnson, and Tony Foleno with Ann Duffett and Patrick Foley, *For Goodness' Sake: Why So Many Want Religion to Play a Greater Role in American Life* (New York: Public Agenda, 2001), 40, http://www.publicagenda.org/research/research_ reports_details.cfm?list=25.
5. Jim Wallis, "Compassion, Not Politics, for Refugees," *Sojourners* 8, no. 9 (September 1979): 5.
6. E. J. Dionne Jr., "Why the Culture War Is the Wrong War," *The Atlantic* 297, no. 1 (January–February 2006): 132.
7. See Steven Waldman and John C. Green, "Tribal Relations," *The Atlantic* 297, no. 1 (January–February 2006): 136.
8. Baldwin, "No God, No Guns, No Guts."
9. Harris, *End of Faith*, 221.
10. Ibid., 15.
11. Ibid., 225.
12. Natalie Angier, "'The End of Faith': Against Toleration," *New York Times Sunday Book Review*, September 5, 2004, http://www.nytimes.com/2004/09/05/books/review/ 05ANGIERL.html?ex=1146024000&en=9e6d7089919ef8a4&ei=5070.
13. Farkas et al., *For Goodness' Sake*, 43.
14. See also chapter 5, "All the Presidents' Faith," p. 92.

Chapter 2: What Liberals Are Missing

1. John F. Kennedy, commencement address, Yale University, New Haven, CT, June 11, 1962, http://www.jfklibrary.org/Historical+Resources/Archives/ Reference+Desk/Speeches/JFK/003POF03Yale06111962.htm.
2. The "Religious Right" and the "Religious Left" are both phrases that have taken on such pejorative baggage through negative stereotyping in the God-and-country shouting match that their legitimate usage to describe those of religious faith on the "liberal" and "conservative" side of social public policy issues such as abortion, homosexual marriage, war and peace, environmental issues, wealth distribution, etc., has now been severely marginalized. Please note that while I find the usage of these phrases necessary to describe the two groups and their differences, this should in no way be taken to imply acceptance of the pejorative attacks and negative epithets far too often associated with them.
3. Sam Harris, *The End of Faith: Religion, Terror, and the Future of Reason* (New York: W. W. Norton, 2005), 14.

4. Ibid., 14.
5. Jim Wallis, *God's Politics: Why the Right Gets It Wrong and the Left Doesn't Get It* (San Francisco: HarperSanFrancisco, 2005), 3.
6. Jimmy Carter, *Our Endangered Values: America's Moral Crisis* (New York: Simon & Schuster, 2005), 3.
7. Jimmy Carter, "Just War—or a Just War?" *New York Times*, March 9, 2003, sec. 4, p. 13.
8. Peter Slevin, "'St. Jack' and the Bullies in the Pulpit; John Danforth Says It's Time the GOP Center Took On the Christian Right," *Washington Post*, February 2, 2006, C01.
9. Ruth Bader Ginsburg, "Speaking in a Judicial Voice," 67 New York University Law Review, 11185 (1992).
10. Jim Wallis, *Who Speaks for God? An Alternative to the Religious Right—a New Politics of Compassion, Community, and Civility* (New York: Delacorte/Bantam Doubleday Dell, 1996).
11. Abraham Lincoln, "Second Inaugural Address," March 4, 1865, in *The Collected Works of Abraham Lincoln*, ed. Roy S. Basler, vol. 8 (New Brunswick, NJ: Rutgers University Press, 1953), 332–33.
12. "Republican Budget Meets Greed of Special Interests Instead of Needs of the American People," *U.S. Newswire*, December 19, 2005, http://releases.usnewswire.com/Get Release.asp?id=58369.
13. Paul Kengor, *God and George W. Bush: A Spiritual Life* (New York: HarperCollins/ReganBooks, 2004), 183–84.
14. Chautauqua Institution, Chautauqua, NY, July 3–9, 2005, "Faith and Politics" Week.
15. See Deuteronomy 6.
16. Madeleine Albright, *The Mighty and the Almighty: Reflections on America, God, and World Affairs* (New York: HarperCollins, 2006), 32.
17. Ibid.
18. Ibid.
19. The editors, "The Great Debate of Our Season," *Mother Jones* (December–January 2006), http://www.motherjones.com/news/feature/2005/12/great_debate.html.
20. John Adams, "Address to the Military," October 11, 1798.
21. Kennedy, commencement address.
22. Richard John Neuhaus, *The Naked Public Square* (Grand Rapids: Eerdmans, 1986).

Chapter 3: What Conservatives Are Missing

1. John Weaver, "The Truth about the Confederate Flag," posted online at radio host Chuck Baldwin's Web site, http://www.chuckbaldwinlive.com/ rebel_flag.html. Weaver's biographical information states that he is a graduate of Bob Jones University and a preacher of "God's whole Word."
2. See Luke 20:20–26.
3. Weaver, "Truth about the Confederate Flag."
4. Ibid.
5. Eugene D. Genovese, *The Southern Front* (Columbia, MO: University of Missouri Press, 1995).
6. For history on Roger Williams and Native Americans, see Edwin S. Gaustad, *Roger Williams* (New York: Oxford University Press, 2005).
7. For a discussion of Roger Williams's metaphor of the garden and the wilderness, see Stephen L. Carter, *God's Name in Vain: The Wrongs and Rights of Religion in Politics* (New York: Basic Books, 2000), 75–79.
8. Francis Schaeffer, *The Church at the End of the Twentieth Century*, in *The Complete Works of Francis A. Schaeffer: A Christian Worldview* (West Chester, IL.: Crossway Books, 1982), 4:71.
9. Gregory S. Paul, "The Great Scandal: Christianity's Role in the Rise of the Nazis," *Free Inquiry Magazine* 23 no. 4, http://www.secularhumanism.org/index.php?section= library&page=paul_23_4.

Notes

10. Much of the material in the following section of this chapter is adapted from the film *Theologians under Hitler*, produced and directed by Steven D. Martin, copyright 2005 by Vital Visuals, Inc. See also *A Question of Power*, ed. Steven D. Martin (Oak Ridge, TN: Vital Visions, Inc., 2006, www.vitalvisions.org), a study guide accompanying the film *Theologians under Hitler*.
11. Martin, *Theologians under Hitler*; and also Ericksen, *Theologians under Hitler: Gerhard Kittel, Paul Althaus and Immanuel Hirsch* (Yale: Yale University Press, 1987), 5–14.
12. Ibid.
13. Martin, *Theologians under Hitler*.
14. Ibid.
15. Ibid.
16. Ibid.
17. Ibid.
18. Ibid.
19. Ibid.
20. Ibid.
21. David P. Gushee, "When Christians Don't Make a Difference," in *Christians in the Public Square: Faith in Practice?* ed. Richard D. Land and Lee Holloway (Nashville: ERLC Publications, 1996), 63.
22. Ericksen, *Theologians under Hitler*, 199.
23. The Nazis never received a majority of the votes in a fair German election. Their peak popularity was about 37 percent of votes cast, and within just a few months of gaining power, any true democracy was stamped out by the emerging Nazi police state.
24. Ericksen, *Theologians under Hitler*, 85.
25. Ibid.
26. Martin, *Theologians under Hitler*.
27. Ibid.
28. Ibid.
29. Ibid.
30. Ibid. It should be noted that after November 8, 1938, *Kristallnacht*, "the Night of Broken Glass," in which hundreds of synagogues and Jewish businesses were burned and more than one hundred people were killed, Althaus never spoke favorably of the Nazis again.
31. Ibid.
32. Ericksen, *Theologians under Hitler*, 123.
33. Ibid., 137.
34. Ericksen, *Theologians under Hitler*, 166.
35. Ibid., 144.
36. Ibid.
37. Ibid., 145.
38. Martin, *Theologians under Hitler*.
39. Ibid.
40. Quotations from the Barmen Declaration are from Arthur C. Cochrane, *The Church's Confession under Hitler* (Philadelphia: Westminster Press, 1962), 237–42. For the full text of the Barmen Declaration, see appendix B.
41. Martin, *Theologians under Hitler*.
42. Statement from D. James Kennedy on Pledge of Allegiance ruling, June 26, 2002, http://www.coralridge.org/PledgeofAllegiance.htm.
43. Carter, *God's Name in Vain*, 3.
44. The Clinton Global Initiative, September 15–17, 2005, New York City.

Chapter 4: Where Has God Been in America?

1. Joseph Lieberman, from an interview on NBC News' *Meet the Press*, Tim Russert, host, titled "Faith in America with Reza Aslan, Rev. Robert Drinan, Dr. Richard Land, Sen.

Joseph Lieberman, Jon Meacham and Rev. Jim Wallis," March 20, 2005, http://www.msnbc.msn.com/id/7284978/from/ET/.

2. C. S. Lewis, "On the Reading of Old Books," in *God in the Dock: Essays on Theology and Ethics* (Grand Rapids: Eerdmans, 1970), 202.

3. C. S. Lewis, "Learning in War-Time," in *The Weight of Glory and Other Essays* (New York: Macmillan, 1980), 28–29.

4. For reading on the history of the Puritan settlements, see Alden T. Vaughan, ed., *The Puritan Tradition in America, 1620–1730* (Lebanon, NH: University Press of New England, 1997).

5. The preamble to the Declaration of Independence of the Thirteen Colonies in Congress, July 4, 1776.

6. Lieberman, "Faith in America."

7. Ibid.

8. Alexis de Tocqueville, *Democracy in America*, vol. 1, chap. 17, sec. 5, "Indirect Influences of Religious Opinions upon Political Society," n.p., http://xroads. virginia.edu/~HYPER/DETOC/1_ch17.htm.

9. Robert Bellah, "Religion and the Legitimation of the American Republic," *Society* 15, no. 4 (1978): 16–23; reprinted in Robert Neelly Bellah, *The Broken Covenant: American Civil Religion in Time of Trial*, 2nd ed. (Chicago: University of Chicago Press, 1992), 164.

10. Mark A. Noll, George M. Marsden, and Nathan O. Hatch, *The Search for Christian America*, expanded ed. (Colorado Springs: Helmers & Howard, 1989), 156.

11. Gavin Newsom, San Francisco's mayor in 2005, was issuing marriage licenses to same-sex couples in open defiance of California state law. In doing so, he was asserting the right to ignore a state law with which he disagreed, a decision well beyond his mayoral authority and jurisdiction.

12. "Chief Justice Vows to Fight Monument Order," *CNN News*, August 22, 2003, http://www.cnn.com/2003/LAW/08/21/ten.commandments/.

13. See Ephesians 6:5; Colossians 3:22.

14. Ephesians 5:22; see also vv. 23–24.

15. Michael Novak, "Religion and Liberty: From Vision to Politics," *The Christian Century*, July 6–13, 1988.

Chapter 5: All the Presidents' Faith

1. Abraham Lincoln, quoted in George C. Rable, "Lincoln's Civil Religion," *History Now* 1, no. 6 (December 2005), http://www.historynow.org/12_2005/historian4.html.

2. Jim Wallis, *God's Politics: Why the Right Gets It Wrong and the Left Doesn't Get It* (San Francisco: HarperSanFrancisco, 2005), 141.

3. Kevin Phillips, *American Theocracy: The Perils and Politics of Radical Religion, Oil, and Borrowed Money in the Twenty-First Century* (New York: Viking/Penguin, 2006), 205–6. Ross Douthat, an associate editor at the *Atlantic Monthly* and author of *Privilege: Harvard and the Education of the Ruling Class* (2005), has demolished the hysterical rants of Kevin Phillips, Randall Balmer, et al. concerning a burgeoning "theocratic" and Dominionist movement among American Evangelicals in "Theocracy, Theocracy, Theocracy," *First Things* (August–September, 2006): 23-30.

4. Bruce Lincoln, *Holy Terrors: Thinking about Religion after September 11* (Chicago: University of Chicago Press, 2003).

5. Paul Kengor, *God and George W. Bush: A Spiritual Life* (New York: ReganBooks/ HarperCollins, 2004), 348n28.

6. Ibid., 182–84.

7. Ibid., 195–96.

8. Information in this section is from "Bibles and Scripture Passages Used by Presidents in Taking the Oath of Office," compiled by the Office of the Curator, Architect of the Capitol, http://memory.loc.gov/ammem/pihtml/pibible.html. Passages quoted are from the King James Version unless otherwise indicated.

9. According to the inauguration staff, George W. Bush had hoped to use the Masonic Bible that had been used both by George Washington in 1789 and by the president's father, George H. W. Bush, in 1989. This historic Bible had been transported, under guard, from New York to Washington for the inauguration, but because of inclement weather, a family Bible was substituted instead.

10. Michael Gove, "Thank God for Politicians Who Take Their Cue from Above," *London Times*, May 6, 2003.

11. Abraham Lincoln, "Meditation on the Divine Will," in *The Collected Works of Abraham Lincoln*, ed. Roy S. Basler, vol. 5 (New Brunswick, NJ: Rutgers University Press, 1953), 404n.

12. Abraham Lincoln, "Second Inaugural Address," March 4, 1865, in *The Collected Works of Abraham Lincoln*, ed. Roy S. Basler, vol. 8 (New Brunswick, NJ: Rutgers University Press, 1953), 332–33.

13. Ibid.

14. Lincoln, quoted in Rable, "Lincoln's Civil Religion."

15. Cf. chapter 1, "What's God Got to Do with America?" p. 3.

16. Abraham Lincoln, remarks made during the Lincoln-Douglas debate on October 15, 1858, at Alton, Illinois.

17. See Hebrews 4:16.

18. Ira Chernus, "Eisenhower: Faith and Fear in the Fifties," http://spot.colorado.edu/~chernus/Research/EFaithAndFear.htm.

19. Ibid.

20. Ibid., 2.

21. Ibid.

22. *Inaugural Addresses of the Presidents of the United States.* Washington, D.C.: U.S. G.P.O.: for sale by the Supt. of Docs., U.S. G.P.O., 1989; Bartleby.com, 2001. www.bartleby.com/124/press54.html. [August 30, 2006].

23. Ibid.

24. Ibid. I am grateful to Dr. Nancy Gibbs of *Time* magazine for many helpful insights into the role faith played in Eisenhower's presidency.

25. John F. Kennedy, "Address to the Greater Houston Ministerial Association," Rice Hotel, Houston, TX, September 12, 1960, http://www.jfklibrary.org/j091260.htm.

26. John F. Kennedy, inaugural address, January 20, 1961, http://www.jfklibrary.org/Historical+Resources/Archives/Reference+Desk/Speeches/JFK/003POF03Inaugural0120 1961.htm.

27. Lyndon B. Johnson, *Congressional Record,* House (March 15, 1965), 4924, 4926.

28. Paul Kengor, *God and Ronald Reagan: A Spiritual Life* (New York: Reagan Books, 2004).

29. Ibid., 152.

30. Ibid., 153.

31. Ibid., citing Maureen Reagan, "A President and a Father," *Washington Times*, June 16, 2000, A23.

32. Ibid., 154, speech delivered November 13, 1979.

33. Ibid.

34. Ibid.

35. Ibid.

36. Ibid.

37. Ibid., 155, quoting Peggy Noonan, then a CBS radio crew member and future Reagan speechwriter. Noonan recounts this story in her book *When Character Was King: A Story of Ronald Reagan* (New York: Viking Adult, 2001), 130–131.

38. Ronald Reagan to Terrence Cardinal Cooke, Good Friday, 1981, quoted in Kengor, *God and Ronald Reagan*, 197.

39. Kengor, *God and Ronald Reagan*, 235.

40. Ibid., 236.

41. Ibid.

42. Ibid., 239.
43. Ibid., 217. As Kengor explains, "He said this often as president. This quote was offered at least three times." See Reagan, "State of the Union Address," February 6, 1985; Reagan, "Remarks at a Ceremony Marking the Annual Observance of Captive Nations Week," July 19, 1983; and Reagan, "First Inaugural Address," January 20, 1981.
44. George W. Bush and Karen Hughes, *A Charge to Keep* (New York: William Morrow, 1999), 45.
45. Remarks quoted here are from a transcript of NBC News' *Meet the Press*, Tim Russert, host, titled "Faith in America with Reza Aslan, Rev. Robert Drinan, Dr. Richard Land, Sen. Joseph Lieberman, Jon Meacham and Rev. Jim Wallis," March 20, 2005, http://www.msnbc.msn.com/id/7284978/from/ET/. The statements by President Bush that were the subject of the media's questions were made in a private, face-to-face meeting while he was governor of Texas.
46. Jim Wallis, misled by media accounts, perpetuates this distortion by quoting the media quoting me—out of context. See his *God's Politics*, 140–41.
47. Kengor, *God and George W. Bush*, 173–96.

Chapter 6: Why We're So Confused about Church and State

1. Chris Hedges, "Soldiers of Christ II: Feeling the Hate with the National Religious Broadcasters," *Harper's*, May 2005, http://www.harpers.org/FeelingTheHate.html.
2. Claudia Winkler, "On Evangelicals and Theocrats: The Example of James Madison Shows Why Liberals Who Continue to Conflate the Taliban with Religious Conservatives Are Wrong," *The Daily Standard*, January 22, 2002, http://www. weeklystandard.com/Content/Public/Articles/000/000/000/813bbcfy.asp?pg=1.
3. Jeff Sharlett, "Soldiers of Christ I: Inside America's Most Powerful Megachurch," *Harper's*, May 2005, http://www.harpers.org/SoldiersOfChrist.html.
4. See Princeton University's Web site, 2005–2006 courses in the American Studies Program, http://web.princeton.edu/sites/amstudies/course0506.htm. The course description reads, "The Christian Right and the Open Society will explore the role of the radical Christian Right in American society, how it functions as a political and religious movement and what its possible ramifications will be for the United States. Students will be expected to do some field research on the Christian Right and report on their findings." One might wish that the professor would do some of his own field research.
5. Hedges, "Soldiers of Christ II."
6. From a PBS interview hosted by David Brancaccio with Chris Hedges and Roy Moore, June 10, 2005, http://www.pbs.org/now/transcript/transcriptNOW123_full.html.
7. Roy Moore with John Perry, *So Help Me God: The Ten Commandments, Judicial Tyranny, and the Battle for Religious Freedom* (Nashville: Broadman & Holman, 2005), 7.
8. PBS interview, June 10, 2005.
9. Winkler, "On Evangelicals and Theocrats."
10. Bruce Gourley, "The Baptist Index: Outline of Baptist Persecution in Colonial America," March 17, 2006, http://www.brucegourley.com/baptists/persecutionoutline.htm.
11. Danbury Baptist Association, letter to Thomas Jefferson, October 7, 1801.
12. Thomas Jefferson, letter to the Danbury Baptists, January 1, 1802.
13. See Stephen L. Carter, *God's Name in Vain: The Wrongs and Rights of Religion in Politics* (New York: Basic Books/Perseus, 2000), 75–76.
14. Daniel L. Dreisbach, "Thomas Jefferson, a Mammoth Cheese, and the 'Wall of Separation Between Church and State,'" in *Religion and the New Republic*, ed. James H. Hutson (Lanham, MD: Rowman & Littlefield, 2000), 65.
15. Ibid.
16. Ibid. (July 20, 1801).
17. Ibid.
18. Ibid., 66, citing numerous contemporary newspapers.
19. Lyman Butterfield, "Elder John Leland, Jeffersonian Itinerant," in William L.

Lumpkin, *Colonial Baptists and Southern Revivals: An original Anthology* (New York: Armo Press, 1980), 224.

20. Ibid. This reference undoubtedly reflects the strong anti-slavery sentiments of John Leland. The major reason Leland left Virginia and returned to his native Massachusetts in 1791 was Virginia Baptists' more ambivalent attitude toward slavery, which Leland abhorred and believed to be "a violent deprivation of the rights of nature." John Bradley Creed, "John Leland, American Prophet of Religious Individualism" (PhD diss., Southwestern Baptist Theological Seminary, 1986), 103, quoting Leland's "Letter of Valediction on Leaving Virginia".

21. Dreisbach, "Thomas Jefferson," 71.

22. James Huston, "A Wall of Separation: FBI Helps Restore Jefferson's Obliterated Draft," *The Library of Congress Information Bulletin* 57, no. 6 (June 1998): 137, quoted in Dreisbach, "Thomas Jefferson," 72.

23. Jon Butler, "Coercion, Miracle, Reason: Rethinking the American Religious Experience in the Revolutionary Age," in *Religion in a Revolutionary Age*, ed. Ronald Hoffman and Peter J. Albert (Charlottesville: University Press of Virginia: United States Capitol Society, 1994), 29–30, quoted in Dreisbach, "Thomas Jefferson," 75.

24. Butterfield, "Elder John Leland," 226, citing W. P. and J. P. Cutler, *Life, Journals and Correspondence of Rev. Manasseh Cutler* (Cincinnati 1888), 2:66–67.

25. Ibid.

26. Ibid, 227.

27. "*Dignitatis Humanae*: Declaration on Religious Freedom on the Right of the Person and of Communities to Social and Civil Freedom in Matters Religious Promulgated by His Holiness Pope Paul VI on December 7, 1965," http://www.vatican.va/archive/hist_councils/ii_vatican_council/documents/vat-ii_decl_19651207_dignitatis-humanae_en.html#top.

28. From an interview on National Public Radio's *Morning Edition*, December 14, 2005, http://www.npr.org/templates/story/story.php?storyId=5052876.

29. For examples of how these three positions would be applied to specific issues, see appendix F.

30. Douglas Kmiec, remarks made in an interview with host Tim Russert and fellow guest Mario Cuomo, former governor of New York, on NBC News' *Meet the Press*, August 16, 2005, http://www.msnbc.msn.com/id/8714275/.

31. Abraham Lincoln, "Address Delivered at the Cemetery at Gettysburg," November 19, 1863, in *The Collected Works of Abraham Lincoln*, ed. Roy S. Basler, vol. 7 (New Brunswick, NJ: Rutgers University Press, 1953), 23.

32. Richard W. Garnett, "Two Justices Who 'Get' Religion," *USA Today*, January 22, 2006, http://usatoday.com/news/opinion/editorials/2006-01-22-religion_x.htm.

Chapter 7: Is There a New Religion Penalty in America?

1. Stephen L. Carter, *God's Name in Vain: The Wrongs and Rights of Religion in Politics* (New York: Basic Books/Perseus, 2000), 192–93.

2. Jim Wallis, *God's Politics: Why the Right Gets It Wrong and the Left Doesn't Get It* (San Francisco: HarperSanFrancisco, 2005), 69.

3. Ibid., 242.

4. Bruce Bartlett, "As Tax Rates Fall, Wealthy Pay More," *Budget and Tax News*, February 1, 2006, 1. This data is based on tax rates from 1980 through 2003, compared with percentage of taxes paid by the top 1 percent of taxpayers.

5. Ibid.

6. Bill Frist, "Tax Cuts Make Money," *USA Today*, February 21, 2006.

7. Stephen Moore, "Real Tax Cuts Have Curves," *The Wall Street Journal*, June 13, 2005, A13.

8. David Brooks, "Fear and Rejection," *New York Times*, June 2, 2005, A27.

9. Ibid.

NOTES

10. AP/Ipsos poll, "Religious Fervor in U.S. Surpasses Faith in Many Other Highly Industrial Countries," June 5, 2005, http://wid.ap.org/polls/050606religion.html.
11. Janet Folger, *The Criminalization of Christianity* (Sisters, OR: Multnomah, 2005), 55.
12. Ibid., 101–2. President Bush signed into law on August 14, 2006, legislation to protect San Diego's Mount Soledad cross as a memorial to military veterans. The case is under litigation in the courts and will no doubt ultimately be decided by the Supreme Court.
13. John Gibson, *The War on Christmas* (New York: Sentinel/Penguin, 2005), xxiii.
14. Associated Press, "Reeve: Keep Religious Groups Out of Public Policy," April 3, 2003.
15. Dana Milbank, "Religious Right Finds Its Center in Oval Office," *Washington Post*, December 24, 2001.
16. Katherine Yurica and Laurie Hall, "The Despoiling of America: How George W. Bush Became the Head of the New American Dominionist Church/State," http://www.axisoflogic.com/cgi-bin/exec/view.pl?archive=43&num=5160&printer=1.
17. Jim Allison, "The Rise of the Theocratic States of America," http://members.tripod.com/~candst/theocracy.htm.
18. Jeremy Learning, "Americans United for Separation of Church and State," *Religious Right Watch*, August 24, 2005, http://blog.au.org/religious_right_watch/index.html.
19. Quoted by Adam Nagourney in "G.O.P. Right Is Splintered on Schiavo Intervention," *New York Times*, March 23, 2005.
20. Bill Moyers, "9-11 and the Sport of God" (speech, Union Theological Seminary, New York City, September 9, 2005).
21. Supreme Court chief justice nominee John Roberts, appearing before the U.S. Senate Judiciary Committee, September 12–13, 2005, transcript courtesy Morningside Partners/FDCH (Morningside Partners, LLC 2005, 4200 Forbes Blvd., Suite 200, Lanham, MD 20706).
22. William Martin, "With God on Our Side: Reflections on the Religious Right" (presentation, annual forum of The Center for Progressive Christianity, 1997), http://www.religion-online.org/showarticle.asp?title=1658.
23. William J. Clinton, introduction to *The Mighty and the Almighty: Reflections on America, God, and World Affairs* by Madeleine Albright (New York: HarperCollins, 2006), xi.
24. Joseph Lieberman, "Scoop Jackson Democrat," interview by Adam Meyerson, *Policy Review*, no. 53 (Summer 1990), http://www.policyreview.org/summer90/lieberman.html.
25. Quoted by Gary Tanner in "Supreme Court Changes Inspire Card Choice," Associated Press, December 3, 2005.
26. John Adams, *The Works of John Adams, Second President of the United States*, ed. Charles Francis Adams, vol. 9 (Boston: Little, Brown, & Co., 1854), 229.

Chapter 8: What Happens When You Mix God and Country—and What Happens When You Don't?

1. Ronald M. Green, Beliefnet.com debate with Nigel Cameron, "Scholarly Smackdown: The Stem Cell Debate," http://www.beliefnet.com/story/152/story_15286_3.html.
2. Nigel Cameron, Beliefnet.com debate with Ronald M. Green "Scholarly Smackdown: The Stem Cell Debate," http://www.beliefnet.com/story/152/story_15286_4.html.
3. Russell Kirk, *The Roots of American Order* (Wilmington, DE: ISI Books, 1974), 29.
4. Steve Farkas, Jean Johnson, and Tony Foleno with Ann Duffett and Patrick Foley, *For Goodness' Sake: Why So Many Want Religion to Play a Greater Role in American Life* (New York: Public Agenda, 2001), 43, http://www.publicagenda.org/research/research_reports_details.cfm?list=25.
5. Cited in Stephen L. Carter, *God's Name in Vain: The Wrongs and Rights of Religion in Politics* (New York: Basic Books, 2000), 72–73.
6. Norton Garfinkle and Daniel Yankelovich, eds., *Uniting America: Restoring the Vital Center to American Democracy* (New Haven: Yale University Press, 2006). Quotations here are from a portion of the book posted online in an essay by Yankelovich,

"Overcoming Polarization: The New Social Morality," http://www.publicagenda.org/aboutpa/aboutpa_articles_detail.cfm?list=28.

7. Ibid.

8. Green, in "Scholarly Smackdown."

9. Cameron, in "Scholarly Smackdown."

10. See Stephen L. Carter, *The Culture of Disbelief: How American Law and Politics Trivialize Religious Devotion* (New York: Basic Books, 1993).

11. Bruce Bartlett, "As Tax Rates Fall, Wealthy Pay More," *Budget & Tax News*, February 1, 2006, 1–2.

12. Thomas L. Friedman, "A Race to the Top," *New York Times*, June 3, 2005, A27.

13. "Reaganomics at 25," *Wall Street Journal*, August 12–13, 2006, A8.

14. Ibid.

15. Documented in W. J. Smith, *Culture of Death: The Assault on Medical Ethics in America* (San Francisco: Encounter Books, 2000), 150.

16. Ron Reagan Jr., in a speech at the Democratic National Convention, Boston, July 27, 2004.

17. See Robert Jay Lifton, *The Nazi Doctors: Medical Killing and the Psychology of Genocide* (New York: Basic Books, 2000).

18. See Peter Singer, *Animal Liberation* (New York: Ecco Press, 2001).

Chapter 9: Does America Have a Special Role in the World?

1. Kevin Phillips, *American Theocracy: The Peril and Politics of Radical Religion, Oil, and Borrowed Money in the Twenty-First Century* (New York: Viking/Penguin, 2006), 220.

2. Madeleine Albright, *The Mighty and the Almighty: Reflections on America, God, and World Affairs* (New York: HarperCollins, 2006), 31.

3. Ibid.

4. Phillips is also the author of *American Dynasty: Aristocracy, Fortune, and the Politics of Deceit in the House of Bush* (New York: Viking/Penguin, 2004).

5. Elaine L. Chao, in a speech at a Citizenship Day naturalization ceremony at Ellis Island, New York, September 16, 2005, http://www.dol.gov/_sec/media/speeches/20050916_citizenship.htm.

6. Albright, *Mighty and the Almighty*, 5.

7. Ibid., 31.

8. Ibid., 32.

9. For the fascinating story of how Madeleine Albright was raised Catholic but discovered her Jewish heritage later in life, including the shock of learning that three of her grandparents and multiple family members had died in the Holocaust, see her previous book *Madam Secretary: A Memoir* (New York: Miramax, 2005), 235–49.

10. Abraham Lincoln, "Address Delivered at the Cemetery at Gettysburg," November 19, 1863, in *The Collected Works of Abraham Lincoln*, ed. Roy S. Basler, vol. 7 (New Brunswick, NJ: Rutgers University Press, 1953), 23.

11. *Congressional Record*, 1941, vol. 87, pt. 1.

12. John F. Kennedy, inaugural address, January 20, 1961, http://www.jfklibrary.org/Historical+Resources/Archives/Reference+Desk/Speeches/JFK/003POF03Inaugural01201961.html.

13. Ibid.

14. George W. Bush, first inaugural address, January 20, 2001, http://www.whitehouse.gov/news/inaugural-address.html.

15. Jim Wallis, *God's Politics: Why the Right Gets It Wrong and the Left Doesn't Get It* (San Francisco: HarperSanFrancisco, 2005), 139–40.

16. Phillips, *American Theocracy*, 219–20.

17. Jan Winiecki, "American Unilateralism: A Personal Perspective," *The Tocquevillian Magazine*, August 30, 2006, http://www.tocquevillian.com/articles/0123.html.

18. Colin Powell made this statement in his address to the World Economic Forum, Davos, Switzerland, January 26, 2003.
19. See *Americans Struggle with Religion at Home and Abroad* (Washington, DC: Pew Research Center/Pew Forum on Religion & Public Life, 2002), 7.
20. Kevin R. den Dulk, "Evangelical Elites and Faith-Based Foreign Affairs," *The Review of Faith and International Affairs* 4, no. 1 (Spring 2006): 23.
21. Jimmy Carter, *Our Endangered Values: America's Moral Crisis* (New York: Simon & Schuster, 2005), 113–14.
22. See Richard Land, *Real Homeland Security: The America God Will Bless* (Nashville: Broadman & Holman, 2004), section titled "What If the End Is Near?" 190ff.; and *Imagine! A God-Blessed America: How It Could Happen and What It Would Look Like* (Nashville: Broadman & Holman, 2005), 182.
23. In the absence of such evidence, one must conclude that the Bush administration's policies concerning Israel and the Middle East are based upon the same prudential considerations concerning national security, Israel as the only stable democracy in the Middle East, and Israel's right to live within secure borders that have been the continuous policy of American presidential administrations from the Truman administration forward. Personally, I have never met anyone at any level in the Bush administration who has given any evidence that issues of biblical prophecy have had any impact on their decision making concerning the Middle East, nor have I ever seen any copies of the Left Behind series on the shelves of any West Wing offices I've visited.
24. Joseph Lieberman, "Scoop Jackson Democrat," interview by Adam Meyerson, *Policy Review*, no. 53 (Summer 1990), http://www.policyreview.org/summer90/lieberman.html.

Chapter 10: Soul Freedom—a Divine Mandate?
1. George W. Bush, second inaugural address, January 20, 2005, http://www.whitehouse.gov/news/releases/2005/01/20050120-1.html.
2. For history on the Anabaptist movement, see William R. Estep, *The Anabaptist Story: An Introduction to Sixteenth-Century Anabaptism* (Grand Rapids: Eerdmans, 1996).
3. Philip Schaff, *Creeds of Christendom* (Grand Rapids: Calvin College/Christian Classics Ethereal Library, n.d.), vol. 1, §104, http://www.ccel.org/ccel/schaff/creeds1.x.v.html.
4. Walter Shurden, *The Baptist Identity: Four Fragile Freedoms* (Macon, GA: Smyth & Helwys, 1993), 23.
5. Stephen L. Carter, *God's Name in Vain: The Wrongs and Rights of Religion in Politics* (New York: Basic Books, 2000), 75–76.
6. Ibid., 76.
7. Michael Novak, "Religion and Liberty: From Vision to Politics," *Christian Century*, July 6–13, 1988, http://www.religion-online.org/showarticle.asp?title=955.
8. United Nations Universal Declaration of Human Rights, article 18, http://www.un.org/Overview/rights.html.
9. Philip Schaff, *History of the Church*, vol. 7, *Modern Religious Intolerance and Liberty in England and America* (Grand Rapids: Calvin College/Christian Classics Ethereal Library, n.d.), http://www.ccel.org/ccel/schaff/hcc7.ii.i.xii.html?#highlight.
10. Bush, second inaugural address.
11. R. James Woolsey, chairman, Center for Religious Freedom, testimony before the U.S. Senate on "Constitutionalism, Human Rights, and the Rule of Law in Iraq," June 23, 2003, http://freedomhouse.org/religion/country/Iraq/Testimony_June%2025.htm.
12. James Key, "War and Faith," *USA Today*, November 13, 2005, http://www.usatoday.com/news/opinion/editorials/2005-11-13-faith-edit_x.html.
13. Ibid.
14. Gary Langer, "Poll: Four Years after the Fall of the Taliban, Afghans Optimistic about

the Future," an ABC News Special Report, December 7, 2005, http://abcnews.go.com/International/PollVault/story?id=1363276.

15. Editorial, "Hobbes in Sudan," *Wall Street Journal*, March 23, 2006, A16, http://online. wsj.com/article_email/SB114308102839205954-lMyQjAxMDE2NDIzNDAyODQx Wj.html.

16. Ibid.

17. Ibid.

18. Richard V. Pierard, "Why the Time Is Right for God's Politics," *The Review of Faith and International Affairs* 4, no. 1 (Spring 2006): 55–56.

19. William M. Pinson Jr. and Doris A. Tinker, eds., "Is Soul Competency *The* Baptist Distinctive?" article 5 in *Baptist Distinctives*, http://www.baptistdistinctives.org/ textonly5.html (italics in original).

20. Philip Schaff, "Church and State in the United States," essay written in 1888 for the American Historical Society, http://candst.tripod.com/1888.html.

21. Bush, second inaugural address.

Chapter 11: What Does It Mean to Say, "God Bless America"?

1. Abraham Lincoln, "Proclamation Appointing a National Fast Day," issued March 30, 1863, in *The Collected Works of Abraham Lincoln*, vol. 6 (New Brunswick, NJ: Rutgers University Press, 1953), 155–56.

2. Jim Wallis, *God's Politics: Why the Right Gets It Wrong and the Left Doesn't Get It* (San Francisco: HarperSanFrancisco, 2005), 4.

3. Paul Marshall, "Jim Wallis' Politics—or Lack Thereof," *Review of Faith and International Affairs* 4, no. 1 (Spring 2006): 49–50.

4. Manjit Singh, remarks made during a discussion sponsored by the Pew Forum on Religion & Public Life, "God Bless America: Reflections on Civil Religion after September 11," Washington, DC, February 6, 2002, http://pewforum.org/events/ index.php?EventID=22.

5. Madeleine Albright, *The Mighty and the Almighty: Reflections on America, God, and World Affairs* (New York: HarperCollins, 2006), 32.

6. See John Donne's Meditation XVII, from *Devotions upon Emergent Occasions* (1624).

7. Stephen L. Carter, *The Culture of Disbelief* (New York: Anchor/Doubleday, 2003), 22.

8. Stephen L. Carter, *God's Name in Vain: The Wrongs and Rights of Religion in Politics* (New York: Basic Books, 2000), 79–80.

9. Rita Spillenger, "Reasons to Fear the Religious Right," http://www.positiveatheism.org/ writ/ccandgop.htm#FEAR.

10. Peter Berkowitz, remarks made during a discussion sponsored by the Pew Forum on Religion & Public Life, "God Bless America: Reflections on Civil Religion after September 11," Washington, DC, February 6, 2002, http://pewforum.org/events/ index.php?EventID=22.

11. See Matthew 7:24–27.

12. Lincoln, "Proclamation Appointing a National Fast Day."

13. Joseph Lieberman, from an interview on NBC News' *Meet the Press*, Tim Russert, host, titled "Faith in America with Reza Aslan, Rev. Robert Drinan, Dr. Richard Land, Sen. Joseph Lieberman, Jon Meacham and Rev. Jim Wallis," March 20, 2005, http://www.msnbc.msn.com/id/7284978/from/ET/.

14. Chronicled in Carter, *God's Name in Vain*, 93–94.

15. Ibid.

16. Ibid.

17. Ibid.

18. A description of the 96th Assembly posted on the American Assembly's Web site, http://www.americanassembly.org/programs.dir/prog_display_ind_pg.php?this_ filename_prefix=uas_religion&this_ind_prog_pg_filename=descr.

19. "Uniting America Series—Matters of Faith: Religion in American Public Life," Final

Report of the Ninety-sixth American Assembly (Harriman, NY, March 23–26, 2000), 7, http://www.americanassembly.org/programs.dir/report_file.dir/uas_religion_report_report_file_ReligionRpt.pdf.

20. See Philip Longman, *The Empty Cradle* (New York: Basic Books, 2004). An excerpt from this book was reproduced in the article "The Global Baby Bust," *Foreign Affairs*, May–June 2004, http://www.foreignaffairs.org/20040501faessay83307-p0/phillip-longman/the-global-baby-bust.html.

21. "Barna Survey Reveals Significant Growth in Born-Again Population," press release from the Barna Group Ltd., Ventura, CA, March 27, 2006, www.barna.org.

22. For an in-depth exploration of such a tipping point for God's blessing, see Richard Land, *Real Homeland Security: The America God Will Bless* (Nashville: Broadman & Holman, 2004). For an extended treatment of what America might actually look like under God's blessing, see Richard Land, *Imagine! A God-Blessed America: How It Could Happen and What It Would Look Like* (Nashville: Broadman & Holman, 2005).

23. Lincoln, "Proclamation Appointing a National Fast Day."

Appendices

1. Reprinted from Arthur C. Cochrane, *The Church's Confession under Hitler* (Philadelphia: Westminster, 1962), 237–42.

2. Clarence W. Bowen, *The History of the Centennial Celebration of the Inauguration of George Washington* (New York, 1892), 72, illustration.

3. Listed in the files of Legislative Reference Service, Library of Congress, source not given.

4. John Wright, *Historic Bibles in America* (New York, 1905), 46.

5. List compiled by Clerk of the Supreme Court, 1939.

6. One source (*Chicago Daily Tribune*, September 23, 1881, 5) says that Garfield and Arthur used the same passage but does not indicate which one.

7. Stilson Hutchins, *The National Capitol* (Washington, DC, 1885), 276.

8. *Harper's Magazine*, August 1897.

9. Senate Document 116, 65th Congress, 1st Session, 1917.

10. *New York Times*, April 13, 1945, p. 1, col. 7.

11. *Facts on File*, January 16-22, 1949, 21.

12. *New York Times*, January 21, 1953, 19.

13. *New York Times*, January 22, 1957, 16.

14. *New York Times*, January 21, 1961, p. 8, col. 1.

15. Booth Mooney, *The Lyndon Johnson Story*, 1.

16. Office of the Clerk of the Supreme Court via phone July 1968.

17. *Washington Post*, January 20, 1969, A1.

18. *New York Times*, August 10, 1974, A1.

19. *Washington Post*, January 21, 1977, A17.

20. White House Curator's Office.

21. *Washington Post*, January 21, 1997, A14.

22. Inauguration staff. George W. Bush had hoped to use the Masonic Bible that had been used both by George Washington in 1789 and by his father, George H. W. Bush, in 1989. This historic Bible had been transported, under guard, from New York to Washington for the inauguration, but because of inclement weather, a family Bible was substituted instead.

23. Posted online at http://www.whitehouse.gov/news/releases/2005/01/images/20050120-1_3-p44290-376-515h.html.

24. American Historical Documents, 1000–1904. Vol. XLIII. The Harvard Classics. New York: P. F. Collier & Son, 1909–14; Bartleby.com, 2001. www.bartleby.com/43/36.html. [8/29/2006].

25. Inaugural Addresses of the Presidents of the United States. Washington, D.C.: U.S. G.P.O.: for sale by the Supt. of Docs., U.S. G.P.O., 1989; Bartleby.com, 2001. www.bartleby.com/124/press32.html. [8/29/2006].

Notes

26. Franklin D. Roosevelt Presidential Library and Museum, http://www.fdrlibrary. marist.edu/4free.html.
27. Franklin D. Roosevelt Presidential Library and Museum, http://www.fdrlibrary.marist.edu/odddayp.html.
28. John F. Kennedy Presidential Library and Museum, http://www.jfklibrary.org/ Historical+Resources/Archives/Reference+Desk/Speeches/JFK/JFK+Pre-Press/ Address+of+Senator+John+F.+Kennedy+to+the+Greater+Houston+Ministerial+ Association.htm.
29. John F. Kennedy Presidential Library and Museum, http://www.jfklibrary.org/ Historical+Resources/Archives/Reference+Desk/Speeches/JFK/ 003POF03Inaugural01201961.htm.
30. John F. Kennedy Presidential Library and Museum, http://www.jfklibrary.org/ Historical+Resources/Archives/Reference+Desk/Speeches/JFK/ 003POF03TradeMart11221963.htm.
31. See Luke 2:14.
32. Posted online at http://www.whitehouse.gov/news/inaugural-address.html.
33. Posted online at http://www.whitehouse.gov/news/releases/2005/01/20050120-1.html.
34. Posted online at http://www.un.org/Overview/rights.html.
35. Excerpt from *The Baptist Faith and Message* (adopted by the Southern Baptist Convention as its confession of its faith, June 2000).

★ Index ★

Index

Index

Index

INDEX

Index

INDEX

★ Scripture Index ★